# Education for Inclusive Citizenship

*Education for Inclusive Citizenship* contributes to theoretical thinking on inclusive citizenship education through a detailed and lively account of the different concepts of citizenship held by some of the key players involved, and the extent to which these concepts accommodate ethnic and religious diversity.

The book focuses on the policy and curriculum development process of citizenship education in the English secondary school contemporary context, and is based on original first-hand accounts from interviews with the key players involved, including David Blunkett, Sir Bernard Crick and other high-profile policymakers and those working in the fields of citizenship and diversity. Four main models of citizenship underpinned by political philosophy are proposed, and the theoretical and practical implications for diversity of these four models are explicated. While the 'participatory' conception of citizenship emerges as the most dominant conception, Kiwan argues that it does not substantively accommodate a diversity of identities. In response, she proposes an inclusive model of citizenship, which consists of two main components: 'institutional' multiculturalism, and a greater emphasis on the relationship between citizen and state.

*Education for Inclusive Citizenship* provides readers with a conceptual understanding of citizenship in a broader policy, societal and global context. It informatively and provocatively illustrates how policymakers, teachers and other practitioners can use and modify the four models of citizenship to realistically promote an inclusive citizenship in practice.

**Dina Kiwan** is an Academic Fellow/Lecturer in Citizenship Education at Birkbeck College, University of London, UK.

# Education for Inclusive Citizenship

Dina Kiwan

Routledge
Taylor & Francis Group

LONDON AND NEW YORK

First published 2008
by Routledge
2 Park Square, Milton Park, Abingdon, Oxon OX14 4RN

Simultaneously published in the USA and Canada
by Routledge
270 Madison Avenue, New York, NY 10016

*Routledge is an imprint of the Taylor & Francis Group, an informa
business*

Typeset in Times New Roman by Keyword Group Ltd
Printed and bound in Great Britain by TJ International Ltd, Padstow,
Cornwall

*British Library Cataloguing in Publication Data*
A catalogue record for this book is available from the British Library

*Library of Congress Cataloging in Publication Data*
A catalog record has been requested for this book

ISBN10: 0-415-42367-8 (hbk)
ISBN10: 0-415-42368-6 (pbk)

ISBN13: 978-0-415-42367-0 (hbk)
ISBN13: 978-0-415-42368-7 (pbk)

**To Hibou**

# Contents

| | | |
|---|---|---|
| *List of tables* | | ix |
| *Preface* | | x |
| *Foreword* | | xii |
| *Acknowledgements* | | xvi |
| *List of abbreviations* | | xviii |
| | | |
| Introduction | | 1 |

**PART 1**
**The development of citizenship education**      11

| | | |
|---|---|---|
| 1 | Citizenship education in England: setting the scene | 13 |
| 2 | Key players' perceptions: influences, processes, aims and contributions | 22 |

**PART 2**
**Conceptions of citizenship**      43

| | | |
|---|---|---|
| 3 | 'Moral' conceptions | 49 |
| 4 | 'Legal' conceptions | 62 |
| 5 | 'Participatory' conceptions | 74 |
| 6 | 'Identity-based' conceptions | 84 |

**PART 3**
**Developing theory and practice** 105

7 Developing a theory of inclusive citizenship 107

8 Practical implications for policy, curriculum and pedagogy 116

*Notes* 128
*Bibliography* 131
*Index* 143

# Tables

2.1 Influences on initiative as perceived by interviewees, ranked in
descending order of frequency                                                    24

2.2 Aims and outcomes as perceived by interviewees, ranked in
descending order of frequency                                                    30

2.3 Number of interviewees at each stage of the development process,
by gender and ethnicity                                                          33

# Preface

This book has grown out of my doctoral research, which examined conceptions of citizenship in the policy and curriculum development process of citizenship education in the English secondary school contemporary context, from the perspectives of the 'key players' who were involved in its formulation. I was interested in two related issues: first, the nature of the inter-relationship between theory and policy. And second, the 'processes' of citizenship – the dynamics of participation of those designated 'powerful' key players acting in the public domain of policy and curriculum development.

When I first started this research, I was somewhat overwhelmed by the vast literature on citizenship from a wide range of disciplinary perspectives, with numerous competing conceptualizations of citizenship from within any given discipline. As I grappled with these literatures, I began to realise that I was interested primarily in the politico-philosophical literature on citizenship, in that it examines philosophical conceptions of what it is to be a human being, and the relationship between individuals and their political community or state. Inherent in the relationship between the individual and their political community is the role that identity, or a sense of belonging plays within this relationship. If citizens are motivated to be active and participate in the wider societal context, then logically they must 'identify' with, or feel a sense of belonging to, the context where they are participating. Similarly, just as a sense of belonging or identity may promote participation, the experience of participating can enhance a sense of belonging. In my research, I was interested in how the politico-philosophical literature on citizenship is reflected in conceptions of citizenship throughout the policymaking process, with a particular focus on the extent to which these conceptions address ethnic and religious diversity, both in terms of their theoretical and practical implications.

While I am committed to a model of participatory citizenship that is inclusive with respect to a diversity of identities defined in terms of gender, social class and age, as well as ethnicity and religion, my focus is on ethnic and religious diversity in the context of citizenship. This was in part a pragmatic decision, so as to define a manageable scope. It was also influenced by the national and international contemporary socio-political context over the last five years, where issues relating to ethnic and religious diversity have taken on an increasingly heightened profile in the media, as well as within education and public policy agendas. Indeed, on submitting evidence to the House of Commons Education and Skills Select Committee Inquiry into Citizenship Education in June 2006, I noted that when I carried out my interviewing of key players in 2002, perceptions regarding the aims of citizenship education were framed primarily in terms of voter apathy, and perceived 'deficits' in young peoples' behaviour and attitudes. There has been a significant shift over more recent years with the aims of citizenship education linked to discourses on community cohesion, identity, diversity, 'shared values' and 'Britishness' (Kiwan 2006a).

This book is also informed by my direct involvement in Home Office and Department for Education and Skills (DfES) policy development, relating to citizenship. In 2002–3, I served on a Home Office Advisory Group , the 'Life in the UK' Advisory Group, chaired by Sir Bernard Crick where our focus was on citizenship in the legal sense – developing policy recommendations for those applying for British citizenship. I was subsequently seconded to the Home Office from 2004–6 to head the Secretariat of a newly created independent advisory board to advise on the implementation of the Advisory Group recommendations. In 2006, I was asked by the Department for Education and Skills (DfES) to work with Sir Keith Ajegbo to carry out a curriculum review of diversity and citizenship; our report was published in January 2007. The government has welcomed the recommendations and these recommendations are reflected in the Qualifications and Curriculum Authority's (QCA) revised Programmes of Study.

# Foreword

Not merely the first but for a long time, this will surely be seen as the most comprehensive and judicious analysis of 'Citizenship' as a subject in the national curriculum for England, and also the account of how it came to be. Dina Kiwan has herself been an actor in the events in two different but not unrelated ways (as have I), as she explains: a member of the advisory group on 'Living in the United Kingdom', then as first executive secretary of the Advisory Board for Integration and Naturalization; but also the colleague of Sir Keith Ajegbo in the January 2007 report that arose when ministers asked for more concentration in schools on teaching and learning about diversity and for the citizenship curriculum to place some emphasis on British values through historical examples. Their balanced report put to rest many fears of what might have been intended.

Dina Kiwan sees identity questions at the heart of citizenship. 'Multiculturalism' has become, as she points out, a much contested term. A few wish it *should* mean separate communal recognition, while others simply fear that this is what is happening – almost segregation; but others still use it descriptively, sociologically and historically, and firmly distinguish integration from assimilation. She argues well that multiculturalism is both a description of our society and contains a value, indeed, an acceptance of cultural, religious and ethnic diversity. This is one of the key contexts of active citizenship. We should accept multiculturalism as a revealing concept and not shelter behind the vaguer 'diversity' more favoured in ministers' speeches, some of whom have, in my opinion, too readily adopted the segregationist and invidious connotation of multiculturalism favoured by many editors and journalists.

The linkage of theory to policy is Dina Kiwan's great strength and primary focus. Her discussion of academic theories is thorough and balanced. Most of these are today unknown to both politicians and civil servants. However, even as I began to write this Foreword, the report of the House of Commons Education and Skills Committee (March 2007) on *Citizenship Education*, together with these views distilled with admirable clarity from at times somewhat esoteric academic debates, brought us all down to earth on public policy. Teaching and learning about diversity is not simply for schools in ethnically and religiously mixed areas, it is for all our schools to understand the realities of our changing society. Thus, citizenship should be a part of *all* initial teacher education and professional development programmes. I add that both schools' citizenship and preparation for legal citizenship (the two senses of 'citizenship') are badly underfunded. As with so many promising New Labour initiatives, the aims and ideas have outpaced the resources available for effective implementation. So this book will be welcomed as a wake-up call that the ambitious aims of the citizenship curriculum – to create a culture of citizenship in Britain – are a long way from achievement.

My great admiration for this book's seriousness and achievement may permit me to debate and mildly differ on some always contentious points. Kiwan is rightly critical that the original advisory group put too little emphasis on learning for diversity, on questions of identity and on explicit anti-racism. There was, indeed, less stress on content in general than on developing the skills and attitudes needed for tolerant and informed discussion of whatever appear as real issues – 'political literacy'. But the opportunity was there, even in the formal language of the official order. 'Pupils should be taught about ... the origins and implications of the diverse national, regional, religious and ethnic identities in the United Kingdom and the need for mutual respect and understanding'. But, she and others are right; diversity and anti-racism were not emphasized enough. To some extent, however, this is to be wise, and wise she is as well as thorough in her research; but wise after the event. The context looks different after July 2005 than it did in 1998.

She sees this clearly and reports from her interviews that some of the advisory group saw our underplaying these sensitive themes as political prudence. While one does not surrender to a sometimes grossly uninformed and prejudiced public opinion, one must consider carefully how to persuade it. Perhaps she may underestimate both the political opportunity that had to be seized quickly, with a minister who supported active citizenship, and the potential for political, media and public hostility to the whole project. 'Was the tail wagging the dog? Was citizenship an overload, a threat to standards and a non-subject? Was New Labour trying to politicise the schools?' A door had to be opened that would be hard politically ever to close again; but it would be best not to provoke opposition unnecessarily or hope to get it all right, all at once.

My admission when interviewed was that my theoretical approach was firmly that of civic republicanism as contrasted to rule-of-law liberalism. She sees my *In Defence of Politics* as underlying the way I led from the front, but is surprised to find that none of those on the advisory group had read the book and that civic republicanism did not figure explicitly in our committee. I only saw the need for a constant pressure and bias to stress – what is to me the heart of the matter – 'active citizenship' more than just 'good citizenship'. We were writing a report for politicians, the press and the general public, not for academic colleagues.

I cannot agree with Dina Kiwan that civic republicanism necessarily relegates ethnic and religious diversity to the private sphere. Perhaps so in pure theory, or perhaps in France, with a virtual national religion of secularism, but I see civic republicanism as always responding to contexts and as fully compatible with pluralism, both as a philosophy of politics and as a description of most civilised societies. The boundaries between what is private and what is public are themselves always contestable and changing – as in fact most of this book demonstrates. But some distinction is always there.

It is true enough to say that the composition and proceedings of the advisory group were 'not very democratic' nor 'transparent'. But how could they be? The only fully representative body for policy is parliament, and there is some difficulty about how democratic that is, except in a narrow institutional sense. An advisory group is appointed by a minister. The composition must inspire public confidence. It cannot be all experts or subject specialists. The late Stephen Tumin was on the group. He turned out to know nothing about ordinary schools. But the good judge had been a Chief Inspector of Prisons who had rebuked famously and boldly the policies of Michael Howard when he was Home Secretary. His support was most helpful. That of a Professor of Education at Brummage might not have been. The former Conservative Secretary of State for Education, Kenneth Baker (Lord Baker) was not a man for educational theory, but he was willing to serve because he said that he had wanted Citizenship to be part of his original national curriculum, but 'she had said no' – and that settled it. A *more* representative group there could have been, most certainly – just as schools can be more democratic but never just democratic; and the group could have commissioned original research and travelled around to see how others did it; but then we might not have reported in time to be turned into law in the life of a parliament or possibly a minister.

The reader might infer that there was too great a closeness (at that time) between David Blunkett and myself. But that was the opportunity to get things done. A clear and quick report to government can be rejected or savaged by the media (we were gently mocked), but a lengthy report that takes the time-scale of academic research grants either gets forgotten or kicked into touch. A flurry of New Labour reports set up in 1997 went that way. We were a rare survivor because we were quick, brief and clear. A political theorist, unlike a sociologist, but very like a historian, is all too well aware of contingency. The republican realist Machiavelli treated 'Fortuna' as a real force, never to be discounted. If John Smith had not died or if the governor of Florida had not been the brother of the Republican candidate, would there have been a war in Iraq? Most unlikely? The conditions for social or educational change have to be right but individuals have to seize the opportunity. Perhaps this weak defence against a well meant and telling criticism of personal dominance could be, however, another kind of theory: Popperian. A clear hypothesis has to be formulated before anything can be modified, decided or refuted and progress made.

'For Crick, the process is more important than the end result' – yes, indeed for the end results of education are always particular and often contrasting in different contexts. Common standards should not lead to common results. That indeed is what we should value in a diversity of dual identities.

This book's depth of research and final recommendations for policy are admirable – not just to tolerate diversity but to make it integral to civil culture. This book will be the standard account and analysis for a long time. But, of course, like the citizenship report itself, it is written at a moment in time. A second edition might come at an easier time when the government will press for the right thing for better reasons. A heightened sense of 'Britishness' and linking it to revisions of the Citizenship curriculum and teaching may be good in themselves but they are no immediate answer to terrorism – as some ministers say. In any case, attitudinal change is not achievable through school education alone, and even that contribution is on a generational, not a parliamentary time-scale.

Certainly 'diversity' needs defending against those who, at best, press for more British (usually meaning English) uniformity, or at worst see all those post-windrush immigrants as a threat to 'our way of life', rather than sharing and gradually modifying it. But the best defence may be to think more historically. For we have been a multinational state since 1707 and a multicultural one since the Industrial Revolution brought both internal and external migration. The Poor Irish flooded into the English industrial cities and then followed by the poor Jews. Some of their descendants have vanished – assimilated; but most, still visible but integrated, have kept a distinct identity while being free citizens of a reasonably free society. Basically, I have no disagreement with the broader construction of Britishness that some thoughtful voices of new Britons favour. But I think they often miss the most convincing line of argument against the suspicions and false resentments of old Brits mirrored or stirred by the popular press: that we have been here before with the Irish and the Jews. But now the time-scales needed for social integration need not be so long, with an active and participative citizenship being taught and evaluated in our schools and with (hopefully) more targeted social policies towards discrimination, health differentials, poverty and housing.

This in-depth and stimulating book raises and faces all these issues. I am happy, despite my dialogic reservations, that if this author should now come to lead the citizenship debate, it will be in strong and independent-minded hands.

Sir Bernard Crick

# Acknowledgements

I am indebted to a number of people who have supported and encouraged me – first while doing my PhD, and subsequently in writing this book. I am grateful to Professors Andy Green and Alex Moore who supervised my PhD and provided me with detailed feedback and guidance throughout its numerous drafts. I would also like to thank all the interviewees who kindly agreed to my interviewing them and using the interview data for the purposes of my research. A special thanks to Sir Bernard Crick who has provided intellectual and professional mentorship to me throughout the time I have known him. I have also been greatly supported and encouraged by Professors John Annette and Sue Jackson of Birkbeck College, since I joined Birkbeck in September 2006. I would also like to thank Sir Keith Ajegbo and Seema Sharma with whom I worked on the Diversity and Citizenship curriculum review for the DfES.

Parts of this book have been published in the forms of articles and chapters. Chapter 2 is an expanded and revised version of Kiwan (2006c) 'Constructing citizenship in the education policymaking process in England: an act of citizenship?', *International Journal of Learning* 13(6): 131–8; readers must contact Common Ground publishing for permission to reproduce. The first part of Chapter 4, which focuses on human rights is an expanded and revised version of Kiwan (2005) 'Human rights and citizenship: an unjustifiable conflation?', *Journal of Philosophy of Education* 39(1): 37–50. 'Uneasy relationships? Conceptions of "citizenship", "democracy" and "diversity" in the English citizenship education policymaking process', forthcoming in *Education, Citizenship and Social Justice*, further develops themes around democracy, participation and diversity in Chapter 5.

Parts of Kiwan, D. and Kiwan, N. (2005) 'Citizenship education: the French and English experience', in C. Pole, J. Pilcher and J. Williams (eds.) *Young People in Transition: Becoming Citizens*, Basingstoke: Palgrave Macmillan have been reproduced and further developed in Chapters 1, 4 and 6 of this book with permission of Palgrave Macmillan. Chapter 7 is an expanded and revised version of Kiwan (2007a) 'Developing a model of inclusive citizenship: "institutional multiculturalism" and the citizen-state relationship', *Theory and Research in Education* 5(2): 225–40, reprinted by permission of SAGE Publications Ltd.,

Copyright (© SAGE Publications and the Slovene Society of Researchers in the School Field, 2007). In addition, Kiwan (2007b, forthcoming) 'Citizenship Education in England at the Cross-roads? Four Models of Citizenship and their Implications for Ethnic and Religious Diversity', *Oxford Review of Education* addresses in a more concise form a number of themes that are addressed throughout the book. Finally, Kiwan (2007c, forthcoming) 'Towards a theory of inclusive participative citizenship', a chapter in a Council of Europe publication examining themes relating to human rights, diversity and participation, which arise in particular in Chapters 4, 5 and 7, who have given permission for this material to be used in this book.

This book could not have been written without the support and love of my husband Nader El-Bizri. My son Hibou and his future have given me the motivation to keep going throughout. And last and most importantly, my mother and father's belief in me over the years has been unwavering, and their gentle love, support and encouragement has given me the confidence to see this project through.

# Abbreviations

| | |
|---|---|
| **CRE** | Commission for Racial Equality |
| **DfES** | Department for Education and Skills |
| **KS3/4** | Key Stage 3/4 |
| **QCA** | Qualifications and Curriculum Authority |

# Introduction

In recent years, there has been an upsurge of interest in citizenship and citizenship education, not only in the UK, but throughout Europe, and indeed globally. While citizenship as an educational aim of the state is not a new idea, citizenship education has never formally been part of the school curriculum in England (Fogelman 1997). It was introduced as a new statutory subject in England in 2002, following the policy review of citizenship education by the 'Crick' Advisory Group in 1998 (QCA 1998). The case for explicitly examining diversity in the context of citizenship and citizenship education is increasingly pertinent, not only given the current national context in the UK, but the current socio-political climate globally. The UK has witnessed a number of legal and political events, including the political and legal recognition of institutional racism (Macpherson 1999), and the introduction of new requirements for the acquisition of British citizenship and permanent settlement (Home Office 2005, 2006), set against a backdrop of increased globalization, migration and social pluralism (Home Office 2001a) and the occurrence of key international events such as 11 September 2001, and the London bombings in July 2005. In 2006, reflecting these concerns, the DfES commissioned a review of diversity and citizenship, which the government framed in terms of concerns with community cohesion, and linked to discourses on identity and diversity, 'shared values', and 'Britishness' (Rammell 2006). At the same time, the House of Commons Education and Skills Select Committee conducted an Inquiry into Citizenship Education, which included the following terms of reference: how citizenship education might promote 'shared values', an understanding of identity and diversity, and 'Britishness' (Education and Skills Select Committee 2006). There has also been much associated media attention and indeed sensationalized debate around these issues, with an article in the *Times Educational Supplement* (TES) exemplifying this: 'Can a citizenship lesson once a week stop British children growing up to become suicide bombers? It seems an ambitious goal for a subject that became compulsory in secondary schools only four years ago' (TES 23 June 2006).

Internationally there is also a heightened policy focus on the inter-relationship between citizenship, integration and diversity. This reflects a central tension in balancing unity and diversity, not only evident in discourses in England, but indeed internationally in a number of different nation-state contexts (Banks 2004), including the USA (Ladson-Billings 2004), Canada (Joshee 2004; Kymlicka 1999), Denmark (Mouritsen 2006), France and Germany (Brubaker 1998; Kastoryano 2006; Luchtenberg 2004). For example, the Transatlantic Task Force on Immigrant Integration has been set up by Antonio Vitorino, the former European Commissioner for Justice and Home Affairs, and Rita Sussmuth, the former President of the Bundestag (parliament) of Germany. The aim of this Task Force is to influence the 2007 EU Presidencies of Germany and Portugal, with particular recommendations in three core areas: education, civic and political participation and workplace integration (Papademetriou 2006). The rationale for this Task Force is urgently presented in terms of a need for effective integration, otherwise 'we face social strife, political polarization, potential security threats, and economic stagnation'; Papademetriou (2006: 1) points to the recent 'urban unrest in France, and August's [2006] attempted London bomb plots are just two warning signs that our societies must heed'. The Council of Europe has also launched a youth policy initiative around the themes of diversity, human rights and participation, where priorities include social cohesion, inclusion and participation of young people (Council of Europe 2006). Banks *et al.* (2006), in their 'Democracy and Diversity' Report, propose a set of principles and concepts for teachers to use in the USA, and indeed elsewhere, in order to further develop their citizenship education curricula to simultaneously address issues of unity or 'shared values' and diversity in the local, national and global contexts.

Until fairly recently, the literatures on citizenship and on diversity have historically, tended to be distinct from each other.[1] Indeed, civic republican models of citizenship take, as an explicit premise, that cultural diversity must not operate within the public sphere. France is often cited as the classic example of the 'civic republican' model where citizenship is formulated in abstract universal terms, with no reference to personal or group attributes, such as ethnicity or religion (Brubaker 1998). Historically, citizenship has been, by definition, an exclusionary concept (Heater 1990), with citizenship typically being conferred to only a subset of people within a society. Ancient Greek conceptions of citizenship were conceived of as a privilege, not just excluding women, but also excluding various other categories of men, for example, the very young, the very old, and those of certain occupations (Heater 1990). However, with the relatively recent expansion of citizenship to include all members of society, especially in the case of multicultural societies, there is an increasing interest in considering citizenship and diversity in a theoretically more explicit and integrated way (e.g. Kymlicka 1995; Parekh 2000).

## Focus and methodology

This book provides a case study of policy and curriculum development in citizenship education in a Western multicultural democratic society, of interest and relevance to those in other countries also facing the challenges of increased social pluralism, immigration and constitutional change, and where there is an interest in moving towards more inclusive forms of citizenship. My methodology entailed interviewing 30 participants involved at different stages of the policymaking process, including David Blunkett, Sir Bernard Crick and others, actively involved in the policy process, subsequent curriculum development stages and also related initiatives. Interviewees were identified and selected from three main categories: first, those who have had substantial influence in developing policy, curriculum and/or developing teaching resources in relation to citizenship education in England; second, those who have a 'stake' in the issue but were not involved or included in the process, and third, those who have been involved in related initiatives or domains, which may have theoretical and/or practical implications for the citizenship education initiative.

Potential participants in the first category were initially identified as a result of their membership in the Crick Advisory Group on Citizenship, and subsequently set-up working groups, focusing on curriculum development, teacher training and the development of resources for schools. With regard to the second and third categories, these potential participants were identified through established networks and consultation with others in the field. Once potential participants in the above three categories were identified, participants were selected so that a wide range of perspectives would be reflected. These included: government officials, teachers, academics and members of various non-governmental organizations and charities. In addition, the selection also included approximately equal numbers of men and women, a range of ages, and as far as possible, people from a range of ethnic and religious backgrounds.[2] The sample, consisting of 30 participants (15 men and 15 women), was drawn from a wide range of backgrounds involved at different stages of the process:[3]

- David Blunkett, former Secretary of State for Education and former Home Secretary
- Eight (out of 15) members of the Crick Advisory Group on Citizenship (four male, four female, including the Chairman; this also included two 'ethnic minority' members)
- Three individuals with whom the Crick Advisory Group consulted ('high profile' individuals in the field)
- One QCA curriculum development specialist
- Ten individuals/organizations involved in development of resources (including both DfES-funded and non-DfES-funded teaching resources, teacher-training resources, community involvement resources)
- Seven individuals/organizations involved in affiliated initiatives (e.g. community cohesion, 'race' relations).

Interviewing can be conducted from different epistemological standpoints, e.g. traditional social survey approaches take a realist position, where it is assumed that the interview data represents the social world independent of the language used by the interviewee (Seale 1998). In contrast, an idealist position views interview data as just one of many possible accounts of the social world, and that what is interesting is not just accessing what is assumed to be the 'truth', but rather the value of the interview data is that it allows the interviewer to access the interviewee's thoughts, feelings and values. I would propose that my approach to interviewing was similar to what Seale (1998) refers to as interview 'topic' – in which the activities of the participants are investigated through the analysis of the language they use (idealist approach). This is because I am particularly interested in the perspectives of the interviewees, with multiple accounts that vary according to their differing values and interests, and at different points throughout the development process of citizenship education. This reflects my ontological stance on the form and nature of reality (Cresswell 1998; Guba and Lincoln 1998), which I understand to be construed as being subjective and multiple, reflected by the range of participant perspectives in the study (Cresswell 1998; Mertens 1998; Pring 2000). These semi-structured interviews were conducted over a 9-month period, from April to December 2002. They were semi-structured in order to allow for flexibility, so that interviewees could talk about what they considered to be relevant, while still covering certain topics/issues, and maintaining some structure within each interview. Interviews were typically 45 minutes to 1 hour in length, with all but two interviews having been tape-recorded, with the consent of interviewees. Interviews were then transcribed, in order to allow for a detailed analysis, and attention to detail of the language used by the interviewees.

My approach to data analysis draws on key features of a grounded theory approach to data analysis; an approach first articulated by Glaser and Strauss (1967). The primary outcome of this approach is the generation of theory, where theory should primarily be grounded in data from the field. In addition, grounded theory articulates a systematic approach with a specific number of steps, consisting of 'open', 'axial' and 'selective' coding (Corbin and Strauss 1990). Although the distinction between theory generation and theory verification is a useful one, I would argue that this distinction is not always so clear-cut. Although grounded theory is predominantly based on induction, it also uses deduction, given that theory generation requires progressive verification as well (Punch 1998). So, while my data analysis approach is based on induction, fulfilling a theory generation role, there is an interplay and mutual verification between the theoretical literature on citizenship, and the coding of conceptions of citizenship arising out of the interview data. With regard to the analysis of policy and curriculum documentation, this was also conducted using the grounded theory approach (Corbin and Strauss 1990). However, analysis of this documentation played more of a 'verification' role, supporting the central theory generation role of the interview data.[4]

In Chapter 2, the data that I am drawing on in particular relates to the responses interviewees gave to the following questions I posed to them: (1) their perceptions of why citizenship education came onto the agenda at this time and became statutory in English secondary schools; (2) their perceptions of the aims and outcomes of citizenship education; (3) their perceptions regarding the workings of the Crick Advisory Group and (4) their perceived expertise and contributions. Interviewees were also asked about their understandings of 'citizenship' and 'diversity' and how these may inter-relate, which is the focus of Part 2 of this book. In addition, this is supplemented by an analysis of the Crick Report (QCA 1998), as well as the Key Stage 3 (KS3) curriculum documentation – the KS3 Programme of Study (QCA 2000) and KS3 Schemes of Work (QCA 2001).[5] This is also interpreted in light of new policy developments in citizenship education (Ajegbo *et al.* 2007; QCA 2007).

## Methodological reflections: interviewee confidentiality/anonymity and researcher positionality

Given that this sample of participants are 'policymakers', many of whom hold, or who have in the past held, significant positions of power, with respect to the research topic under investigation, the common concern that the researcher, in the interview situation, is in a relative position of power over the participants plays out somewhat differently. A number of dynamics emerged over the course of the interviewing, including the researcher as 'guest' (Kvale 1996); researcher as 'student'; and researcher as 'journalist'. Researcher as 'guest', refers to a dynamic that emerged as a result of being invited in some cases to the home of a participant, where an ethos of 'politeness' and 'not being on one's own turf' can unconsciously affect the tone of the interview. The second metaphor, researcher as 'student' emerged where the participant typically of senior standing, in some cases, 'tested' the knowledge of the interviewer. This power dynamic, whereby the participant asserted their power over a situation where they were being asked questions, may also have been affected by the physical characteristics of both the interviewer and interviewee: where the researcher in many cases was much younger than those being interviewed, and in addition, female and of 'ethnic minority' appearance, and in contrast, the participants, in many cases were older, male and 'white'. Finally, by the third metaphor, researcher as 'journalist', I am referring to the idea that the participant, although in a relative position of power with respect to myself as interviewer, was concerned with the notion of confidentiality and the form that the reporting would take. These concerns emerged for various reasons, e.g. when a participant attempted to 'represent' the views of their organization, and hence there was a perceived sense of responsibility to the organization. In addition, certain participants were concerned that what they had said about others in the field would get back to them.

Given the nature of this sample of 'key players', I propose that the usual approach of the researcher automatically confirming anonymity and confidentiality is not necessarily appropriate in this case. Indeed, support for this approach can be found in the field where research has been conducted on the 'elite' in education (Ball 1994a; Mickelson 1994; Walford 1994). The standard approach of automatically conferring anonymity and confidentiality may not necessarily be appropriate, given that the sample was not a homogenous sample drawn from a larger sampling frame, but rather consisted of a heterogeneous group of individuals coming from a range of backgrounds bringing with them different interests. In addition, a number of the participants are well-known to the public, and it is often difficult to avoid identifying them given their key roles. As a consequence, when it comes to data analysis, it is arguable that it is particularly important to be able to attribute certain beliefs, views and attitudes to particular people, in order to make sense of the data. In addition, the typical power dynamics of the researcher in position of power in relation to the participants is somewhat different in the context of interviewing 'elites', or those in positions of relative power.

Nevertheless, the researcher does have an ethical responsibility to their interviewees in terms of the potential consequences of the interview on their participants (Punch 1998). Therefore, I decided that I would discuss the issue of confidentiality and anonymity individually with each participant. A sizeable majority stated that they were comfortable with me attributing the interview data to them personally, although a sizeable minority stated they would prefer it to be framed in terms of 'representative' of their organization. Other suggestions that arose included that I as the researcher, should make an appropriate judgement, and in some cases name them individually, and in other cases, in terms of organizational affiliation. A very small minority of participants stated that they would like to be able to approve the quotations and interpretations. Such requests have to be handled sensitively, as on the one hand, the researcher has an ethical duty to respect the views of the participant, yet on the other hand, the researcher must not be put in a position where the data is being censored inappropriately, or interpreted by the participants. Indeed, Cookson (1994), in his study of education decision-makers in the USA, argues that while interviewees have rights with regard to the ethical treatment of the interview data, these rights do not extend to the interpretation of the data itself. While it is important to act responsibly toward the participant and protect the participant, at the same time, the researcher has a responsibility towards the research community to accurately report research findings. I have endeavoured to act responsibly towards all participants by treating each case individually, and by making judgements with regard to attributing research findings at the most appropriate level of attribution in each case.

Given that I have been directly involved in policy developments relating to citizenship and citizenship education, this necessarily raises the question of my dual positioning as both 'researcher' and 'actor' in the policy domain. Being involved in developing policy – the original focus of my research means that I am no longer standing 'outside' the research frame. It could be argued that such dual positioning results in a loss of objectivity and could lead to bias in analysis and interpretation. In a related vein, the question of whether having a particular political position necessarily makes the research biased has been discussed in the literature (Griffiths 1998). Walford (2001) believes that 'partisanship' is compatible with social science research, arguing that research is conducted based on subjective political evaluations of what is important. This argument could also be extended to the question of involvement in the policy or practice under research investigation. It is important that the researchers be explicit and acknowledge their dual positioning. The primary aim of my research is that it contributes to developing theory, and therefore provides a potential contribution to the development of policy and practice.

## Scope, structure and content

Part 1 of this book examines the situational context of the development of citizenship education in England, which is important in order to understand the different conceptions of citizenship held by the 'key players' involved in the policy development process – the focus of Part 2 of the book. Chapter 1 situates the development of citizenship education in England in its 'multicultural' context, providing a brief historical overview to its development. In Chapter 2, I examine key players' understandings and perceptions of the development of citizenship education, including their perceptions of societal and other contextual influences, aims and outcomes, policymaking procedures and individual contributions. I discuss three main themes that emerged from the interview data. First, I note that interviewees emphasized the role of individuals relative to societal influences in their explanations of why citizenship education came onto the agenda, and I provide three explanatory models. Second, I examine the apparent lack of clarity with regard to expected aims and outcomes of citizenship education, and third, I illustrate that the workings of the Crick Advisory Group were not always perceived to be democratic or representative of diversity. Chapter 2 provides the context to understanding the key players' perceptions of citizenship, examined in Chapters 3, 4, 5 and 6.

In Part 2 'Conceptions of Citizenship', I provide an overview of the Crick Report's conceptions of citizenship in terms of the 'three strands', as well as considering its proposed 'distinctiveness' as a subject in the curriculum. I explain that I have identified and classified four main models of citizenship based on the views of the key players as well as analysis of key policy and curriculum documentation – which are the focus of the following four chapters. There are three 'dominant' conceptions, which I refer to as 'moral', 'legal' and 'participatory' conceptions of citizenship, with the 'participatory' conception being the most dominant of these conceptions. In contrast, interviewees also referred to 'underplayed' conceptions of citizenship – which I call 'identity-based conceptions' – as they are inherently concerned with 'identity', or forms of identification at different levels.

In Chapter 3, 'Moral' conceptions, I examine interviewees' different and sometimes conflicting understandings of citizenship framed in 'moral' terms. This includes such themes as perceptions of society in moral crisis (Beck 1998) and a perceived need to discover 'shared values' (Talbot and Tate 1997). Conflicting understandings of the nature of values also emerged, namely whether values refer to more 'procedural' aspects, e.g. respect for certain public institutions and the rule of law, or whether these refer to more personal, social and cultural values. Moreover, the concept of 'shared values' is used to challenge the support and endorsement of diversity. This chapter examines these themes in relation to contemporary societal and educational discourses and events, and other educational policies, exploring implications for theory and practice. I argue, however, that support for 'shared values' should not necessarily be problematic in an ethnically and religiously diverse society.

Chapter 4, 'Legal' conceptions illustrates conflicts arising from the different understandings of the key players regarding the relationship between citizenship and human rights. In contrast to the Crick Report, some of the interviewees propose a model of citizenship explicitly underpinned by human rights. This chapter cri- ( tiques the tendency among some human rights educators to conflate human rights and citizenship (Kiwan 2005), and argues for a clear conceptual understanding of these different although related concepts. Policy developments in relation to citizenship as a legal status – citizenship as nationality, are also examined. As in Chapter 3, theoretical and practical implications for ethnic and religious diversity are examined and discussed.

Chapter 5, 'Participatory' conceptions focuses on arguably the most dominant conception of citizenship, which I examine in relation to other related concepts, including 'democracy'. I show that there are differing views on the relationship between citizenship and democracy; furthermore, there were concerns expressed about a lack of conceptual clarity with regard to how democracy relates to such concepts as liberty, individualism and equality. I examine the theoretical and practical implications for diversity, and I argue that in order to be motivated to participate, citizens must be able to identify with, or feel a sense of belonging to the larger community.

In Chapter 6, 'Identity-based' conceptions, this set of underplayed conceptions include national, European, and global framings of citizenship, as well as citizenship presented as a framework for anti-racist education, and finally, 'multicultural' citizenship. A key theme that emerges is that diversity is often perceived to be conceptually and politically problematic. In addition, diversity is conceptualized differently at different stages of the policy and curriculum development process. I examine the implications for ethnic and religious diversity of the different identity-based conceptions of citizenship.

Developing themes from Parts 1 and 2 of the book, Part 3 develops a theory of inclusive citizenship and outlines implications for practice. In Chapter 7, I propose an inclusive model of citizenship, by drawing both on my empirical data, and developing certain relevant themes raised in the politico-philosophical literature on citizenship (Kymlicka 1995, 2003; Parekh 2000; Spinner-Halev 2003). This model consists of two main components: 'institutional' multiculturalism, constituted as a process, and a greater emphasis on the citizen-state relationship, relative to the emphasis on the relationship between individuals and groups from different backgrounds and cultures which is the predominant focus of 'interculturalism' (Gundara 2003; Kymlicka 2003).

In the final chapter, Chapter 8, I provide practical examples at the level of policy, curriculum and pedagogic practice of how to achieve a more inclusive citizenship, based on my theoretical model developed in Chapter 7. I illustrate how policymakers, teachers and other practitioners can draw on the four models of citizenship examined in Chapters 3–6 in Part 2, to promote an inclusive citizenship in practice.

It is expected that this book will primarily be of interest to academics and postgraduate students in the fields of educational studies (philosophy and sociology of education), as well as those in politics and sociology departments with interests in the interdisciplinary fields of citizenship, multiculturalism, social justice and ethnic studies. It may also be useful for students and teachers on postgraduate (PGCE) and Continuing Professional Development (CPD) courses in citizenship education, and other practitioners and policymakers in the field.

# Part 1

# The development of citizenship education

# 1 Citizenship education in England

## Setting the scene

> Multiculturalism is not about difference and identity per se but about those differences that are embedded in and sustained by culture; that is a body of beliefs and practices in terms of which a group of people understand themselves and the world and organise their individual and collective lives. Unlike differences that spring from individual choices, culturally derived differences carry a measure of authority and are gathered and structured by virtue of being embedded in a shared and historically inherited system of meaning and significance
>
> (Parekh 2000: 23)

## The UK as a multicultural society?

The UK is both a 'multination' state and a 'polyethnic' state, in that there are a large number of different ethnic and religious groups, largely a result of mass immigration[1] since the Second World War. In the seventeenth century, citizenship in Britain could be understood in terms of the aristocracy dissolving feudal ties and promoting the notion of equality of opportunity; this was further challenged in the nineteenth and twentieth centuries by the working classes fighting for not only equality of opportunity but equality of outcome (Rex 1991). T. H. Marshall's social democratic conception of citizenship, developed within the socialist tradition in the context of class struggle (Marshall and Bottomore 1992) built on this, arguing that the national identity of citizenship would replace class identity (Rex 1991).

British national identity has historically been formulated implicitly rather than explicitly (Grillo 1998). In the eighteenth century, the concept of national identity was one that was superimposed over internal differences between Wales, Scotland and England, and arose reactively as a consequence of contact with France; British identity was construed as a Protestant as opposed to a Catholic identity (Colley 1992, cited in Grillo 1998). However, British nationalism has not managed to supersede Scottish, Welsh or Irish nationalism (Rex 1991). With regard to English nationalism, despite England's dominant position within the Union, the English did not, to the same extent, develop a separate English identity, as in Scotland, Wales or Ireland. While Scottish and Welsh nationalism have been encouraged and celebrated, English nationalism has been treated with suspicion and associated with the politics of far-Right groups (Colley 1992, cited in Grillo 1998). However, over the last few years, there has been a significant change, with such symbols as the flag of St George being re-claimed from far-Right groups, and the notion of 'Englishness' being openly discussed (e.g. Blunkett's talk to the Institute of Public Policy Research (IPPR) on 'Englishness', March 2005). This lack of a unified concept of 'Britishness' has been explained in terms of globalization, Britain's declining economic power coupled with the collapse of the Empire, Britain's changing relationship with Europe, devolution and increased pluralism (Runnymede Trust 2000).

Grillo (1998) proposes that 'Britishness' has been defined by means of contrast with an 'other', as well as through reference to certain values and institutions within the historical tradition, which provides a framework for understanding what it means to be 'British' in the contemporary context. He goes on to argue that these ways of defining 'Britishness' were not inherently racialized, although from the mid-twentieth century onwards, racialized discourses have been implicitly coupled to discourses on national identity (Grillo 1998). This can be understood in the context of post-war mass immigration predominantly from the former colonies of the British Empire (Runnymede Trust 2000), and more recently, perceived threats to liberties arising from international terrorism (Pattie *et al.* 2004).

A shift in approach can be noted with the introduction of the first Act to Control Commonwealth Immigration in 1962 (Rex 1991). Before this time, immigrants of the Commonwealth who were British could settle in Britain, but after 1962, controls became much more restrictive. However, a selective immigration rule was introduced whereby those immigrants who could illustrate a long-established family connection with Britain, were allowed to settle (Rex 1991). In practice, this was a means of exclusion on the basis of skin colour, as it allowed white Commonwealth immigrants in, while excluding predominantly black and Asian immigrants (Rex 1991). However, this did not alter the fact that there was by this time, already a large non-white population settled in Britain, and hence the government was concerned with the 'integration' of these immigrants. The Race Relations Act was passed in 1976, and the Commission for Racial Equality was set-up with the remit to promote 'race relations' and tackle racial discrimination.

In contrast to the relation between 'race'/ethnicity and state, the relation between religion and state is less explicit, as Britain is not a completely secular state, with the Anglican Archbishop of Canterbury crowning the monarch, and having high profile on many public occasions (Rex 1991). Islam has been high on the public agenda both nationally and internationally, particularly more recently, given the events of 11 September 2001, and the London Bombings in 7 July 2005. It could be argued that the position of Islam and Muslim immigrants in contemporary Britain is similar to the position of Catholicism in Britain in the nineteenth and early twentieth century. The British nation was characterized by Protestantism, as opposed to Catholicism, and Protestantism was the foundation of English liberties (Ballance 1995). In contrast, Catholicism was not only considered alien to being British, but Catholics were considered disloyal, as their loyalty was to the Pope, rather than to the state (Ballance 1995). Public discourses on Islam echo some of these same assumptions. Islam is typically cast as being in opposition to Britain's liberal ideals, exemplified by the Rushdie Affair (Modood 1992). The loyalty of British Muslims has also continued to be a topic of debate, with a concern that British Muslims' loyalty is first and foremost to Islam, rather than to the state. There is also a concern that Islam cannot restrict itself to the private sphere, and hence is fundamentally opposed to secularism in the public sphere, in contrast to Protestantism. Indeed, Ballance (1995) has noted the inextricable link between Protestantism and secularism, arguing that secularism arose from within Protestantism, rather than as a radical break with Protestantism. However, British attitudes towards Islam cannot simply be understood in terms of an analogy with Catholicism in the nineteenth and early twentieth century. Islam is also presented in public discourse as dangerous and violent, especially since the events of 11 September 2001. Yet at the same time, this has highlighted the problem of 'Islamophobia', with the British government making a point of stressing that the contemporary 'war on terrorism' is not a war or crusade on Islam.

It has been argued that Britain's approach to its immigrant communities has moved from 'assimilation' towards 'integration' over the last 50 years (Grillo 1998). Grillo (1998) notes that the term, 'integration' has been used ambiguously and inconsistently in public discourse; e.g. Enoch Powell using it as a synonym for 'assimilation', whereas Roy Jenkins, Labour Home Secretary in 1966, explicitly defined it as 'not as a flattening process of assimilation but as equal opportunity, coupled with cultural diversity, in an atmosphere of mutual tolerance' (Jenkins 1967, cited in Grillo 1998: 267).

### Policy discourses – 'multiculturalism' or 'integration with diversity'?

Discourses of multiculturalism can be seen in educational policies dominant in the 1980s, exemplified by a 'multicultural' approach to education. Many teachers were primarily concerned with two issues: the educational underachievement of ethnic minorities, and including non-British culture, literature and history within the British curriculum (Grillo 1998). Ethnic minority underachievement was in part attributed to low self-esteem, so a range of different pedagogical approaches were used with the aim of promoting a more positive identity for ethnic minority students. Likewise in the USA, there has been pedagogical and curriculum reform in the name of multiculturalism. Schlesinger (1992: 17) has criticized these approaches, arguing that the American public education system should not have as its main objective 'the protection, strengthening and perpetuation of ethnic origins and identities', but rather that its aim should be to strengthen the bonds of national cohesion. In a similar vein more recently, also in the US context, Huntingdon (2004) has fervently argued in favour of national identity, advocating that liberals should re-claim this territory.

The rationale behind broadening out the curriculum was that it would benefit both ethnic minority and ethnic majority students, supported by the Swann Report's 'Education for All' (Grillo 1998). Goulbourne (1991) suggests that the

1988 Education Act reflects both the dominant ethnic nationalism of the majority population, evident in the formulation of a 'National Curriculum', and also the commitment to new pluralism, as represented in the Swann Report, with concern for provision for religious education. This form of 'soft' multiculturalism, associated with the Swann Report, has since fallen from favour in schools, as it is perceived to merely exoticize ethnic minorities, rather than effectively addressing structural disadvantage and inequalities (Watson 2000). Human rights and anti-racist education approaches have often been embraced in light of such criticisms. However, these approaches do not allow for a critical dialogue between the dominant and minority cultures, and tend to focus on outcome, rather than process.

Gillborn (1999) argues that New Labour's policy narrative 'remakes Thatcher's "Britain" in all key aspects' – with its conception of nation similarly drawing on the 'new racism' framed in terms of cultural difference rather than racial superiority (Barker 1981, cited in Gillborn 1999: 89); he also notes that race equality was absent as an issue in the 1997 general election. With regard to educational policies more specifically, the DfEE White Paper 'Excellence in Schools' made explicit references to racial inequalities in education (DfEE 1997). Gillborn (1999) notes, however, that this consists of only two paragraphs in an 80-page document, and that it is limited in scope to 'ethnic minority achievement' and 'racial harmony' rather than relating to all the proposals within the document such as teacher education, testing and selection, which continue to be treated in colour-blind terms.

In contrast to these approaches, Watson (2000) highlights the role of 'critical' multiculturalism (as opposed to 'soft' multiculturalism), citing as examples, the revision of curricula and the establishment of faith schools. The state has historically funded Christian and Jewish faith schools, and there is currently a commitment to do the same for Islamic schools; an issue raised by the Runnymede Trust in 1997, in its consultation paper on 'Islamophobia' (Grillo 1998). Annette (2005) suggests that government commitment to faith schools reflects the influence of communitarian thinking, and also the belief that faith schools have a role in increasing social capital and contributing to active citizenship. However, this government support has resulted in much debate, with those supporting the maintenance of faith-based schools arguing in terms of equality of treatment between different religious groups (Pring 2005); parents' rights to a diversity of choice with respect to the education of their children, that such schools provide a strong moral framework; and also that they are often academically successful (Parker-Jenkins 2005). Although the number of requests for such stated-funded Islamic schools are very small (Gates 2005), critics argue that separate faith schools are divisive and not conducive to community cohesion (Mason 2005), and indeed antithetical to the liberal aims of education (Brighouse 2005; Pring 2005). The British Humanist Association opposes religious schools on the grounds that they are discriminatory, and that religion should remain within the 'private' sphere; instead they propose inclusive pluralist community schools 'to meet the requirements of both the religious and non-religious without compromising the human rights and educational entitlements of all pupils' (Mason 2005: 74). While the Cantle Report (Home Office 2001a) does not argue against separate faith schools, it does in general favour a multi-faith approach with proposals of partnerships between different communities and schools, and that faith schools be required to accept a quota of pupils from other faiths.

There has been a growing discontent in popular discourses with the term, 'multiculturalism' (e.g. Alibhai-Brown 2000; Blunkett, quoted in *The Independent on Sunday*, 9 December 2001: 4; Trevor Phillips, quoted in *The Times*, 3 April 2004; Polly Toynbee, *The Guardian*, 7 April 2004). 'Multiculturalism' is a contested term and there is no agreed-upon definition of what it pertains to or represents. Multiculturalism has come to be misconstrued as about, and for minorities, and in effect, has supported the image of a homogeneous majority and small pockets of 'unmeltable' minorities (Anthias and Yuval-Davis 1993). This is sometimes referred to as 'mosaic' multiculturalism – where a number of different communities or cultures live side-by-side with one another, with differences seen to be kept distinct (Joppke and Lukes 1999). Here, culture is conceptualized in a relatively deterministic, bounded way. This is contrasted with 'hodgepodge' multiculturalism, which is conceptualized in terms of hybridity and mixing, with an acknowledgement that culture is not static, but is in a state of flux (Joppke and Lukes 1999). Multiculturalism as a concept is increasingly being cast as unhelpful and inappropriate: 'speaking to the past, not the future' (Alibhai-Brown 2000: 11), that it is 'static and divisive' and it is being accused of 'woolly liberalism' (Alibhai-Brown 2000: 7).

One reason may be that multiculturalism has come to be seen as a critique of Western universalism and liberalism (Joppke and Lukes 1999). In this type of account, multiculturalism is conceptualized as a reaction against the dominant discourse of universalism and 'shared values'. This is exemplified when Blunkett, the former Home Secretary called on ethnic minorities to adopt British 'norms of acceptability', when he said: 'and those that come into our home – for that is what it is – should accept those norms' – where he was presumably referring to new immigrants (*The Independent on Sunday*, 9 December 2001: 1). This suggests a conception of culture as static, with an underlying assumption that the priority is to maintain the status quo.

Delanty (2003: 93) explains that European multiculturalism emerged in the 1960s and 1970s, as an 'extension of liberal tolerance rather than aiming at participation', and was not meant as a model for bringing about societal change. Parekh (2000) argues however, that there is terminological confusion, proposing that 'multiculturalism' is not merely a *descriptor* of a given society, but rather refers to (or should refer to) the society's *response* to a given multicultural setting. Similarly, Sen (2006) argues that typically what tends to be erroneously labeled as multiculturalism – where different communities live separately side-by-side, is in fact, 'plural monoculturalism'.

There has also been a critique of multiculturalism from within anti-racist discourses, which has been ongoing over the last two decades (Gillborn 2004). These critiques can be traced back to the 1980s, with one of the most well-known catchphrases critiquing multiculturalism coined by Troyna – 'the three S's – saris, samosas and steelbands' (Troyna 1984). This refers to the exoticization of minority cultures and the presentation of only a superficial characterization of the given minority culture(s). Furthermore, multiculturalism is presented as relatively ineffective, as well as tokenistic. Proponents of multiculturalism have attempted to respond to these criticisms by re-inventing and re-naming multiculturalism as 'critical' multiculturalism (May 1994; Watson 2000), which aims to be more pro-active and less 'celebratory' in its emphasis.

The theme of 'Integration with diversity' has become dominant in contemporary policy discourses (Home Office 2001a,b, 2002), presented in the form of the concepts of 'shared values', 'community cohesion' and 'integration with diversity'. The 2002 Home Office White Paper, *Secure Borders, Safe Haven: Integration with Diversity in modern Britain*, emphasizes the public/private sphere distinction, with promulgation of citizenship as 'shared' public culture, and the practice of minority cultures occurring in the private sphere of family and local community (Rex 1995). Similarly, in the Community Cohesion Review ('Cantle Report') – set up after inter ethnic group violence in the summer of 2001 in a number of cities in England, the idea of achieving 'shared' values is framed in terms of social cohesion and linked to discourses of social capital, social inclusion and citizenship (Home Office 2001a), with calls for citizenship education to address these issues (Home Office 2001a,b, 2002). In a speech on community cohesion given by Minister Bill Rammell in May 2006, he launched the DfES Diversity and Citizenship review in terms of 'examining how we can incorporate modern British cultural and social history into the curriculum within our secondary schools' (Rammell 2006). Since November 2006, a new statutory requirement (Education and Inspections Act 2006) has been introduced putting a duty on schools to promote community cohesion (DfES 2006), with a requirement on OFSTED to inspect schools in relation to promoting community cohesion from September 2007. This requirement was seen as a compromise after the failure to secure agreement that all faith schools must accept a 25 per cent quota of pupils from other faiths (*The Independent*, 31 October 2006). Prime Minister Blair's speech 'Our Nation's Future – multiculturalism and integration' (8 December 2006) exemplifies the continuing theme of balancing integration with diversity.

## The development of citizenship education in the UK 'multicultural' context

The history of citizenship education in England is often typically traced back to the nineteenth century Victorian context (Batho 1990; Lawton 2000). Education in general had clear social and moral purposes, with public schools preparing the upper classes for leadership in England and the Empire, in contrast to education for the poor serving a quite different purpose – in effect, teaching them to accept their position in society, with a clear moral purpose, which is explicitly articulated in the Elementary Code of 1904:

> The purpose of the Public Elementary School is to form and strengthen the character and to develop the intelligence ... assisting both girls and boys,

according to their different needs, to fit themselves, practically as well as intellectually for the work of life

Gordon and Lawton 1978, cited in Batho 1990: 92

In relation to citizenship more specifically, at the turn of the century, a book entitled *The Teaching of History and Civics in the Elementary and the Secondary School*, by Bourne was published, in which he proposed that pupils must be taught both about the structure of government, and the individual's related duties, and also the application of these duties in the school context as training for adult life (Batho 1990). The former was generally accepted, however the latter was more controversial, with few schools approving of this or putting it into practice (Batho 1990).

The importance of local community was a prominent theme by the 1920s, influenced by Dewey (Batho 1990). In the 1920s, it was widely thought that citizenship should be taught through traditional school subjects such as History, Geography and Religious Knowledge, what Lawton (2000) refers to as the 'indirect training' approach. But by the 1930s, the climate had changed, with a 'direct training' approach being advocated, with a more traditional 'civics' curriculum involving describing British institutions and outlining related rights and duties, rather than teaching citizenship in context.

However, the Spens Report (1938) and the Norwood Report (1943) did not support the direct training approach, and instead proposed that pupils under 16 should study History and Geography (Lawton 2000). In 1945, the direct training approach was revived by the Council for Curriculum Reform, which advocated social studies as a compulsory core subject, but this view did not have much influence in post-war England (Lawton 2000), and in fact, social studies (and citizenship) were associated with the lower achievers in the 1950s and 1960s (Batho 1990). During the 1960s, there were moves to explicitly develop Social Studies teaching in schools – including the subjects of sociology, economics and political science (Lawton 2000). This tended to focus on teaching older pupils, but some advocated much earlier teaching, e.g. Bernard Crick – who was involved in the 'Programme for Political Education' (PPE) in the 1970s (Davies 1999a; Lawton 2000). In part, the development of political education was accepted because of the lowering of the voting age to 18 in 1970 (Davies 1999a). This programme aimed to develop critical knowledge and promote skills for active participation (Crick and Porter 1978). However, this political literacy project did not come to fruition with the Conservatives coming into power in 1979, and a range of new education programmes broadly committed to social justice took hold in the 1980s, for example, 'peace education', 'anti-sexist education' and 'anti-racist education', reflecting wider public debates (Davies 1999a).

After the 1988 Education Reform Act introducing the National Curriculum, the National Curriculum Council (NCC) proposed citizenship as one of a number of cross-curricular themes. But as this was non-statutory, it got squeezed out of the curriculum (Lawton 2000). In the early 1990s, in the context of a climate of rising moral panic with traditionalists mourning the situation that religion no longer provides an agreed morality framework in England's now increasingly multicultural society (Beck 1998), the Schools Curriculum and Assessment Authority (SCAA) in 1996, set-up the National Forum for Values in Education and the Community in order 'to discover whether there are any values upon which there is agreement across society', and 'to decide how best society in general, and SCAA in particular might support schools in the task of promoting pupils' spiritual, social and cultural development' (Talbot and Tate 1997: 2). There were 150 members drawn from across society, who drew up a statement of values relating to: the self, relationships, society and the environment. The statement, paradoxically, came under bitter attack from neo-conservatives, who were scathing that such a disparate group of individuals came up with what they considered to be a weak and meaningless set of watered-down, 'politically correct' values (Beck 1998).

Nick Tate, then Chief Executive of SCAA, was particularly concerned with the idea of national identity and the need for 'social cohesion', arguing that the National Curriculum should play a key role in fostering a national identity (Beck 1998). It has been argued that Tate's views illustrate support for, and attempts made to 'preserve' majority culture (Beck 1998); there was a diagnosis of society in moral decline, explained in terms of a move away from 'traditional values', with the assumption that this had resulted in a moral vacuum. The solution to society's troubles was assumed to lie in resurrecting or reconstructing 'shared values' for society (Beck 1998). Osler (2000) has also highlighted that there is a dominant discourse of a deficit model of young people, citing extreme cases sensationalized in the press, such as the Jamie Bulger case in the 1990s, and the murder of Stephen Lawrence. There has also been a rising concern with perceived political apathy, particularly of young people (Pattie *et al.* 2004).

A historical shift occurred with the policy review of citizenship education undertaken in 1998 by the Advisory Group on Education for Citizenship and the Teaching of Democracy in Schools, chaired by Bernard Crick (Kerr 2000a). This Group was set up by David Blunkett in 1997, and managed by QCA, following the decision to strengthen the teaching of citizenship in schools, which was presented in the 1997 Education White Paper, *Excellence in Schools* (Kerr 2000b). The Advisory Group was intended to be non-partisan, and was made-up of practitioners with relevant experience, teachers, members of relevant organizations and those with political expertise.

Some of the main recommendations of the Advisory Group included that citizenship education would be a statutory 'entitlement', and also that it would be a separate subject rather than a cross-curricular theme (QCA 1998). The conceptualization of citizenship in the Crick Report, defined in terms of the three 'strands' of social and moral responsibility, community involvement, and political literacy, largely derives from T. H. Marshall's conceptualization of citizenship as being made up of three elements: civil, political and social citizenship (Marshall and Bottomore 1992), although it lacks Marshall's emphasis on rights. The explicit emphasis on 'shared values', the central preoccupation of the National Forum for Values, was subsequently downplayed in the Crick Report (QCA 1998). Learning outcomes for each key stage were outlined in terms of four elements: (1) concepts, (2) values and dispositions, (3) skills and aptitudes and (4) knowledge and understanding (QCA 1998). The proposed learning outcomes in the curriculum materials, the Programmes of Study and Schemes of Work are presented in terms of three categories: 'knowledge and understanding', 'skills of enquiry and communication' and 'skills of participation and responsible action' (QCA 2000, 2001).

The Crick Report highlights as particularly important, the recognition of the importance of the ethos, organization and practices of schools as having a significant impact on the effectiveness of citizenship education (Scott 2000). In addition, it identifies a number of key concepts, including: 'democracy and autocracy', 'cooperation and conflict', 'equality and diversity', 'fairness, justice and rule of law', 'rules, law and human rights', 'freedom and order', 'individual and community', 'power and authority', 'rights and responsibilities' (QCA 1998).

The 1998 Report of the Advisory Group (Crick Report) was largely welcomed by government and 'Citizenship' was introduced as a new statutory foundation subject in secondary schools, and part of the non-statutory framework within Personal, Social and Health Education (PSHE) in primary schools in September 2002. Most recently, the DfES Diversity and Citizenship review recommended the addition of an additional 'fourth' strand, entitled 'Identity and Diversity: Living together in the United Kingdom' (Ajegbo *et al.* 2007). This has been incorporated into the newly drafted QCA Programmes of Study launched for public consultation in February 2007 (QCA 2007), to be published in September 2007, and to be implemented in schools from September 2008.

# 2 Key players' perceptions

Influences, processes, aims and contributions[1]

The focus of this chapter – based primarily on the analysis of interview data, is on key players' understandings of how citizenship education developed, which entailed exploring the range of perspectives of those involved in the citizenship education development process. It examines key players' understandings of a number of themes, including: Why did citizenship education come onto the agenda at this time? What are the aims and outcomes of citizenship education? What are the perceptions on representation and decision-making of those involved within the policy development process? What do they consider their perceived expertise and contributions to be? This chapter aims to provide a context to understanding key players' conceptions of citizenship and diversity, the focus of Part 2 of this book (Chapters 3–6), which similarly draws on the interview data but also includes an analysis of the concepts of 'citizenship' and 'diversity' in key policy and curriculum documentation (QCA 1998, 2000, 2001). These conceptions are examined in light of the newly proposed changes to the citizenship education curriculum (Ajegbo *et al.* 2007; QCA 2007).

## Reasons behind the 'initiative': why now?

### The power of the individual

What is immediately striking from the analysis of the interview data in relation to interviewees' perceptions of the reasons behind the initiative, is that almost two-thirds of those interviewed referred to the political will of certain key individuals as being of central importance. In particular, David Blunkett and Sir Bernard Crick were named by the majority of those who stressed the central importance of certain individuals in this process. While there was acknowledgement of a range of other factors involved in precipitating this most recent citizenship education initiative in England, interviewees emphasized the significance of *individuals*, rather than *societal* factors. This is exemplified by the comments of 'B', a member of the Advisory Group on Citizenship, when asked specifically about this relative emphasis:

> Yes, but then I'm a politician if you like, or political science is my background.
> I see the outcome of politics being the result of inputs, and inputs being the

people doing things behind the scenes. I don't see ... a kind of sociologically cultural climate that brought that about ... because I know more about what conversations took place in the corridors of power

(Interview with 'B', member of Crick Advisory Group: 3)

This was also the perception of the named individuals themselves. Crick referred to the 'will of Blunkett' (Interview with Sir Bernard Crick: 4) in precipitating the initiative. Distinguishing between theory and practice, there is an implicit echo of 'B's relative emphasis on personal as opposed to societal influences: 'I can give you all kinds of reasons why it should have come as we stated in the Report, but ... alas, politics doesn't move through reason. I wish it did' (p. 4). Yet there is an acknowledgement of intellectual influences in his assertion that 'It's a coincidence of *ideas* [italics added] and individuals' (p. 4), possibly a specific reference to his own intellectual influence both on Blunkett, and the actual conception of citizenship itself in the policy and curriculum documentation (QCA 1998, 2000, 2001).

David Blunkett also stressed the role of individuals, including himself:

Well, a lot of people have been battering at the door on this for decades, so I don't pretend that I've invented something new or solely been responsible. What I've done is I've made possible what others have pressed for ... so I got hold of my old professor, Bernard Crick, and said, "let's go for it"

(Interview with David Blunkett: 1)

The importance of Crick, and Blunkett, then Secretary of State for Education in 1997 with New Labour coming into power, is certainly considered to be of key importance in the literature (Kerr 2000a,b). Yet the role of these individuals is set in the wider context of a range of socio-political forces and events (Osler 2000; Pattie *et al.* 2004). One interpretation for why interviewees placed a greater emphasis on certain key individuals' roles than on societal issues/context could be an artefact of the order of the interview's questions or themes. While the interview was semi-structured, and each interview was tailored to each individual interviewee, in general interviews began by asking about the nature of the interviewee's involvement in the citizenship education development process, before asking them for their views on the impetus for the citizenship education 'initiative'. The rationale behind this was that beginning the interview in this way would put interviewees at ease. However, this approach focuses on them as individuals, and perhaps may have unconsciously biased them into framing their answers to the subsequent question at the level of the person/individual, rather than taking into account, broader societal factors. It may also be, that given that many of those interviewed are 'powerful' actors within the citizenship education domain, they may have a heightened sense of personal agency, with a tendency to play down the role of societal influences.

Similarly, emphasis on the perceived importance of certain key individuals is also evident in the 2006 Department for Education and Skill's (DfES) review of Citizenship. Having consulted extensively throughout 2006 with academics, policymakers, practitioners, subject associations and other 'experts' working in the field of citizenship and other related domains, we noted that there was a dominant perception among interviewees that Gordon Brown, Chancellor of the Exchequer, had played a major role both in initiating the review at this time, and particularly in influencing the framing of its terms of reference of the review (Ajegbo *et al.* 2007). Indeed, Brown has given a number of high-profile speeches on Britishness emphasizing the role of history in defining 'Britishness' and 'shared values' (Brown 2004, 2006).

### *Societal influences*

From the previous section, what we learn from interviewees who had both direct and indirect involvement in the process, as well as the named key individuals themselves, is that 'powerful' individuals were clearly perceived to have been central in getting citizenship and citizenship education onto the agenda. Individuals however did also refer to a range of other influences in the context of getting citizenship education onto the agenda in the late 1990s, which I have coded into seven main categories. Table 2.1 ranks in descending order of most frequently referred to, the range of influences considered to be influential by interviewees:

*Table 2.1* Influences on initiative as perceived by interviewees, ranked in descending order of frequency

*Reasons given*

1. Political apathy of young people
2. Society in moral crisis
3. Democratic crisis/low voter turnout
4. Legal changes (e.g. Europe/HR Act)
5. Diversity/Immigration issues
6. Education – move away from 'standards' emphasis
7. Re-negotiation between 'citizen' and 'state'

Diversity/immigration issues are ranked relatively low, coming fifth out of seven main categories. Only four out of the 30 interviewees referred to societal diversity at all as an explanatory factor. All four were women and three of the four were of ethnic minority. What is also of note is that only one out of the four was directly involved as a member of the Advisory Group. According to this interviewee, she stated that 'For me the context was the kind of Stephen Lawrence and the morality of that, and how it brought to the fore many issues. One is how vulnerable are young people to the issue of race' (Interview with 'I': 2).

One possible interpretation of this is that those individuals who are members of groups who may have been traditionally excluded from the full rights of citizenship, may have a greater awareness of the relationship between citizenship and diversity and the potential role of citizenship in empowering those from traditionally excluded groups. These interviewees noted that the themes of diversity, identity and 'race' were relatively underplayed in relation to citizenship in policy and curriculum documentation (QCA 1998, 2000, 2001).

These interviewee perceptions echo multicultural and feminist critiques of liberalism and liberal conceptions of citizenship, which argue that the theoretical conceptions of citizenship are only partial and biased representations based on the needs and defining features of only a restricted group within society (predominantly Western white men). This, in turn, relates to the questioning of the public/private sphere distinction that is made in theories of citizenship, which has been raised from a feminist perspective (Jones 1998). Jones (1998) argues for space for the private within the political scope of an understanding of citizenship, an argument which can also be applied to ethnic and religious diversity, and other personal aspects of an individual's identity that may affect how they exercise, experience and conceptualize citizenship. Blunkett's commitment to political literacy and how this can facilitate 'how you bring about change' (Interview with David Blunkett: 4) reflects his concern with personal empowerment. This can be understood in terms of Blunkett's personal experience and characteristics, given his own personal story of overcoming adversity and achieving great success (*The Times T2* 18 August 2004: 4–5). Indeed, one interviewee explains David Blunkett's commitment to citizenship in these terms:

> David Blunkett initiated it as a Minister of Education, but what triggered it in his mind … comes from his own disability … I wonder whether it would be anything more than paying lipservice for Estelle [Morris] … cause she's not disabled. I think his disability … [or for example] minority ethnic grouping … you're much more aware of where you feel society is not catering to your needs individually, and where society is not tolerant of the problems you have
>
> (Interview with TTA employee: 10)

However, while Blunkett's personal experiences and identity are reflected in his commitment to personal empowerment, this does not lead him to question the public/private sphere distinction. His commitment to liberalism's distinction between the public and private spheres can also be seen in the 2002 Home Office White Paper, *Secure Borders, Safe Haven: Integration with Diversity in modern Britain* (Home Office 2002), when David Blunkett was Home Secretary.

With regard to the theme of immigration, only two of the interviewees referred to the issues surrounding immigration and asylum seekers as explanatory factors, arguing that, typically these issues are framed as a problem:

> I think with the increase in concern and anxiety and focus on issues around migration of asylum seekers, issues of citizenship are being raised in terms of who isn't a citizen, as well as who is … they shot up to the centre of the agenda
>
> (Interview with 'C': 3)

In part, the relative lack of reference to this issue in relation to citizenship may be related to political sensitivities at the time relating to the contentiousness surrounding the introduction of citizenship education itself, as well as regarding 'race' and diversity in the context of talking about citizenship. It may also relate to the fact that the complexity of issues surrounding citizenship, immigration, asylum seekers and refugees is not explicitly addressed in either the policy or curriculum documentation, which Crick argued was a deliberate strategy.[2]

Over the last 5 years, there has been an increasing awareness among current 'key players' and in public discourses of the importance of addressing issues of identity and diversity within citizenship, in contrast to interviewees' perceptions in 2002 (Education and Skills Select Committee 2006; Ajegbo *et al.* 2007). It is also interesting to note that the new priorities of the Commission of Racial Equality (CRE) over the last 2–3 years entail that citizenship and nationality have been made a significant focus of work, explicitly bringing together work on 'race', the CRE's traditional focus with a new focus on citizenship (CRE 2006). These conceptual shifts are discussed in Chapter 6, which focuses on 'identity-based' conceptions of citizenship.

## *Explanatory models*

While the issue of societal, as well as personal influences that have contributed to citizenship and citizenship education coming onto the contemporary agenda is discussed in the literature (e.g. Beck 1998; Osler 2000; Pattie *et al.* 2004), what is of note, however, is *how* contemporary societal discourses and events have actually impacted on, or resulted in citizenship education coming onto the political agenda, and the form it takes is not substantively addressed.

Interviewees often cited more than one of the seven domains of influence (see Table 2.1) and hence these categories are not mutually exclusive. How the various influences as listed in Table 2.1 actually culminated in the citizenship education initiative coming onto the agenda when it did in the late 1990s is not self-evident. I do not attempt to provide causal explanations with regard to how factors have influenced the form of citizenship; rather, I am interested in the *perceptions* of key players with regard to these issues, and based on these perceptions, I propose three types of explanatory model.

The first model is the 'cocktail' model. This is where a complex interaction of personal and societal influences is referred to:

> It's actually a complex process which is dependent on characters, luck, lots of different factors come together, some long term factors and some initial ones ... but basically the underlying thing was sufficient head of steam within the public arena. The Secretary of State for Education is very keen on the area and has a past record in it, so you need a political push and all that comes together in that mix of character and personalities and luck and judgement
> (Interview with David Kerr, Professional Officer at QCA and Secretary to the Crick Advisory Group: 2)

The 'mixing' of these influences was perceived to culminate in bringing the initiative onto the agenda. In addition to key individuals being referred to, references were made to the *perceived* disengagement from the political process – particularly by the young – constitutional change and diversity. It was also suggested that citizenship's heightened profile on the public agenda can, in part, be explained in terms of 'the anxiety of politicians worrying that there is some kind of threat to democracy and in particular because of lack of voting amongst young people' (Interview with 'C': 2).

Politicians' perceptions, however, do not wholly correspond to empirical evidence. While there is evidence that there has been a decline at the level of formal political participation in the form of voting in general and local elections over the last 20 years (Pattie *et al.* 2004), this cannot simply be attributed to the apathy of the young. Pattie *et al.* (2004) in their UK ESRC-funded study on 'Democracy and Participation' with a sample of over 12 000, showed that while those aged over 65 are relatively more satisfied with how British democracy works[3] than those under 65, there is no statistical difference in attitudes between those under age 24 and those over aged 24. Therefore, this suggests that the young (under age 24) are not necessarily more cynical about democracy than older adults, as assumed by politicians. In addition, if political participation is construed more broadly to include such activities as contacting an MP, or contacting the media, for example, the situation is not as straightforward or as bleak as has been portrayed by politicians. Pattie *et al.* (2004) showed that both the old (over age 65) and the young (under age 24) are less politically active than those in 'middle' age (aged between 25–65), yet the young are more likely to engage in collective[4] political actions than their older counterparts.

With regard to ethnicity, Pattie *et al.* (2004) discovered that ethnic minorities are relatively more satisfied with how democracy works than are those of 'white/European' ethnic designation. However, with regard to religion, the 'religious' tend to be less satisfied than the 'non-religious', although this trend was not statistically significant (Pattie *et al.* 2004). This could be interpreted that the public/private sphere distinction is less accommodating of religion than ethnicity, resulting in those designated as 'religious' in this study, being relatively more dissatisfied than the 'non-religious'. Given that public discourses have been increasingly focused on Islam, especially since 11 September 2001 and more recently the 7 July 2005 London bombings, it would have been informative to have a breakdown by religion in order to investigate whether there were differences between religious groups themselves. The finding on ethnicity is counter-intuitive, and raises the question of whether this effect would disappear or indeed be reversed, if other variables such as education and income were controlled for.

The media has a key role in the second explanatory model, the 'trigger' model. In this type of model, there was a perception that there are a large number of influences, but that there was one key incident that is the 'last straw that breaks the camel's back', which triggered public outrage and created a climate conducive to the acceptance of the policy initiative. The media plays a key role in contributing to a public climate of fear and outrage, acting as catalyst. References were typically made to key crime cases in the early 1990s, notably the Jamie Bulger murder, where a 2-year-old boy was murdered by two 10 year olds; the murder of the head teacher, Philip Lawrence, and the Dunblane school massacre. In these cases, children and young people were perceived to have a lack of acceptable standards of behaviour, due to a lack of a values consensus in society (Beck 1998), with the result that there is rising crime and a lack of respect for authority. According to one member of the Crick Advisory Group, the Jamie Bulger murder was the 'trigger' (Interview with 'V': 1), with schools being apportioned some of the blame for not playing 'more of a role'.

While previously, society's perceived moral crisis has predominantly been framed in terms of a lack of acceptable standards of behaviour of the young, the new perceived threat is being increasingly framed in terms of the dangers of diversity. Debates surrounding citizenship and citizenship education, and its relationship to 'shared values', national identity, diversity and immigration have become increasingly high profile in media discourses since 1997. British identity is constructed as culturally Christian (Anthias and Yuval-Davis 1993), where Muslims are the new and 'dangerous' outsiders. In a comparison of the way that 'Britishness' has been depicted in the press in the past three general elections, issues relating to Islam have appeared with significantly greater frequency and framed more negatively in the 2005 election campaign, compared with the 1997 and 2001 campaigns (Billig *et al.* 2006).

The third explanatory model is the 'fluke' model, where it was perceived that there is an arbitrary nature to how the initiative took hold. For example, David Kerr, as previously mentioned, described the process by which this range of influences interact to culminate in citizenship education coming onto the agenda in the late 1990s in England, in terms of 'luck'. Another interviewee, Jan Newton, the then Director of the Citizenship Foundation, and member of the Crick Advisory Group, referred to 'a coming together of a lot of forces, a kind of, you know, *serendipity* [italics added]' (p. 1). This may be because the processes by which policy issues come onto the agenda lack transparency, and appear to have a certain quality of arbitrariness. For the general public, and also even those actively involved in the citizenship education field, it may appear unclear why some issues capture the public imagination as opposed to others. This can also be seen in the choice of language used by Crick when he describes it as 'a *coincidence* [italics added] of ideas and individuals' (p. 4).

## Aims and outcomes

There was vagueness expressed by many interviewees with regard to what the implementation of citizenship education may achieve: 'I don't know how you would evaluate' (Interview with 'Z': 5). This vagueness in part reflects much of the empirical literature, in that there is scant evidence of a direct correlation between the implementation of citizenship education and increased formal political participation, or indeed a promotion of 'shared values' and national identity.

Furthermore, the policy and curriculum development have taken place without empirical evidence of the potential impact of these policies at the student level (Kerr 1999). There have been several large-scale studies conducted on citizenship education, such as the International Association for the Evaluation of Educational Achievement (IEA) Civic Education Project, which is one of the most high profile studies covering 24 countries (Torney-Purta *et al.* 1999), a UNESCO study in 1994, with the aim of improving educational strategies for citizenship education (Albala-Bertrand 1997) and a 1997 European Commission study reviewed by Osler and Starkey (1999) across 18 European countries, which aimed to identify features of projects in education, training and youth programmes, which contribute effectively to political education and 'active citizenship'. Osler and Starkey (2005) have also conducted a review of research, policy and practice of citizenship education in England from 1995 to 2005. In the English school context, Kerr (2001) notes a positive correlation between levels of civic knowledge and *expectation* to participate. However, neither this study nor the above-mentioned studies explicitly address the effects of citizenship education at societal level, e.g. in terms of whether there is *actual* increased formal political participation. David Kerr, who is currently coordinating a longitudinal study funded by DfES on the impact the implementation of citizenship education, suggested that: 'It's going to be difficult to measure these outcomes, the way to link it in that sort of way. I think there will be soft indicators and they might impact on hard indicators' (Interview with David Kerr: 9). Indeed, the reports published to date from this study do not explicate what outcomes are expected from the implementation of citizenship education, nor are expected outcomes measured; instead the stated aim is to 'identify, measure and evaluate the extent to which effective practice in citizenship education develops in schools so that such practice can be promoted widely' (Kerr *et al.* 2004).

The tentativeness of many of the interviewees stands in marked contrast to David Blunkett, who argued that citizenship education is 'crucial to the life of a democracy', as democracy is 'threatened by apathy and disengagement' (Interview with David Blunkett: 1). His explanation was that if people are well-informed and actively participating, 'the more likely they are to participate in formal things like voting, but more crucially than that, the more likely they are to take part in civil and civic activity in terms of their own community'. However, this authoritative statement is not supported by empirical evidence, with no evidence to date that there is a direct correlation between citizenship education and formal political participation (Albala-Bertrand 1997). Similarly, there is also a lack of empirical evidence that there is a direct correlation between citizenship education and the promotion of national identity and 'shared values'.

The aims and outcomes of citizenship education as perceived by interviewees can be grouped under a number of themes. The key themes referred to by interviewees in order of frequency are presented in Table 2.2.

The aims and outcomes of citizenship education as perceived by interviewees reflect their conceptions of citizenship, which are analysed in Part 2. For the majority of interviewees, their understandings of citizenship are framed in terms

*Table 2.2* Aims and outcomes as perceived by interviewees, ranked in descending order of frequency (codings not mutually exclusive*)

---

*Aims and outcomes of citizenship education*

---

1. Political literacy
2. Supporting democracy and formal political participation
3. Empowerment/change
4. Community involvement
5. Democratic schools with increased pupil self-esteem
6= 'Better' society and 'better' citizens
6= Social Order
8= Community cohesion/resolving conflict
8= 'Do-gooding' (volunteering) agenda
10. Race equality, human rights

---

*Interviewees in many cases gave more than one aim and/or outcome of citizenship education.

of the Crick Report's three 'strands' – 'social and moral responsibility', 'community involvement', and 'political literacy' – with particular emphasis on political literacy and active participation (QCA 1998). It is therefore to be expected that the aims and outcomes were framed most commonly in terms of political literacy, supporting democracy and community involvement.

The list of perceived aims and outcomes in Table 2.2 suggest that interviewees perceived that the citizenship education policy initiative serves more than one type of aim. While policies may often serve more than one aim, there may be inherent tensions between the above-mentioned aims and outcomes;[5] e.g. between the aim of empowerment and change in contrast to the aim of social order. Similarly, diversity-related aims (framed as 'race equality/human rights') may require a different set of measures than aims that focus exclusively on supporting formal political participation, for example.

However, it could be argued that this initiative predominantly aimed to serve what Malen and Knapp (1997) refer to as a 'rational' perspective on policy, where it is assumed that there is a problem to solve, or what McLaughlin (2000: 442) refers to as a 'detailed prescription for action aimed at the preservation or alteration of ... institutions or practices'. Diversity-related aims are at the bottom of Table 2.2, referred to by only two of the interviewees, both of whom were not directly involved in the initiative. The two most frequently cited aims of political literacy and supporting democracy assume that citizenship education will solve the perceived problem of political apathy and its potentially negative implications for democracy. Pattie *et al.* (2004) found that two-thirds of participants donated money to a political organization – what they classify as an 'individual' act of participation (e.g. voting or signing a petition). This challenges the assertion that citizens in the UK are politically apathetic (QCA 1998). Although there is support for the idea that citizenship education is important in order to support democracy, a number of interviewees, in contrast to Blunkett, did express scepticism with regard to citizenship education resulting in greater participation in formal politics in the form of voting. 'E' joked: 'More votes, falling crime rates, all live harmoniously, no ... I mean' ... (p. 9).

The theme of empowerment also came up frequently with interviewees, but it is interesting to note that this was more often referred to by those interviewees involved either indirectly through the consultation process, or indirectly through general involvement and less likely to be referred to by members of the Crick Advisory Group.[6] This is reflected in the Crick Report, which is relatively less concerned with the idea of empowering citizens for change, than with maintaining the status quo (Osler and Starkey 2001). Indeed, Crick, in his interview, did not refer to this as an aim of citizenship education, although in contrast, Blunkett asserted that 'it's very much about personal empowerment, about giving people confidence to know that they can make a difference' (Interview with David Blunkett: 5).

'B', a member of the Crick Advisory Group, referred to empowerment, which he described in terms of a conception that citizenship education that can help protect the citizen 'against' the state:

> not just to empower people, but to equip people to be strong against the society in which they live ... a very radical agenda ... to equip people to see how they're ... having the wool pulled over their eyes, how they're being manipulated, how they're being exploited and so on, so that's always been my agenda ...
>
> (Interview with 'B': 6–7)

This framing of the aims of citizenship education implies an understanding of the contract between the state and citizens to be one where the state should have minimal intervention in the lives of its citizens (Held 1993), where citizens have rights 'against' the state. Inherent to this liberal conception of citizenship is the public/private sphere distinction, where 'difference' is kept out of the assumed 'neutral' public sphere. It is not a coincidence that there is no mention of ethnic and religious diversity in relation to empowerment in this interviewee's account of the need for empowerment, nor is there any acknowledgement of the differential power of different groups and as a consequence, differential rates of participation.

When interviewees referred to the issue of diversity in the context of aims and outcomes of citizenship education, this was presented predominantly in terms of raising awareness of race equality and human rights issues. Two interviewees expressed concern that these issues were not perceived to be aims of citizenship education by the Crick Advisory Group and those involved subsequently in the curriculum development process. In the IEA study, England scored below the international mean on positive attitudes towards immigrants, and also on national identity and patriotism with girls more supportive of immigrants' and women's rights in all countries (Kerr 2001). Similarly, 'community cohesion' is ranked towards the bottom of the table with relatively few interviewees making reference to this. As noted in Chapter 1, over the last 5 years, the themes of integration and multiculturalism have also taken on a heightened profile in the broader policy agenda, presented in the form of the concepts of 'shared values', 'community cohesion' and 'integration with diversity'. Increasingly, there have been calls for citizenship education to address these issues (Home Office 2001a,b, 2002; Rammell 2006).

## Workings of the Crick Advisory Group: democratic and diverse?

Given that David Blunkett, as the then Secretary of State for Education set up the Advisory Group for the 'Teaching of Citizenship Education and Democracy in Schools', and that Sir Bernard Crick was the appointed Chairman of this Advisory Group, the emphasis on these particular individuals is unsurprising. However, what is of interest is to contrast the actual workings of the Advisory Group, with the *idea* or understanding of citizenship and citizenship education. From the name of the Advisory Group itself, we can see that the concept of democracy is explicitly linked to the concept of citizenship. In this section, I examine whether the workings of the Advisory Group were 'democratic'; I examine this in terms of the constituents, the means by which individuals were selected to be involved, and then the management of the Group itself. The conceptual relationship of democracy to citizenship is addressed in Chapter 5.

### Constituents of the policy development process: a diverse membership?

The Crick Advisory Group consisted of: 15 members, Sir Bernard Crick as Chairman of the Group, the Rt Hon Betty Boothroyd, MP (then Speaker of the House of Commons), as Patron, and three Observers to the Group, consisting of representatives of the Office for Standards in Education (OFSTED), the Teacher Training Agency (TTA) and the Department for Education and Employment (DfEE, now DfES). The Group was managed by the Qualifications and Curriculum Authority (QCA), with three QCA employees directly involved in the management and coordination of the Advisory Group's work (QCA 1998). Membership also included Lord Baker, former Conservative Secretary of State for Education and Home Secretary, suggesting cross-party support for the initiative, a representative of the Speaker of the House of Commons, three teachers, a member of the General Synod of the Church of England, Head of the think-tank *Demos*, Chief Executive of Community Service Volunteers (CSV), Chief Executive of the Citizenship Foundation, former Chief Inspector of Prisons for England and Wales, Chair of the Parole Board, two lecturers and a local education officer (QCA 1998).

According to 'B', a member of the Crick Advisory Group, there were two particularly strong 'lobbies' on the Group, with 'a very strong lobby from Community Service Volunteers (CSV)' and 'the other voice that was strong was for the personal and social education side of things, and there was a strong institutional voice for that as well, coming from outside the group' (Interview with 'B': 7). With regard to both these 'lobbies', it is interesting to note their strength given Crick's views with regard to both volunteering and Personal Social and Health Education (PSHE) in relationship to citizenship, which I discuss in the following chapter. How these differences in views played out in making group decisions is discussed later in this chapter in the section on decision-making.

My interview sample comprised of 15 men and 15 women. Nine of the 15 women were from 'ethnic minorities', whereas none of the men were.[7]

While the numbers in Table 2.3 are not necessarily representative of all those involved at the different stages of the citizenship education development process, they may reflect certain aspects of involvement relating to ethnicity. What became evident through the process of interviewing was that there was a relatively greater involvement of those from ethnic minority designations at later stages in the development process. This could be interpreted as those from ethnic minorities being involved at later stages having been less able to exert 'power' over the form that citizenship education takes. What is also of interest to note is that the interests of ethnic and religious diversity as represented by such organizations as, e.g. the Refugee Council, or Commission for Racial Equality were relatively more likely to be involved at a later stage. An alternative explanation is that this pattern of involvement could be seen to reflect a growing recognition in policy circles of the pertinence of engaging with issues of diversity, given the changing sociopolitical context both in the UK and globally since 1998.

That the Group was perhaps not ethnically or religiously diverse enough is referred to by Crick himself, acknowledging: 'I think we might have worked out ideas on what we've been talking about [diversity] a little more quickly or more clearly if there had been a better ... more representation of minority communities' (Interview with Sir Bernard Crick: 10). This perception was also shared by a number of members of the Crick Advisory Group. According to one member of

*Table 2.3* Number* of interviewees at each stage of the development process, by gender and ethnicity

| Stage of development process | Numbers involved | Gender | Ethnicity |
|---|---|---|---|
| Overview[†] | 1 | 1M | 1W |
| Policy development[‡] | 15 | 8M, 7F | 12W, 3E |
| Curriculum development | 5 | 2M, 3F | 5W |
| Resources development | 10 | 5M, 5F | 6W, 4E |
| Related initiatives | 8 | 2M, 6F | 5W, 3E |
| No direct involvement | 1 | 1F | 1W |

*Numbers in the different categories are not mutually exclusive, as several interviewees were involved at more than one stage, so numbers do not add up to 30.

[†]I am referring to Blunkett's role as 'overview'.

[‡]This includes both members of the Crick Advisory Group and those who were consulted with. M, male; F, female; W, white; E, ethnic minority.

the Group:

> I think possibly and I guess I wouldn't be saying this necessarily on a very public platform, I think the diversity strand wasn't strong enough. I mean, Usha Prashar was there who was incredibly good, very conscious of all the issues and very committed to social justice for groups, but I think she was someone who ... I mean, she's now a civil service commissioner, but she was on lots of things, so I think it would have been really good if we'd had maybe a sort of radical Black lawyer. The only thing is, against myself I would say, would we have come up with the conclusion that were possible to put into practice, I don't know ...
>
> (Interview with 'K': 8–9)

There are two issues of particular interest raised in this excerpt. The first is that there is the suggestion that although there was a degree of ethnic minority representation on the Group, this presence was 'establishment', and hence the range of views reflected in the Group were not necessarily particularly diverse. This is not to advocate that groups be diverse merely for the purpose of being representative, but rather that a process for a real negotiation between different views and interests is initiated. The second and related issue is that reaching group consensus might have been undermined if views were too diverse. These issues are discussed in the following section on the 'selection process', where it emerges that 'like-minded' individuals working in the area were selected, so that achieving consensus would be facilitated.

Some interviewees referred to the consultation process as a means by which a diverse range of views were sought by Crick. According to David Blunkett, when asked if he thought that there may have been any missing voices, he stated that:

> I didn't hear people acclaiming that we'd missed the agenda because we did a very, I think, extensive consultation process, and I think that was very important and Bernard himself traversed the whole length and breadth of Britain and I think did an excellent job of drawing people together
>
> (Interview with David Blunkett: 6)

Looking at the appendices of the Crick Report, there is a long list of organizations and individuals consulted. However, there is no transparency with regard to the methodology of how, or the extent to which comments from those consulted might have been addressed. It would appear that in the Crick Report, certain arguments are supported with selective use of submissions from certain individuals or organizations whose views coincided with those of Crick, e.g. the use of extensive quotes from the British Youth Council on the relationship between Citizenship and PSHE (QCA 1998: 20).

The representation of ethnic and religious diversity within the citizenship education process is an issue that was often not referred to at all by interviewees. For many interviewees, there was a perception that the issue of diversity was not something of relevance to them, and there was therefore a lack of engagement with the issue of diversity: 'It's not my area basically' (Interview with 'E': 10). Diversity for many was synonymous with ethnic minorities. This lack of engagement with the issue of ethnic and religious diversity in a multicultural society is at odds with the whole enterprise of citizenship being inclusive of all types of people. When diversity was referred to in the context of representativeness in the policy development process, it was perceived to be an inappropriate variable:

> There was a definite attempt not to get on that Group, representatives of any constituency, because the constituencies were huge and there was a lot of outcry from a number of constituencies that they weren't there. If you're looking for the voice of, shall we say, people from the Asian sub-continent ... well, I'm not sure you could say ... I forget her surname ... Usha, the person from the Parole Board, I don't think she would have seen herself speaking as an Asian, I don't know, it's a wider issue as to how groups should be composed
>
> (Interview with 'B', member of Crick Advisory Group: 8)

The issue of a tension between striking the right balance between representativeness and tokenism was raised specifically in the context of talking about ethnic and religious diversity:

> Too many people are put on groups, not because of their intrinsic merit, but because it makes the representation of the group look better [*laughs*]. Never happens to me because I'm a white male, but I see it happen to other people
>
> (Interview with 'O', former senior QCA employee: 8)

'O''s quote above indicates scepticism of representativeness, in particular with respect to ethnic diversity. There is an implication that there is tokenistic inclusion of non-whites and females on such Advisory Groups out of a concern to appear representative, and that in doing so, there may be an erosion of standards.

Not only is there concern raised with regard to including a diverse membership, but there is confusion[8] regarding categories of nationality and ethnicity. For one member of the Advisory Group, ethnicity or 'race' is synonymous with nationality:

> I also don't think there was anybody of another nationality on the Group, was there ... I'm casting my mind around the table and I can't see anyone of colour there. Oh yes, I can, one of the head-teachers was black, yeah, but I think she was the only ... she was certainly the only non-white person, whether she was the only non-English person ...
>
> (Interview with 'N': 5)

In this account, to be English is to be 'white'. There is a dominant schema that 'Englishness' is synonymous with 'white-ness', therefore, anyone of non-white designation cannot authentically be English. Who authentically may belong to the national community is discussed by Gilroy (2002). He quotes Enoch Powell: 'The West Indian does not by being born in England, become an Englishman. In law, he becomes a United Kingdom citizen by birth; in fact he is a West Indian or an Asian, still' (Powell 1968, cited in Gilroy 2002: 47). 'N''s quote above exhibits this form of thinking, an unconscious perception that being black is not an authentically English trait. However, a moment later, 'N' realised the 'error', saying, 'Actually she is English' (p. 5).

There is relatively less comment on the issue of *religious* diversity in the context of citizenship. Again, like ethnic diversity, religious diversity is deemed by many interviewees to be an inappropriate variable in the context of group membership. This may be due to a civic republican approach to citizenship expressed by a number of the interviewees, where it is deemed important to keep ethnicity and religion out of the public sphere of citizenship (Brubaker 1998). 'N', a member of the Crick Advisory Group stated that religious diversity was not a consideration with respect to Group membership: 'I seem to remember there was rather a large chunk where religion should have been' (p. 4). 'N' further noted the lack of Jewish and Catholic representation saying: 'There should have been, if not Jonathan Sacks, there should have been a representative from Jonathan's office … I mean Elaine [Appelbee, National Synod of Churches] … but there wasn't anyone from Catholic churches' (p. 5).

### Selection of constituents

When asked about how individuals were chosen to be involved in the policy development process, what emerged was that even for those individuals involved, the process lacked transparency, with interviewees unclear as to the nature of how these decisions were made. In some cases, there was a perception that the Group aimed to be representative, although there were limits placed on the extent of this. According to David Kerr, Secretary to the Crick Advisory Group, he referred to the perceived need to represent different interests, such as the Church, LEAs and a cross-political party balance. In contrast, 'O', a former senior employee of QCA argued that representativeness was not an aim:

> I remember there being a discussion about representation and I think the argument would have been, we are gathered together, a range of people, who were involved in this area, and likely to contribute to sensible discussion, weren't trying to create a simulacrum of the wider society, probably would have been the argument
>
> (Interview with 'O': 8)

What emerges from the excerpt above, is the notion of those 'who were involved in the area'. However, what is not mentioned is who decides 'who is involved in the area'. It clearly would not have been of benefit to Crick to have had to manage a Group where the views of members were too conflicting. Therefore, decisions regarding membership may not necessarily have been based on 'who is involved in the area' so as to engage in debate of the issues, but in terms of who is 'like-minded' in the area, in order to minimize the potential contentiousness of citizenship education at a time when political sensitivities around the introduction of citizenship education were very real. According to 'N', excluding diversity was a pragmatic choice that had to be made in order to ensure that the Group had 'shared values' and reached consensus: 'I think what was wanted was a group of people who would nod through what it had already decided was the case' (p. 4).

### Decision-making

The general format of the meetings of the Crick Advisory Group was that there was a meeting approximately every 6 weeks, where the group worked on drafts brought forward by Crick.[9] I asked one member of the Advisory Group close to Crick if these drafts were always authored by Crick, the answer being:

> Towards the interim report, yes. He would show me drafts from time to time, but I'm sure he'd be showing ... I know he was showing other people, he used to show parts of drafts. Later, on ... we divided ... produced working groups so aspects of the report were given over to other people, then they came back to the centre and Bernard and others were ... and obviously David [Kerr] became ... more strongly involved
>
> (Interview with 'B': 9)

Another member of the Crick Advisory Group also referred to Crick's authority as 'Crick very much being the driving force' (Interview with 'V': 2). Crick's dominance in terms of group dynamics was referred to by 'B' off the record in his account of how he stood up to Crick in one of the Group meetings, which escalated into shouting across the table. That Crick, and also Kerr dominated the authorship of the Crick Report was expressed by Crick himself: 'Sometimes I joke too much, but the joke I made, as it were, I wrote the report and he [David Kerr] did the thinking, isn't too far off the truth' (Interview with Sir Bernard Crick: 3).

With regard to how decisions were made, especially regarding contentious issues within the Crick Group, David Kerr asserted that this was done in a 'generally democratic and harmonious way' (p. 5). This view was reiterated by some of the members of the Advisory Group. In contrast to this view, however, was that, according to one member of the Crick Advisory Group, one member was asked to leave as he had broken 'the confidences of the Group' (Interview with 'B': 6). According to 'B', this was Phil Turner who wrote a letter to the Yorkshire Post. 'B' argued that this wasn't so much an issue of 'dissent' as much as 'impatien[ce] with the way in which the Group was going' (p. 5). This distinction between 'dissent' and 'impatience' is not a clear one, however.

Other frustrations with the workings of the Group related to decisions regarding Citizenship as statutory subject: 'Quite a few of us didn't want citizenship to be a subject, but that was decided fairly early on. It wasn't really a democratic organisation at all, you must have heard this from others' (Interview with 'N': 5). 'B' explained that this issue was resolved not through the democratic workings of the Group, but rather, that 'eventually those decisions were taken outside of the meetings' (p. 8). Crick also referred to the antagonism surrounding citizenship becoming a statutory subject and its perceived relationship to PSHE: 'QCA's attitude, and on the whole, they were agin it … first of all they didn't want it compulsory … and they wanted to put it in a pot with PSHE' (p. 11). This issue was not resolved through democratic decision-making at Group-level; instead 'They'd [QCA] got at least two rather stern letters from Blunkett saying that he wanted citizenship to have a separate articulation' (p. 12).

That democracy, more generally is potentially compromised by the (perceived) power of certain key individuals and their relationships or alliances with other powerful actors in other spheres of public life was raised by one interviewee. He asserted that it is these relationships rather than democratic processes that determine society's preoccupations.

> Democracy is a very odd being because in many ways, the only point it's democratic, is when you put an 'X' on the piece of paper, and the rest of the time it's not very democratic at all; it's friendships, it's networking … depending on society's perceived demands which tend to reflect the Sun's newspaper's latest whim, or *Daily Mail, Daily Mirror*, unpacking how society behaves, it tends to be an editor, so you come down to an editor. The group editors know the MPs very well – they're all friends. When you peel back all the layers … some are still for a dictatorship really [*laughs*]
>
> (Interview with TTA employee: 10)

The relationship between democracy and citizenship is elaborated further in Chapter 5.

## Perceived expertise and contributions

### *Closeness to Crick and Blunkett*

What emerged from the interview data was that a close relationship to either Crick and Blunkett was presented as a means of validating expertise in the field of citizenship. Blunkett referred to Crick and *vice versa* in their accounts of their involvement and expertise in the field. Blunkett described that when he became Secretary of State for Education:

> I had the opportunity of pulling all that together and giving people what they'd long wanted … I got hold of my old professor, Bernard Crick, and said let's go for it. He'd been arguing for it ever since he wrote *In Defence of Politics*, in the early sixties, so this was a long longstanding agenda of 40 years standing with him
>
> (Interview with Blunkett: 1)

According to Crick, his interests date back to the early 1970s when the:

> Politics Association was founded, a group of lonely people who were interested in citizenship education or political education as they more often called it at that time
>
> (Interview with Crick: 1)

He declared that:

> my book, *In Defence of Politics*, obviously influenced him [Blunkett] quite a lot but I didn't know him particularly well, so that was the first I knew that Blunkett had these interests, and it must have stayed with him for a very long time, talking about '81, '82 then ...
>
> (Interview with Crick: 2)

What is of note is that only David Blunkett and Bernard Crick made reference to Crick's book, *In Defence of Politics* (Crick 2000). For others, it was deemed sufficient to declare closeness to either David Blunkett or more commonly Sir Bernard Crick. For example, 'B', a member of the Crick Advisory Group, explained:

> Well, I've known Bernard Crick since about 1969 ... had formed a very close working relationship with him ... and then also got to know David Blunkett from about 1972 when he was teaching in further education and a member of the Subject Association ... Bernard talked with me informally at very early stages about the whole nature of the enterprise
>
> (Interview with 'B': 1)

Approval by Crick was expressed by Yasmin Alibhai-Brown, columnist for *The Independent*, and member of Working Party subsequently set-up taking forward the work of the Crick Advisory Group: 'Crick just liked the way I thought ... and it was him and a couple of other people who thought I should be on it ... I don't think there was anyone else who was black who was on it' (p. 2).

This suggestion of 'like-mindedness' is raised again here in the above quote. The interview data could be interpreted that those individuals who were chosen to be involved were more likely to have been chosen because they were perceived to be 'like-minded' and unlikely to express strongly opposing views, rather than necessarily having significant expertise in the field. This concurs with comments made in relation to the selection of Advisory Group constituents.[10]

## Diversity

Very few interviewees claimed either expertise or contribution to issues relating to diversity in the citizenship education policy development process. In terms of involvement in the Crick Advisory Group, one member asserted:

> I had an understanding of issues of diversity … I have a holistic approach, not a "vested interest" approach. Just because I am an ethnic minority, I do not have to be the one to "bang the drum" … but rather I played a role to get them to understand the issues. I believe that I had particular influence on the bits relating to diversity, and also in terms of steering how the report went
>
> (Interview with 'V': 2)

Here, this member was concerned not to be seen as the token 'ethnic minority' voice, but rather someone with general expertise in the area first and foremost. Yasmin Alibhai-Brown also claimed to having expertise in the field of diversity and citizenship and to having contributed to how diversity was dealt with within this process. She stressed that this was primarily through her writings, and then subsequently being involved in the process through her membership in the Working Party:

> I was one of the first people in this country about 3 years ago to start asking questions about whether anybody in this country felt actively involved as citizens … and I started writing quite a lot about let's get away from the usual discourse of race relations and ethnic minorities and anti-discrimination. You can't just talk about that, and get people to think about what is their contract with this nation
>
> (Interview with Yasmin Alibhai-Brown: 1)

In her account, not only is her writing on citizenship and diversity distinctive from contemporary discourses in the field, but she perceived that she had played a key role in initiating debate in this area. For Alibhai-Brown, it was not only that Crick 'approved' of her way of thinking, but that she was sought after because she had something unique to contribute.

## Summary

My interview data suggests that those involved in the policymaking process emphasized the role of individuals relative to societal influences in their explanations of why citizenship education came onto the agenda in the late 1990s, and I propose three explanatory models based on the data. My data also suggests that there was a perception that decision-making was strongly driven by certain key individuals. While this might appear as a relative focus on agency at the expense of societal influences or 'structure', this is a function of my focus on the perceptions of those key players themselves. I do not support a simple conceptual dichotomy between agency and structure; indeed, Ball argues that agency and structure are 'implicit in each other, rather than being the two poles of a continuum' (Ball 1994b: 15). This perspective emerges from the interview data, reflected by interviewees providing both 'personal' and 'societal' influences for why they believed the citizenship education initiative had taken hold.

With regard to the workings of the Crick Advisory Group itself, a key theme that emerged was that the Group could not really be considered to be ethnically and religiously diverse or representative. What is of note was that there was certain scepticism or even hostility towards the idea of representativeness with a number of interviewees who raised a concern about the relative balance between representativeness and tokenism in the context of discussing ethnic and religious diversity. It could be argued that the selection of Advisory Group constituents did not aim to achieve representativeness. Given that the introduction of citizenship education was a contentious and politically sensitive issue, it was considered important that high profile and 'like-minded' people were selected, in order to minimize its contentiousness and so that decision-making would not be too arduous to manage. In addition, the outcome as well as process would be perceived to have credibility. Perceptions of those involved suggested that decision-making was not always democratic, that the views of certain key individuals dominated and that sometimes, certain decisions were actually taken out of the Advisory Group meetings.

In Part 2, I examine interviewees' conceptions of citizenship throughout the policy and curriculum development process. Chapters 3, 4 and 5 focus on the 'moral, 'legal' and 'participatory' conceptions of citizenship and their implications for diversity, while Chapter 6's focus is on the relatively underplayed conceptions of citizenship, where identity is a key component of these conceptualizations.

# Part 2

# Conceptions of citizenship

## Introduction

In the following four chapters of Part 2 of the book (Chapters 3, 4, 5 and 6), I examine the four main conceptions of citizenship evident throughout the English citizenship education policy and curriculum development process. These consist of three 'dominant' conceptions, which I refer to as the 'moral', 'legal' and 'participatory' conceptions of citizenship. These conceptions have been designated 'dominant' as they are the three most frequently referred to codings of citizenship conceptions by the 'key players' that I interviewed.[1] A fourth category of conceptions, 'identity-based', refers to a set of relatively 'underplayed' conceptions of citizenship. I have called these types of conceptions, 'identity-based', because they are inherently concerned with identity, or forms of identification at different levels, e.g. at the local, national, European or global level. This set of conceptions was considered to be 'underplayed' by interviewees, and also was relatively less evident in the policy and curriculum documentation, in contrast to the more frequently utilized 'moral', 'legal' and 'participatory' conceptions of citizenship. These categorizations of conceptions of citizenship are not intended to draw sharp boundaries, as it becomes clear that these categories are not necessarily mutually exclusive. For example, I have located discussion relating to 'shared values' under 'moral' conceptions of citizenship, as public and academic (namely conservative communitarian) discourses often explain active participation in the community in terms of a moral force towards integration and 'shared values' (e.g. Etzioni 1995). However, these discourses are clearly also linked to issues of identity and diversity, as becomes evident in Chapter 6. My analysis is supplemented by an analysis of relevant sections in key policy and curriculum documentation (QCA 1998, 2000, 2001). I examine the implications for diversity of the 'moral', 'legal' and 'participatory' conceptions of citizenship, drawing on the politico-philosophical literature on citizenship and diversity.

Almost 5 years on since the statutory introduction of citizenship education in English secondary schools, citizenship education has come under review (Education and Skills Select Committee 2006; Rammell 2006). The DfES

Diversity and Citizenship in the Curriculum Review in its terms of reference entailed an examination of whether a fourth 'pillar' or component of 'modern British social and cultural history' should be added alongside the existing three strands of the Crick Report, framed in terms of promoting 'shared values' in the British context (Rammell 2006). This review was conducted at the same time as the Qualifications and Curriculum Authority (QCA) KS3 review, whose remit was to reduce curriculum content whilst being more conceptually driven. Revised Programmes of Study have been developed by the QCA, launched for public consultation in February 2007 (QCA 2007), to be published in September 2007, and implemented in schools from September 2008. These developments will also be examined, and their implications discussed in Chapters 3–6.

The literature on the development of citizenship education tends to suggest a fairly coherent translation from 'theory' to 'practice', where a particular theoretical model is drawn upon and reflected in policy and curriculum, and subsequently practice. For example, citizenship education in France is typically framed as a logical and coherent reflection of a classic civic republican model (Brubaker 1998), in contrast to Germany's citizenship education, presented as the classic example of 'ethnoculturalism' (Brubaker 1998; Händle *et al.* 1999). While there is a clear link between the practice of citizenship education and conceptions of citizenship held in different politico-philosophical traditions, the picture is not always so clear-cut.

My research findings suggest a far more complex picture. Not only were multiple, and indeed sometimes contradictory theories drawn upon in interviewees' conceptions of citizenship, but contemporary societal discourses and events, and in particular, certain key individuals have influenced how citizenship is presented in the policy development process. I explore *the range* of theoretical conceptions of citizenship that are drawn upon, and how conceptions of diversity relate to conceptions of citizenship.

The remainder of this Introduction provides a holistic overview of the Crick Report's conception of citizenship in terms of the 'three strands', and how these strands relate to one another.

## The three 'strands' of citizenship

The Crick Report presents T. H. Marshall's conception of Citizenship as its centrepiece, referring to his proposed three elements of citizenship – civil, political and social. It states that a 'working definition must be wide … and relate all three of Marshall's dimensions'(QCA 1998: 11), arguing that 'active citizenship' is a 'habitual interaction between all three' (QCA 1998: 11) elements of citizenship. T. H. Marshall's conception of citizenship, a social democratic alternative to liberalism, proposes that civil, political and social rights are acquired in that order, based on his examination of the British context in a historical perspective (Marshall and Bottomore 1992). The section concludes with the understanding of citizenship being presented as 'three heads on one body: *social and moral responsibility, community involvement* and *political literacy*' (QCA 1998: 13), which are supposed to correspond to T. H. Marshall's three elements of citizenship (QCA 1998).

When asked what aspects of citizenship they believed to be emphasized in the report, most interviewees indeed referred to what many call Crick's three strands of citizenship. Yet in terms of explicit reference to any theoretical conceptualizations of citizenship, what is striking is that only Sir Bernard Crick and David Blunkett made any reference to theories of citizenship. Both Crick and Blunkett believed the core of citizenship to be about political engagement and participation. Their references to theory were carefully selected in order to validate these views. Indeed, the use of theory in this way was acknowledged by Crick, when he said: 'I've got a very simple concept of citizenship which I just naughtily say is the Greek and the Roman, the idea of people combining together with skills and knowledge to get something done' (Interview with Sir Bernard Crick: 5). When asked what citizenship meant to him, Blunkett referred to 'mutuality of purpose', of 'political mutuality' and the importance of 'community'. With regard to the report's three strands of citizenship, he gave theoretical references to give weight to his support for this conception of citizenship:

> Yes, I thought they interlink very well together as one logically feeds into another so that you can see from the great philosophers of the past, whether it's rooted back in the Greek polis, or whether it's Rousseau and the common purpose, or whether it's the argument about individuality from John Stewart Mill, you can see the way in which these particular strands have developed over time
>
> (Interview with David Blunkett: 2)

What is interesting and of relevance to note with regard to the issue of diversity, is that, in the Crick Report, although T. H. Marshall is presented as the starting point for the development of the conception of citizenship, T. H. Marshall's central concern with social inclusion is not explicitly developed or emphasized, given its relevance to and potential for broadening the scope of citizenship through active participation. There is acknowledgement of the notion that historically, citizenship has very much been bounded in nature (Heater 1990), with very few people actually qualifying as citizens, and there is fleeting reference to 'constant demands to broaden the franchise ... to achieve female emancipation, to lower the voting age' (QCA 1998: 9). This acknowledgement of the integral nature of diversity within citizenship, with respect to gender and age, is not developed or extended to other excluded or marginalized groups, however. In particular, there is no substantive consideration of ethnic and religious diversity in the context of 'broadening' citizenship.

## The relationship between the 'strands'

What is less clear in the Crick Report and from the interviewees themselves is how the three strands relate to, or fit with one another, either theoretically, or in practice. The report states that 'Active citizenship must be an habitual interaction between all three' (QCA 1998: 11), yet it goes on to propose that each strand needs a 'somewhat different place and treatment in the curriculum' (p. 11), and gives examples from three different schools as exemplars of teaching relating to each of the three strands. The relationship between the three strands, however, is not elucidated.

Although the majority of those interviewed expressed support for Crick's three strands of citizenship, what emerged is that there was concern in relation to how these three strands relate to each other in practice. An employee of the Community Service Volunteers (CSV), while supportive of the conceptualization of citizenship in terms of the three strands, expressed concern over the 'piecemeal approach rather than a more integrated approach' (Interview with 'Q', CSV: 2). He argued that by structuring citizenship in terms of three separate strands, this might lead to teachers having 'discussions about political literacy away from notions of community involvement which is of course a nonsense because political literacy is intricately related to community involvement' (Interview with 'Q', CSV: ?)

Crick himself was worried that, in schools, what might happen in practice is the watering down of the 'political literacy' strand. Although in the report, Crick defined citizenship in terms of the three strands – social and moral responsibility, community involvement and political literacy, it is evident, that for Crick, political literacy remains at the heart of citizenship. Crick's emphasis can be understood given his background of campaigning for political literacy to be taught in schools, throughout the 1970s, which he has subsequently re-packaged more broadly as 'citizenship' (Crick and Porter 1978; Davies 1999b). Crick's concern regarding the possible watering down of political literacy would seem to arise more from his assumptions about teachers than from the curriculum documentation itself, given that, e.g. the KS3 Programme of Study would appear to contain much more relating to political literacy than to the other two strands. Given that the guidance to teachers is 'light touch' rather than being overly prescriptive, it would seem that Crick assumed that teachers will focus on 'social and moral responsibility' and 'community involvement' aspects of citizenship at the expense of 'political literacy'. As predicted by Crick, there have indeed been difficulties with the delivery of the 'political literacy' strand in schools (OFSTED 2006). In part, this has been attributed to the 'light touch' approach of citizenship education advocated by the Crick Report, and also that there has been insufficient emphasis on political literacy in both Initial Teacher Training (ITT) and Continuing Professional Development (CPD) courses (Ajegbo *et al.* 2007).

Crick gives an example from a school to illustrate this point:

> One school told with innocent pride that their kids … had organised a party in an old people's home, they bought all the food themselves, they had arranged the entertainment and negotiated with the delightful matron and held the party. Well … 'T' [OFSTED employee] was obviously very sceptical about this, I rallied and I more wisely said that would have been splendid … if they had set themselves to learn why the old people were there not being looked after at home, what the borderlines are between the person at the

social services and the health service ... If they had gone into that territory then the party would have been splendid ... So training for citizenship, training for empowerment is not normally hard ... political campaign of mine at the moment, been saying to Ministers, chance to say to the Prince himself extremely briefly that all volunteering ... sorry that all citizenship involves volunteering, not all volunteering involves citizenship. Some volunteering is cannon fodder ...

(Interview with Sir Bernard Crick: 6)

What Crick has highlighted in the above extract is that to qualify as citizenship, the activity must necessarily involve actively learning about the relationship of the individual with the larger community – in this case, the State. He advocated that the students engage with the political issues of how the elderly are looked after by the state's social services and health services. This suggests that it is not deemed sufficient that students merely volunteer for 'good works', without a more political intention. Citizenship is *public* and *political* in this account. Crick is greatly concerned that it be distinguished from certain forms of volunteering, asserting that 'a lot of volunteering is giving voluntary bodies, foot soldiers, to do their work for them ... marvellous British tradition of voluntary bodies' (Interview with Sir Bernard Crick: 7).

While Crick applauds 'good works', for it to qualify as citizenship, the *way* in which individuals become involved in their community, is crucial. Crick's disparaging use of the army metaphor of authoritarian voluntary bodies ordering 'foot soldier' volunteers to get things done contrasts with his account of citizenship, where individuals are self-directed and actively involved in their community. Through such activity, individuals become increasingly politically literate, developing critical skills of inquiry, and become empowered citizens through the process. For Crick, the process is more important than the end result, in contrast to his account of some volunteering bodies, where there is a suggestion that the outcome is more important than the means by which it is achieved.

Crick's concern regarding how schools manage the political literacy strand was also echoed by 'K', who had extensive LEA experience. He stated that teachers have greatest difficulty teaching political concepts and issues. As a result, schools tend to focus more on the social and moral responsibility and community involvement components of citizenship, relative to political literacy aspects of citizenship. He explained this in terms of their associating political literacy with the old-style civics teaching, which placed a focus on knowledge. But he argued that there is a distinction between civics and political literacy, in that political literacy is not only 'knowledge', but entails an active and more critical component – 'about how you use those systems, for the benefit of yourself, the community and society as a whole' (Interview with 'K': 4–5). This tension between the strands of citizenship was picked up by a number of other interviewees. Furthermore, there was disagreement with regard to the relationship to, or relative weighting of the strands to one another. 'N', a member of the

Advisory Group, while in agreement with the conceptualization of citizenship in terms of the three strands, perceived social and moral responsibility to be the central concept of citizenship. This perception can be understood in terms of 'values' being placed at the centre of such a conception of citizenship, which is examined in Chapter 3.

# 3 'Moral' conceptions

## Introduction

'Moral' conceptions of citizenship and other related political concepts, such as the state, can be traced back to thinkers in ancient Greece. One of the greatest early contributions can be seen in *Plato's Republic*, where the state was based on a notion of justice, and the argument that there is a close relationship between the just society and just individuals (Irwin 1992). However, Plato's conception was not a legalistic conception, as he did not conceive of individual human beings actually possessing rights in opposition to the state, rather that human nature is inherently social, and what is optimal for the state is also optimal for its citizens (Sabine 1951). Like Plato, Aristotle conceived of human beings, or more specifically, men, as primarily political beings, who, by their very nature, could only be fulfilled by actively participating in the affairs of the 'polis' or city-state (Heater 1990). Aristotle believed that the state served an ethical purpose (Russell 1964) and he conceived of politics as 'good' for man and the community, given that politics is the fulfillment of 'prudence' (Aristotle 1976 edn.: 213). However, citizenship for both Plato and Aristotle was conceived of as a privilege, not just excluding women, but also excluding various other categories of men, e.g. the very young, the very old and those of certain occupations (Heater 1990). So it can be seen that a defining feature of these traditional theories of citizenship is the fact that they draw boundaries, clearly excluding certain categories of individuals from membership. However, Heater (1990) proposes that perhaps the most important feature relates to the moral nature of citizenship, with a stress on the importance of citizens having virtuous characters, and being proud to fulfill their responsibilities. As a consequence, both Plato and Aristotle believed education to play a crucial role in preparing citizens for their role within the state (Sabine 1951) and that education should primarily serve a moral purpose (Russell 1964). The notion of community where participation in the community acts as a moral force is also evident in discourses of modernity, as exemplified by Durkheim's sociology, which aims to address the issue of what kind of integration can exist in modern society (Delanty 2003). This theme is also evident in conservative strands of communitarianism (e.g. Etzioni 1995).

In contemporary educational discourses, there are varying positions on the extent to which morality should be coupled with citizenship. Haydon (2000)

describes two opposing positions: first, the position conflating citizenship education and moral education, seeing no distinction between the two, and second,
the view that citizenship education should only be concerned with the public political realm and so has nothing to do with morality, which is considered to be private
individual choice. He goes on to advocate a third position: that it is the place of
citizenship education to address the understanding of morality (Haydon 2000),
proposing a conception of morality that cuts across the distinction between the
public and private sphere. Haydon (1999: 50) proposes that citizenship education
should embrace morality as a topic, rather than merely as a 'system of constraints
on people's conduct', or what he calls 'morality as virtue', rather than 'morality
using the language of norms' (1999: 50–1). Similarly, Halstead and Pike (2006: 1)
propose that moral education is a part of citizenship education because 'dispositions and values, as well as skills and knowledge are to be fostered'. They argue
that the perceived aims of citizenship involve value judgements, and suggest that
liberalism provides this framework of values in the UK.[1]

## 'Citizenship' as a distinctive subject

One of the key areas of contention relating to the conceptualization of citizenship
was evident in the debates regarding the relationship between PSHE (Personal,
Social and Health Education) and Citizenship. The Crick Report uses an excerpt
from the submission of the British Youth Council to make its case for the conceptual distinction between Citizenship and PSHE, and as a 'warning against
conflating or confusing PSHE (or other forms of values education) and citizenship
education' (QCA 1998: 20):

> Finally, we believe that it is important to set out areas that the [citizen-
> ship] curriculum should not cover, or at least not be dominated or distracted
> by. It would be tempting to allow citizenship education to become simply
> issues based on moral education, revolving around key concepts such as
> drugs, health education, housing and homelessness, careers development and
> employability, etc.
>
> (QCA 1998: 20)

It also uses a submission from the Hansard Society to support the above-
mentioned distinction. The Crick Report is clearly concerned to make its case
strongly for the conceptual distinction, as can be seen by the inclusion in
Appendix A of a four-page letter from Crick himself to Professor Tomlinson,
Chairman of 'Passport Project'[2] on the relationship between PSHE and Citizenship. Also enclosed is Professor Tomlinson's response, agreeing with and praising
Crick's explication.

In the Crick Report, 'values' are presented as a distinct feature of citizenship
education: 'it is not just knowledge of citizenship and civic society; it also implies
developing values, skills and understanding' (QCA 1998: 13). However, it is made
clear that these 'values' refer more to 'procedural' aspects, for example, respect for

certain public institutions and the rule of law, rather than to more personal, social and cultural values: 'we suggest which values are more specific to democratic politics, drawing on, though not restricted by, the values in the context of society identified by the National Forum for Values in Education and the Community' (QCA 1998: 14).

The National Forum for Values in Education and the Community was set up in 1996 by the Schools Curriculum and Assessment Authority (SCAA) in order 'to discover whether there are any values upon which there is agreement across society' (Talbot and Tate 1997: 2). This must be situated in the context of dominant discourses in the early to mid 1990s in the UK, with traditionalists arguing that England's increasingly multicultural society has undermined a framework of shared religious values (Beck 1998). Society was deemed to be in moral decline, with the solution being assumed to lie in reconstructing 'shared values' for society. The statement of values produced by the Forum relate to the domains of 'self', 'relationships', 'society' and the 'environment'. It is of note that the Crick Report highlights that the values of relevance to Citizenship in this statement to be those relating to 'society'. This distinction reinforces the Crick's distinction between Citizenship and PSHE, with more personal values being perceived to be the domain of PSHE rather than Citizenship.

Distinctions between Citizenship and PSHE can be further elucidated by comparing the Programme of Study for Citizenship and PSHE at KS3. Looking at the Programme of Study at Key Stage 3 for Citizenship, which outline expected learning outcomes, there are three main components: first, 'knowledge and understanding about becoming informed citizens', second, 'developing skills of inquiry and communication', and third, 'developing skills of participation and responsible action' (QCA 2000). The first component proposes that pupils should be taught about such things as human rights and responsibilities, national, regional and ethnic diversities within the UK, and central and local government, while the second component, 'developing skills of inquiry and communication', proposes that pupils learn how to think about 'topical, political, spiritual, moral, social and cultural issues', and develop oral and written skills of communication relating to such discussions (QCA 2000). The third component, 'developing skills of participation and responsible action' proposes that pupils develop empathetic skills, learn how to negotiate, and take part in community-based activities (QCA 2000).

The Programme of Study for PSHE has three headings under 'knowledge, skills and understanding': 'developing confidence and responsibility and making the most of their abilities', 'developing a healthy, safer lifestyle', and 'developing good relationships and respecting the differences between people' (QCA 2005). The first heading includes issues relating to personal identity, respecting differences between people, reflecting on their strengths 'in relation to personality, work and leisure, managing money'. The second heading includes learning about physical and emotional changes and puberty, sexual activity and behaviour and related health issues, and facts and laws relating to drugs. The third heading looks at such issues as prejudice, racism, friendship and other relationships (QCA 2005).

Crick argued that the two subjects are conceptually separate, and as such, should be taught separately. He made reference to theory to support his argument that PSHE and Citizenship are conceptually distinct: 'I draw a sharp distinction between ... PSHE and Citizenship. Old Aristotle said the good man is not necessarily the good citizen, good citizen isn't always the good man' (Interview with Crick: 5).

What Crick was referring to here is that the old Greek philosophies conceived of citizenship as being political in nature, occurring in the public domain (Heater 1990; Sabine 1951). According to Crick, PSHE is concerned with issues relating to the *personal* rather than the public and political. So for Crick, the 'personal is [NOT] the political'. Crick expressed his frustration that the distinction between PSHE and Citizenship has been unclearly represented within the DfES, exacerbated by their organizational arrangements, and also where PSHE teachers are seen as the natural choice in schools to take on the teaching of citizenship:

> Far too many Heads are just thinking that this is something the PSHE teachers should take on. I think quite a lot of PSHE teachers have been spending quite a lot of effort to avoid political questions ... I don't know whether it was a fundamental decision at the top of the Department after Blunkett left or whether it was just administrative economy, or the kind of accident that I'm always fascinated by ... economy would be that the head of the Citizenship team was also put in charge of PSHE. To my mind it's sending a bad signal to schools ... very notepaper says that, it worries her, it worries me ... That is my worry
>
> (Interview with Crick: 5)

There is disagreement however, among the interviewees regarding the relationship of PSHE to Citizenship. The views of 'N', one of the members of the Crick Advisory Group, differed greatly from those of Crick about their inter-relationship. This is exemplified in the response to my asking explicitly if citizenship should be conceived as a sub-component of PSHE: 'N' answered saying, 'Yeah, I think so, yeah ... I don't see what else it can mean' (Interview with 'N': 11). What emerged from 'N''s account is that citizenship is defined in personal, or individual terms first and foremost: 'What's really important is the flourishing of the individual' (p. 11). Citizenship in terms of political engagement and involvement in the community are not part of this conception, except as means for the individual to develop personally. 'N' explains that citizenship is a part of a pupil's personal development:

> I think the job of the whole school is promotion of people's spiritual, moral, social and cultural development, so PSHE should be an integral part of a coherent whole school approach ... and you can't promote pupils' personal social development without teaching citizenship, so I think citizenship should be an integral part of a coherent ... PSHE
>
> (Interview with 'N': 11)

'N', however, expressed disappointment and frustration that the w
National Forum did not have a greater impact on the subsequent forr
Citizenship in the Crick Report:

> I was really, really disappointed with the way the government had deaɴ ᵥ.-
> the Values Forum. I think it was a waste of millions of pounds of public
> money ... actually it would be ideal to underpin the citizenship stuff; instead
> it is relegated to the back of the National Curriculum and nobody knows what
> it's even for
>
> (Interview with 'N': 2)

There are renewed debates about the nature of Citizenship and how it should be
framed in the curriculum. A key aspect of this debate centres around the relationship between History and Citizenship, and how this might relate to the notion of
'shared values'. Indeed, history education in the early twentieth century was used
to inculcate certain values of patriotism and loyalty (Board of Education 1905,
cited in Stow 2000). In Kymlicka's (1999) philosophical consideration of what
is meant by 'shared values', he states that it is often argued that social cohesion
and national unity in a liberal democracy depends on 'shared allegiance to political principles; rather than to a "shared identity"' (p. 94). However, Kymlicka
argues that shared principles are not sufficient, illustrating this using the example
of Quebec in Canada, where paradoxically there is increasing nationalism at the
same time as increased allegiance to political principles. He proposes that what is
crucial is the notion of belonging, where history and language must play a central
role within citizenship education.

More recently, it has been proposed that History is a means of induction into
the dominant national culture (Tate 1994, cited in Stow 2000). As noted earlier,
the terms of reference for the DfES Diversity and Citizenship Curriculum Review
were to consider whether and how to incorporate 'modern British cultural and
social history' as a potential fourth component of Citizenship at KS3 and KS4,
and how other subjects might contribute to this (Ajegbo et al. 2007). Gordon
Brown's emphasis on the importance of history in the promotion of 'British shared
values' has played a key role in shaping the debate in this domain (Brown 2004,
2006). In June 2006, a high-level breakfast meeting on this topic was held by the
Chancellor of the Exchequer to which a select circle of eminent and like-minded
historians were invited. Similarly, the House of Commons Education and Skills
Select Committee in its inquiry into Citizenship Education held an evidence session
on 7 June 2006, which included evidence from the historian, Professor Linda
Colley on the role of history in promoting 'shared values' and British national
identity.

This debate regarding the relationship between History and Citizenship in the
curriculum also has a very practical dimension in that it relates to the fact that Citizenship is statutory until KS4, whereas History is not. This debate has in part taken
the form of subjects vying for their place and time in an overcrowded curriculum.
Given that, for political reasons, it is unlikely at this time that History will be made

statutory at KS4, there was a perception and concern with 'key players' in the field that the terms of reference for the Diversity and Citizenship Review – considering whether to add a fourth component of 'modern British cultural and social history' was primarily a means to squeeze History into Citizenship – a subject that is already statutory. Our Review advocated that while learning about history clearly has a place in Citizenship, the distinctive character of Citizenship must retain its critical, practical and active focus. Getting the pedagogical approach right will be critical. This is addressed in Chapter 8.

## 'Values' and 'shared values' in the curriculum

Halstead and Pike (2006: 26) provide a useful definition of values:

> values are principles and fundamental convictions which act as justifications for activity in the public domain and as general guides to private behaviour; they are enduring beliefs about what is worthwhile, ideals which people strive and broad standards by which particular practices are judged to be good, right, desirable or worthy or respect

While they note that citizenship is most frequently associated with political, civic and legal values, they argue that a wide range of values has relevance in understanding citizenship. While values as a theme was 'dominant' in terms of interviewees' perceptions, and (to a lesser extent) in the Crick Report, this is not the case in the KS3 Programme of Study and KS3 Schemes of Work (QCA 2000, 2001). 'Values and dispositions' are identified as one of the four essential elements in the Crick Report (QCA 1998: 44, Figure 1). These include a commitment to such concepts as human rights, respect for rule of law, equal opportunities, volunteering and active citizenship, as well as an openness to developing certain types of skills including working with others, acting responsibly, being tolerant and defending a point of view, but also being open to changing one's views in light of discussion and evidence. However, the learning outcomes for KS3 are divided into 'skills and aptitudes', and 'knowledge and understanding', with 'values' not appearing as a learning outcome, although the Report asserts that 'the values and dispositions which underpin citizenship and democratic politics are clearly set out in the learning outcomes' (QCA 1998: 55).

'Values' are not referred to explicitly in the KS3 Programme of Study, although values are implicit in several of the aspects referred to under 'developing skills of enquiry and communication', and 'developing skills of participation and responsible action' (QCA 2000). For example, it states that 'Pupils should be taught to: think about topical political, spiritual, moral, social and cultural issues problems and events' (under 'developing skills of enquiry and communication'), and also that 'Pupils should be taught to: use their imagination to consider other people's experiences and be able to think about, express and explain views that are not their own' (under 'developing skills of participation and responsible action') (QCA 2000).

Within the KS3 Schemes of Work, there is a unit focusing on human rights, which proposes that it is an expectation that most pupils at the end of this Unit will 'know that the Human Rights Act is underpinned by common values' (QCA 2001, Unit 3: 2). In a section on 'what are my rights and responsibilities?', it explains that 'pupils consider what basic rights all members of the school have, and what values underpin those rights, e.g. fairness, tolerance, respect for others, desire for justice' (QCA 2001, Unit 3: 4). Under the theme, 'What are human rights?', it proposes a discussion of common values, proposing 'respect' and 'tolerance'. It also refers to links with RE (Religious Education): 'This section links with religious and ethical values' (QCA 2001, Unit 3: 5). Human rights, however, are rights of an individual, underpinned by common values for *all* human beings, rather than rights inherently based on or derived from being a member of a political community or nation-state. This linking of human rights and citizenship through a notion of common values is theoretically problematic, which I discuss further in the following chapter on legal based conceptions.

References to values also occur in the KS3 Scheme of Work, Unit 4: 'Britain – a diverse society?', under the theme, 'What are my identities?', where learning outcomes for pupils include: 'appreciate that identity consists of many factors, including values, race and gender' and for pupils to 'explore personal values and attitudes' (QCA 2001, Unit 4: 3–4). It also notes that values can affect opinion (p. 4). However, factors contributing to identity are framed as personal with proposed teaching activities suggesting discussion of examples relating to music, food and sport (p. 4), with the issue of how such values may operate in the public political sphere not referred to at all. This unit is discussed more substantively in Chapter 6, which focuses on 'identity-based' conceptions of citizenship.

In 2006, the Qualifications and Curriculum Authority (QCA) started the KS3 Review across all National Curriculum subjects, with the aim to reduce curriculum content and to introduce a more conceptual approach. In the revised Programme of Study for Citizenship at Key Stage 3, under the section, 'The importance of citizenship', it states that pupils 'engage critically' with and 'explore' the 'values we share as citizens in the UK' (QCA 2007: 1). The Programme of Study then identifies three categories of 'key concepts': 'democracy and justice', 'rights and responsibilities' and 'identities and diversity'.

The notion of shared values is hinted at in the following statement, under the concept 'democracy and justice': 'Understanding that justice, diversity, toleration, respect and freedom are valued by people with different beliefs, backgrounds and traditions within a changing democratic society' (QCA 2007: 2). Freedom, understanding and respect are then presented as the 'shared values' (p. 5). However, the terms, 'values', 'beliefs' and 'traditions' are used interchangeably, and there seems to be a lack of clarity regarding the difference of meaning between these terms. The phrase 'shared values' is also used explicitly under 'range and content', where it states 'the shared values and changing nature of UK society including the diversity of beliefs, cultures identities and traditions that shape identities and make-up of UK society' (p. 5). Human rights are also presented as being underpinned by 'shared values'. These statements would seem to advocate shared political values in the context of diverse social, personal and cultural values. There is an acknowledgement that achieving shared political values is an ongoing process in the phrase: 'changing democratic society' (p. 2). There is an implicit distinction made between public political sphere and private personal values – the classic civic republican approach which is problematic in that the selected particular values are presented as universal values. This notion of balancing unity and diversity is examined in the following section.

## Balancing 'unity' and 'diversity'

It can be argued that, in the context of the London bombings in July 2005, we are witnessing a renewed rhetoric, voicing concern regarding the potential dangers of diversity, and a moral drive towards the promotion of 'shared values'. Delanty (2000, 2003) calls this 'conservative' or 'governmental' communitarianism, exemplified in the politics of the British Labour party's 1997 election campaign where there was an appeal to certain British civic values, with a stress on family, religion, tradition and nation. This is largely a modified liberalism (Delanty 2003). Etzioni (1995) advocates for community in moral terms, in order to create responsibility, identity and participation (see also Delanty 2000). He argues for the need for individualism to be balanced with social responsibility in an age that he depicts as one of social and moral breakdown in many Western countries (Etzioni 1995). He advocates the restoration of morality proposing that people take responsibility within a community setting – starting first at the level of the family, then at the level of the school, then locally, nationally and finally cross-nationally.

Bron (2005) describes how in the Netherlands, the new core objectives for citizenship education in primary schools emphasize the link between Dutch language education and successful participation in society. In addition, citizenship education is linked to the notion of social integration and social cohesion. The objectives outlined also state that pupils learn that there are generally accepted standards and values. The Netherlands, like England, is an example where there increasingly urgent calls for an emphasis on 'shared values' in the context of citizenship. This illustrates what Ben-Porath (2006: 12) calls 'belligerent' citizenship. Drawing on the examples of the Israeli-Palestinian conflict, and the US 'War on Terror', she argues that a narrow conception of citizenship is invoked in response to perceived national threat. This takes the form of restricting rights, and suppressing diverse opinions through a promotion of 'unity of voice and subscription to a narrow form of patriotism'.

Indeed, what emerged from the interviews is that the term, '*shared values*' was used by some interviewees to question and challenge the support and endorsement of 'diversity', with 'diversity' being presented as the opposite of a more favourable 'unity':

> In citizenship terms, probably what we need in this society is a greater emphasis on our unity, than on our diversity, by which I mean a greater emphasis

on the importance of a civic identity, irrespective of class, gender, ethnic background, religious affiliation or whatever

(Interview with 'O', former senior employee of QCA: 6)

What is being referred to here is a civic republican conceptualization of citizenship, exemplified by France's conception of citizenship (Brubaker 1998). In this conception, all individuals have equal citizenship, regardless of ethnic, religious or national origin. In France, however, the 'nation' is conceived in terms of political unity, rather than shared national culture, defined in terms of ethnicity or religion. Minority cultures must assimilate as it is thought that although they have equal citizenship rights, their minority identities threaten French national culture, and therefore they should be discouraged from maintaining their own cultures (Rex 1996).

What is of note is that, in Crick's interview, he did not refer at all to the issue of shared values, even when directly asked about this. Given his understanding of PSHE as being concerned with the 'personal' and dealing with values, this would tend to suggest, that for Crick, values are, first and foremost, a personal issue, and are not conceptually a significant part of his understanding of citizenship. This reflects a civic republican understanding of citizenship where personal identity characteristics, for example, ethnicity and religious affiliation and related values, are kept out, at least in theory, of the public political domain.

In contrast, as already noted, citizenship for 'N' is underpinned by 'values', who argued that 'an idea of *common* values could underpin quite nicely what citizenship means' (Interview with 'N': 3). However, this does not translate into a conceptualization of citizenship accommodating ethnic and religious diversity. Instead, 'N' argued for one set of 'common' values, rather than an accommodation of diversity, where these 'common values' are the solution to a whole range of problems currently facing contemporary Western society:

Actually, this business with terrorism, and Islam, and you know, should we allow immigrants in here whose values are different from ours, etc., etc., actually this is one of the major citizenship problems and its through our common values that we can deal with that

(Interview with 'N': 3)

Here 'terrorism', 'Islam' and 'immigrants' are all presented in terms of the problem of holding different values. 'N''s answer to dealing with diversity is to somehow convert it to unity, although there is no explanation of how this might be achieved in practice. 'O', a former senior QCA employee expressed a similar line of thinking, arguing that there are limits to tolerance, and that it is the role of education to inculcate common values. Like 'N', he also singled out Islam, linking it to terrorism and Al-Qaeda:

The fact that there are sort of young Muslims in the West Midlands, in the north of England and so on, who felt that their loyalties in this state, were so non-existent really that they could go off and fight for the Al-Qaeda in Afghanistan ... if you have large numbers of people within a society who are actively fighting to undermine and destroy that society, then ultimately that society won't ... it cannot allow people like that within it, it has to have an education system that makes sure that you don't produce lots of people with that level of alienation

(Interview with 'O': 7)

'O' did not, however, suggest *how* education might instill such common values, again avoiding the issue of the *process* by which shared values might be reached. Nor did 'O' acknowledge that while education has a role to play in integration, it cannot succeed unless there are concomitant strategies or policies developed at international, national and local levels within society.

It would appear these perceptions reflect a contemporary fixation with Islam, huightunud by the wwwilu uf 11 September 2001, and the London bombings and attempted bombings in July 2005. It is unclear, however, whether their concerns were specifically regarding Islam, or whether they reflect a broader theoretical concern regarding religious diversity in the context of common values, and the public/private sphere distinction. While some interviewees expressed concerns relating to ethnic diversity in the conceptualization of citizenship (as well as within the policymaking process), ethnic diversity, unlike religious diversity was not perceived to be a threat. This may in part be due to a perception that religion, and in particular, Islam cannot be relegated to the private sphere, and that it is a whole way of life, threatening Western values. The events of 11 September 2001 and the July 2005 London bombings are often presented as symptomatic of what Huntingdon (1993) called a 'clash of civilisations', with religion operating in the public sphere (and in particular, Islam) being blamed for violence and terrorism on a global scale. However, what this account does not consider is that conflict may be exacerbated by the marginalization of minority ethnic and religious groups. Mechanisms to explicitly integrate ethnic and religious minorities into the public political sphere has the potential to present these communities with a legitimated and moderate voice, providing role models for the youth in these communities. This could, in turn provide support for these legitimated 'representatives' to have the confidence to condemn and marginalize extremists within their communities. These themes are developed in Part 3.

## Theoretical implications for diversity

In *Rethinking Multiculturalism*, Parekh (2000) highlights themes of pertinence with regard to moral conceptions of citizenship and their implications for diversity in his historical review of moral approaches to diversity. He outlines three main forms of moral monism, including the: (1) rational monist approach of Greek philosophy; (2) the theological monism of Christianity and (3) the monism of classical liberalism; each approach is explicated in terms of a theory of human nature (Parekh 2000). In the first approach, while there was an awareness of different cultures and their contributions to Greek knowledge and way of life, the Greeks were assumed to be superior (Parekh 2000). Second, within Christian theology, diversity is conceptualized as an intrinsic good, but Christianity was assumed to be the only true religion. Third, Parekh (2000: 47) critiques liberalism, arguing that this was shaped by its development in a Christian context:

> The thought of Locke and Mill, like that of Christian thinkers, displays a strange blend of moral egalitarianism and political and cultural inegalitarianism: equality of human beings but inequality of cultures, respect for persons but not their ways of life, rejection of racism but advocacy of cultural domination, equal concern for all as individuals but not as self-determining collective subjects

It has been proposed that citizenship education can provide the 'moral cement that will withstand the strains of being pluralistic' (Hargreaves 1994, cited in Beck 1998: 37). As noted earlier, the National Forum for Values in Education and the Community was set-up in 1996 to discover whether agreement could be reached regarding 'shared values' (Talbot and Tate 1997). While this discourse implies links between morality and diversity, it has been argued that the literature on moral education has contributed little to understandings of 'race' (Blum 1999). Yet pluralism is necessarily implicated in moral education (Nicgorski 1992) and indeed, it has been advocated that an 'acceptance of pluralism should influence the aims of moral education' (Kekes 1999: 167). A dominant contemporary trend has been for the school's role to be presented as helping students to develop *ways of thinking* about moral issues, rather than on what the substantive content should be, which may be a means to avoid dealing with diversity (Crittenden 1999). However, Crittenden (1999: 52) argues that to reduce moral education to 'an intellectual exercise in problem-solving ... would lead to a gross misunderstanding of morality', and does not in fact avoid dealing with the issue of diversity, as process and content cannot be easily separated from one another. Some schools take the approach of teaching *about* morality (e.g. Haydon 1999, 2000), however Crittenden (1999) argues that teaching *to be* moral should be a schools' obligation.

I would argue that 'shared values' need not necessarily be problematic in an ethnically and religiously diverse society. I propose that the educational context must focus on the *process* of inclusive communication and collective problem-solving, rather than focus on trying to achieve the outcome of 'shared values'. While it is important for social cohesion to have substantive commonality of values, what is often not addressed however, is *how* such commonality or 'shared values' are arrived at. That is, the *process* of reaching shared values is at least as important to consider as the shared values themselves. If this is not addressed, then 'shared values' cannot move beyond being merely a synonym for assimilation into a monoculturalism based on a numerical majority. This was part of the problem of the outcome of the National Forum for Values, where those who did not agree with the 'shared values' opted out. Even though only a minority actually dissented, there is still the problem that, technically, the values are no longer 'shared'. I refer to this inclusive process as 'institutional multiculturalism', a concept that I develop in Chapter 7.

## Practical implications for diversity

There is currently underway, an 8-year evaluation of the implementation of citizenship education into secondary schools in England, conducted by the National Foundation for Educational Research (NFER) on behalf of the Department for Education and Skills (DfES). It has been reported that teachers in 2005, compared with 2003, believe Citizenship to be most effective when delivered as a discrete subject (Kerr and Lopes 2006). In 2004, this longitudinal study reported in its second annual report that most schools had implemented Citizenship most frequently in the form of modules in PSHE (Kerr *et al.* 2004). This is not, however, identified as a problem, despite the issues raised in the Crick Report about the importance of distinguishing between Citizenship and PSHE. What are the implications in practice from such a conflation? The NFER Report would seem to suggest that it is preferable that Citizenship has a specific curriculum 'slot', albeit within PSHE, than the assumption by one-quarter of the schools surveyed that Citizenship is already being covered in the 'hidden' curriculum. This may indeed help to distinguish between what Kerr *et al.* (2004) refer to as 'Progressing Schools' – where citizenship education is being developed in the curriculum, school community and wider community, in comparison to 'Implicit Schools' – where there is no explicit focus on citizenship in the curriculum, although some opportunities are provided for active citizenship. However, by conflating PSHE and Citizenship, there is undoubtedly a lack of conceptual clarity regarding understanding the nature of citizenship, as discussed earlier in this chapter. Indeed, it has been reported that teacher confidence in teaching citizenship-related topics is low (Kerr and Lopes 2006). The NFER typology of schools is certainly useful in helping to understand the factors influencing the implementation of citizenship into schools, but it does not enable judgements to be made regarding the actual quality of the delivery of Citizenship, and students' understanding of what Citizenship actually entails, as distinct from other subjects.

The 2006 OFSTED Report on Citizenship: 'Towards Consensus? Citizenship in secondary schools', also tackles the issue of the extent to which Citizenship is a distinctive subject, the relationship between Citizenship and PSHE, and the practical implications of how Citizenship should be taught in schools. It notes that in 2005/6, the majority of schools place Citizenship within PSHE, and that in approximately half of these schools, 'the distinctions between citizenship and PSHE were unacceptably blurred' (OFSTED 2006: 24). The Report goes on to argue that while offering Citizenship within PSHE is perhaps relatively less disruptive in the short-term, it 'can also provide serious obstacles to developing the subject further'. This is in part because PSHE is a non-statutory subject, in contrast to Citizenship, which is statutory. However the Report also asserts that these two subjects do not necessarily sit well together, given their different theoretical underpinnings, discussed earlier in this chapter. In brief, PSHE concerns pupils' private individual development covering such topics as health and sex education, careers education and work-related learning. In contrast, Citizenship is framed in terms of the public political dimension. Therefore, when it comes to addressing issues relating to diversity, this may result in these issues being addressed in the less contentious personal and cultural domain, rather than in relation to the public political domain. Significantly, OFSTED notes that there is often conceptual misunderstanding exhibited by teachers. An example is given where 'lessons of friendship and relationships' are perceived as Citizenship by teachers, with this equated to conflict resolution; it would appear that there are no explicit links made or references to public or political institutions such as the United Nations, parliament or non-governmental organizations with regard to the topic of conflict resolution. This is not to say, that in practice, Citizenship cannot be delivered with PSHE. However, teachers must first and foremost, have a clear conceptual understanding of the differences between Citizenship and PSHE.

The relationship between RE and Citizenship also warrants examination in this context, given the relevance of debates about religion for debates about the nation-state and contemporary political issues (Jackson 2003). There is increasing interest in explicitly considering how religion has impacted on the development of public institutions in the past, and considering how the relationship will develop in the future (Weisse 2003). QCA has detailed how RE can contribute to the teaching of Citizenship, including pupils learning how political and individual choices and actions are linked to religions and moral values and practices (QCA 2001). It also proposes that RE can develop active citizenship by encouraging volunteering in religious charities. It is also important and relevant for pupils to understand the central position Christianity has occupied in British history and how this has influenced the form of its political and legal institutions. It is also relevant to understand how liberalism has grown out of Protestantism (Ballance 1995). These relationship are not examined in the Crick Report (Jackson 2003; Halstead and Pike 2006), despite the potential for encouraging dialogue between a diversity of religious and non-religious perspectives. Jackson (2003: 78) proposes an 'interpretive' approach, which aims to develop 'understanding of the grammar' found in religious traditions. Drawing on different country case studies, a dialogical approach is advocated (Ipgrave 2003; Leganger-Krogstad 2003; Weisse 2003). However, Halstead and Pike (2006) warn that the appropriate pedagogical approaches are crucial if pupils are to truly 'learn from religion' (QCA 2004). They warn against taking ideas out of context ('extraction' method), and also the 'distraction' method, where the original meaning is distorted in an attempt to make religion relevant. This often takes the form of promoting secularism and individualism without promoting understanding of a diversity of religious beliefs and values. The role of religion in the public sphere in terms of implications for policy and practice is examined in Chapter 8.

# 4   'Legal' conceptions

## Introduction

In contrast to Plato's and Aristotle's conceptions of citizenship, a more legalistic conception of citizenship was first developed by the Romans[1] (Heater 1990). The Romans introduced some interesting adaptations to the concept of citizenship. These included a relatively more inclusive citizenship, allowing all free male inhabitants to be citizens, the notion of multiple citizenships at different levels – a local as well as a more 'national' level (i.e. 'Latin' and 'Roman'), and the notion of a form of sub-citizenship, in which individuals were accorded the private but not the public rights of citizenship (Heater 1990).

Drawing on these early legal conceptions, modern liberal conceptions of the state and citizenship are typically located as developing in seventeenth-century Europe, emerging with doctrines of state sovereignty and the need to define allegiance and rights (Held 1993). The meaning of the term, 'liberalism' has gradually shifted over time, becoming associated with the idea of freedom of choice, and with individuals being 'free and equal' with natural rights (Held 1993). This emphasis on individual rights is essentially a legal conception of citizenship.

This tradition can be traced back to Hobbes and Locke. Hobbes emphasized the importance of consent in the making of a social contract between individuals and the sovereign, in order for it to be legitimate. In addition, he proposed that the main purpose of the sovereign is to protect individuals – a central tenet of modern European liberalism (Held 1993). This emphasis on the individual is the modern element in Hobbes that has been carried through to contemporary times (Sabine 1951). Like Hobbes, Locke was also concerned with the question of legitimate government, and also perceived the establishment of any political framework as subsequent to the existence of individuals with natural rights (Held 1993). However, what is fundamentally different with Locke is that the sovereignty remains with the people, rather than a transfer of subjects' rights to the state as proposed by Hobbes; it is this conception that has laid the foundation for the development of liberalism, in that it prepared the way for popular representative government (Held 1993). Following broadly in the tradition of Hobbes and Locke, Bentham (1748–1832) and James Mill (1773–1836) disagreed with the concept of social contract and natural rights as an explanation for why citizens had a duty to the state. Their argument was a utilitarian one – that the state should exhibit minimal interference so as to allow individuals to maximally pursue their own interests, according to the rules of economic competition (Held 1993).

John Rawls' (1971) *A Theory of Justice* is typically seen as *the* defining contemporary statement on liberal theory, which has two main premises: first, the freedom of the individual, and second, equality of opportunity. These two components derive from the idea of 'justice as fairness': that a fair organization of society is achieved by agreeing on principles that people would approve of if they did not know what their situation in society might be – with the assumption that people would logically choose just principles to organize their society if they did not know what their beliefs or what their circumstances might be (Mulhall and Swift 1994).

## Human rights and citizenship

Contemporary conceptions of human rights have their philosophical roots in eighteenth-century Western European theory framed legally in terms of the rights of the individual against the state (Leary 1990). It has been argued that the source of human rights is the individual's moral nature, where human rights are a consequence of 'the inherent dignity of the human person' (Freeman 1994: 30). While international human rights' instruments clearly have been developed in response to, and indeed reflect particular contemporary socio-political concerns and events, they nevertheless reflect a particular philosophical understanding of what it means to be a human being. For example, the 1948 Universal Declaration of Human Rights refers to the human rights of all human beings, linking it to the idea of the dignity of the human person (UN 1948). Hence human rights are conceptualized in terms of a particular understanding of what it means to be a human being – that is, to be a human being is essentially a universal moral experience.

Contemporary human rights discourses are increasingly being coupled to discourses on citizenship and citizenship education. It has been proposed for example, that the UN Convention on the Rights of the Child (CRC) is 'an ideal basis for citizenship education', arguing that 'rights are central to concepts of citizenship and democracy in clarifying the standards which the citizens agree to share' (Alderson 2000: 115). The UN Convention on the Rights of the Child (CRC) is a stronger document, legally, than the Universal Declaration of Human Rights, in that governments have duties on ratifying the CRC (Alderson 2000). Like the Universal Declaration of Human Rights, children's rights are accorded:

> to each child within their jurisdiction without discrimination of any kind, irrespective of the child's or his or her parent's or legal guardian's race, colour, sex, language, religion, political or other opinion, national, ethnic or social origin, property, disability, birth or other status
>
> (UN 1989, Article 2)

This again supports the notion that children's human rights are 'natural', rather than being derived from the state. In terms of practice, however, as opposed to theory, clearly the possession and exercise of human rights can not occur outside of a political community. Yet the state is obliged to provide, protect and promote participation for all, regardless of formal citizenship status.

There is, however, a theoretical confusion regarding whether these CRC rights refer only to 'human rights' to be accorded to all individuals regardless of citizenship status. The UNCRC refers to three types of rights that governments have a duty to implement in law and practice, regardless of citizenship status – 'provision' rights (for example, access to health and education), 'protection' rights (e.g. protection from abuse and discrimination) and 'participation' or civic rights (Alderson 2000). The inclusion of participation or civic rights in the UNCRC are a theoretically different kind of right to other rights in this document, such as the right to life (Article 6), the right to freedom of religion (Article 14) or the right to education (Article 28) (UN 1989). The confusion arises due to the inclusion of 'participation' or civic rights, which are based on being a member of a political community, rather than being a member of common humanity. Given that the CRC includes civic rights, Alderson's suggestion that the CRC be a basis for citizenship education may coincidentally be theoretically sound, although she does not actually address the distinction between the more universalistic human rights accorded to all because of their membership of the human species, and the more particularistic 'citizenship' rights, accorded to those who are members of a political community – that is, accorded to those that have formal citizenship status.

An example of a 'legal' conception of citizenship can be seen in France's citizenship education curriculum,[2] whose conception is underpinned in terms of human rights and political literacy (Kiwan and Kiwan 2005). Citizenship education in France is seen as contributing to the school's key role in the socialization of its citizens into a single national culture based on the human rights principles of freedom, equality and solidarity (Starkey 2000). Human rights feature prominently in the curriculum with human rights and duties, based on the UNCRC addressed in Year 7, and human rights within the European context addressed in Year 9 (Starkey 2000). It is interesting to note that, in Year 11, rights and responsibilities are addressed in the context of naturalization (Starkey 2000), with citizenship and nationality being synonymous in France. The association of these terms dates back to the Revolution when the enjoyment of the rights in the Declaration of the Rights of Man and the Citizen were made dependent on the possession of French nationality (Kiwan and Kiwan 2002). France's formulation of citizenship would suggest that human rights derive from the state, or that having human rights are a characteristic of belonging to a certain political community, in this case, being French. This notion of human rights deriving from possessing nationality however, is contradictory to the idea that human rights are accorded to all human beings based on their universal membership of common humanity. As such, universal human rights as a theoretical underpinning of citizenship is incompatible and incoherent. While it is important to acknowledge the important role of human rights within the practice of active citizenship, and to recognize that the practice of human rights occurs within a political community, it is inaccurate to conflate the two concepts. This is because human rights discourses are located within a universalist discourse, in contrast to citizenship, which is located within a more particularist discourse.

If we examine the terms of the Crick Advisory Group, explicit reference is made to rights:

> To provide advice on effective education for citizenship in schools – to include the nature and practices of participation in democracy; the duties, responsibilities and rights of individuals as citizens; and the value to individuals and society of community activity
>
> (QCA 1998: 4)

Here, rights are an *included* component of citizenship rather than being presented as its theoretical underpinning. What is of particular note is that the phrase 'human rights' is not used – but rather 'rights of individuals *as citizens*' [italic emphasis added]. This is an important distinction between a more universalist approach and an approach where citizenship is defined in political terms. Underpinning human rights is the notion of common humanity, based on ethical and legal conceptualizations of the individual. In contrast, citizenship rights are underpinned in relation to a political community, based on political and legal understandings of the individual. It is appropriate that these terms of reference do not make the theoretical mistake of conflating universalist ethical understandings of the individual with political understandings of the individual.

While the Crick Report refers explicitly to citizenship rights, it does not at any point address the issue of the relationship of citizenship and nationality. However, the implication of having rights in the context of citizenship is that these rights (and also responsibilities) are afforded specifically to the UK citizen as a result of being a UK citizen, that is, on the basis of nationality. The Crick Report does not state what these are, nor does it explicitly distinguish them from the broader notion of universal human rights, afforded to every individual (regardless of their nationality) living in the UK context.

As noted in the previous chapter, the conceptualization of citizenship in the Crick Report makes reference to T. H. Marshall's conceptualization of citizenship (QCA 1998: 10). The British Youth Council is also quoted at some length in the report (QCA 1998: 8–19), where it states that citizenship education should include 'the responsibility of belonging to society – the rights and responsibilities of citizens'. Again, this is a more theoretically accurate focus on citizenship rights as opposed to the more universalist 'human rights' advocated by two of the interviewees whose arguments I consider below.

In contrast to the Crick Report, some of the interviewees propose a model of citizenship explicitly underpinned by human rights. For example, 'C', who submitted evidence to the Crick Group, argues that one of the key aims of citizenship education should be to make people 'aware of issues around human rights' (Interview with 'C': 5), and that 'the whole discourse of public life be of rights' (p. 6).

From her perspective, her emphasis on human rights resulted in human rights having a higher profile in the final Crick Report (as compared with the Draft Initial Report):

> engaged Bernard Crick himself ... to deliberately debate these issues ... and I did see a difference between the initial report and the final report in terms of addressing human rights. I believe they should be fundamental; they're not fundamental but they are introduced in the final report
>
> (Interview with 'C': 6)

Similarly, the journalist, Yasmin Alibhai-Brown, who has had broad engagement in the field and who also had involvement within the initiative through her membership of a Working Party on Citizenship also linked human rights and citizenship, saying that 'it is important for the twenty-first century to develop a culture of citizenship in this country and a culture of human rights, and for me they go very much together, and that actually civil society depends on this' (Interview with Yasmin Alibhai-Brown: 3). She argued that the human rights model is 'about absolute rights and responsibilities in the public sphere' (p. 5), and that the human rights model is 'one that argues for the humanity of all people' (p. 4). She made reference the UN Declaration of Human Rights and the European Convention on Human Rights, proposing a universalist human rights model as a theoretical basis of a model of citizenship in the context of the nation-state.

While the KS3 Programme of Study and KS3 Schemes of Work do not present citizenship as explicitly underpinned by human rights, human rights are nevertheless prominent. In the KS3 Programme of Study, human rights are the first item under the 'knowledge and understanding' heading: 'Pupils should be taught about: (a) the legal and human rights and responsibilities underpinning society' (QCA 2000).

This is explicated in the KS3 guidance to teachers in the Schemes of Work, with Unit 3 entirely devoted to human rights (QCA 2001). It is proposed that pupils examine the Human Rights Act (1998), which protects basic rights for individuals in the UK. It is important to emphasize that this Act protects all individuals living in the UK, regardless of whether or not they are UK citizens. Pupils are taught that the Human Rights Act is 'underpinned by common values' (QCA 2001, Unit 3: 2), with the values of 'fairness, tolerance, respect for others, desire for justice', given as examples of these values (QCA 2001, Unit 3: 4). What this suggests is a conceptualization of citizenship in terms of values. It does not state, however, whose values these values are, nor how they were arrived at. Nor does it explore whether these are universal common values, or whether these are common values for the UK. It is not clear how these common values are distinctive to citizenship in the UK context, in contrast to other nation-state settings. Rights at the level of the school setting are referred to, as are rights at the international level, with reference to the UN Convention on the Rights of the Child, and the Universal Declaration of Human Rights. The issue of human rights is also raised in Unit 11, in the context of their importance in situations of conflict. Under the theme, 'What is really happening to the people involved in the current conflict?', pupils are supposed to learn about the UN Declaration of Human Rights, and to consider the human rights implications of conflict, who is deprived of their human rights, and the kinds of rights that they may be deprived of (QCA 2001, Unit 11: 5). There is also a whole unit, Unit 16, 'Celebrating human rights – citizenship activities for the whole school', devoted to a focus on human rights at the school level.

While the content and activities of these Schemes of Work relating to human rights are laudable, there is no explicit rationale provided regarding how human rights relate conceptually to citizenship. While it is important to acknowledge the important role of human rights in the context of active citizenship, and to recognize that the practice of human rights occurs within a political community, it is important that theoretical distinctions between citizenship rights and human rights are made in the curriculum documentation. The two concepts should not be conflated, if teachers are to have a clear conceptual understanding of citizenship, in order to be able to communicate this effectively to pupils.

The QCA's revised Programmes of Study for Citizenship at KS3 and KS4 go some way to address some of these issues. It states under 'the importance of citizenship', that 'pupils learn about rights and responsibilities, duties and freedoms, laws and justice, and democratic institutions' (QCA 2007: 1). It has 'rights and responsibilities' as a key concept, which it links to living within a democracy, emphasizing the notion of rights of citizens against the state. Pupils are expected to learn about 'political, legal and human rights' and how these rights can compete. While human rights are presented as a 'key theme in citizenship', and that it is important to learn about values underpinning human rights, the Programme of Study does not present human rights as an underpinning of citizenship, which I have been arguing is an important distinction to make.

## Nationality, immigration and citizenship

The complexity of issues surrounding nationality, immigration, asylum seekers and refugees is not explicitly addressed in either the policy or curriculum documentation (QCA 1998, 2000, 2001). That the Crick Report does not explicitly address the issue of the relationship between citizenship and nationality, was, according to Crick, a deliberate strategy: 'We didn't deal with national identity and that was quite deliberate. I said we're not dealing with nationality, we're dealing with a skill, a knowledge, an attitude for citizenship' (Interview with Sir Bernard Crick: 10). Yet, there would appear to be a logical incoherence in the Crick Report with regard to how the relationship between nationality and citizenship is dealt with. Paragraph 3.14 of the report proposes a single national identity, even though it is acknowledging the presence of a plurality of nations:

> 3.14 Responding to these worries, a main aim for the whole community
> should be to find or restore a sense of common citizenship, including a national

identity that is secure enough to find a place for the plurality of nations, cultures, ethnic identities and religions long found in the United Kingdom. Citizenship education creates common ground between different ethnic and religious identities

(QCA 1998: 17)

It is unclear whether this is just a terminological error – did the report mean to propose a single *state* identity – referring to the UK, which is made up of the different nations of England, Wales, Scotland and Northern Ireland? However, there is further confusion with citizenship education being proposed to 'create common ground between different ethnic and religious identities'. The 'nations' is dropped at this point, and it is unclear whether this is because the report is outlining proposals for citizenship education only in English schools, and not the UK as a whole. Given the decentralized control of the constituent education systems within the UK, it is unclear how a single national identity, or even state identity, for that matter, can be agreed upon. This tension and logical incoherence between the scope of citizenship and citizenship education is never explicitly addressed in the report.

In the KS3 Programme of Study, national identity is acknowledged only insofar as a range of other types of identities, and in the context of respecting and understanding diversity. Furthermore, in contrast to the Crick Report's reference to a single national identity, a *plurality* of national identities, rather than a single national identity is referred to, recognizing the national identities of England, Wales, Scotland and Northern Ireland (QCA 2000). These identity-based conceptions of citizenship are examined in more detail in Chapter 6.

With regard to refugees and asylum seekers – in legal terms, those who do not have formal citizenship status, there is no explicit conceptual examination of these issues in relation to citizenship. References arise only in KS3 Schemes of Work Unit 3: 'Human rights', where pupils are expected, as a learning outcome, to know what a refugee is and to be 'aware of local, national and international government and voluntary organisations in supporting refugees and upholding human rights' (QCA 2001, Unit 3: 6). There are no references to immigrants at all. This approach stands in contrast to the French conceptualization of citizenship, where citizenship and nationality are explicitly synonymous. This equating of citizenship and nationality is also reflected in the French citizenship education curriculum, where in Year 7 (6e), pupils are explicitly taught about nationality and naturalization, and what is of particular note is that even in Year 7 (6e), pupils are explicitly taught to distinguish between the individual and the citizen (Starkey 2000).

While this approach to citizenship – making explicit the relationship between citizenship and nationality has, to date, been avoided in the English citizenship education policy and curriculum documentation, an explicit link between citizenship and nationality has been made in a subsequent and related citizenship initiative. Also initiated by David Blunkett (but then in the position as Home Secretary), and chaired by Sir Bernard Crick, a Home Office Advisory

Group was set-up to develop proposals for language and citizenship education for immigrants applying for naturalization to become British citizens. This Advisory Group published its report in September 2003 (Home Office 2003).[3] In this initiative, citizenship education is explicitly linked to nationality, with direct references made to the earlier Crick Report (QCA 1998), and citizenship education in schools.

The rationale for the work of the 'Life in the UK' Advisory Group is set out in the Advisory Group Report: The New and the Old (Home Office 2003). It refers to the government's stated intention in the 2002 White Paper, *Secure Borders, Safe Haven*, of raising the status of becoming a British citizen. It also describes the work as falling within broader government policy aims including 'a wider citizenship agenda' 'encouraging community cohesion' and 'valuing diversity'. The Nationality, Immigration and Asylum Act 2002, requires those applying for British citizenship to be able to show 'a sufficient knowledge of English, Welsh or Scottish Gaelic' and to have 'sufficient knowledge about life in the United Kingdom' (Home Office 2003: 3). In this context, the Life in the UK Advisory Group was set up with the remit 'To advise the Home Secretary on the method, conduct and implementation of a "Life in the United Kingdom" naturalisation test' (p. 3). Since 1 November 2005, applicants for British citizenship have been subject to three new requirements under the Nationality, Immigration and Asylum Act (NIA) 2002 in order to demonstrate sufficient understanding of English (or Welsh or Scottish Gaelic) and of life in the UK. They must either successfully pass a 'citizenship test'[4] or successfully complete an accredited ESOL ('English as a Second Official Language') with citizenship course, and attend a citizenship ceremony.

The 'Life in the UK' Advisory Group Report (Home Office 2003) recommended that language and citizenship education should be made available, outlining the following six broad categories: (1) British national institutions. (2) Britain as a diverse society. (3) Knowing the law. (4) Employment. (5) Sources of help and information. (6) Everyday needs. The Advisory Group Report also proposed the preparation of a handbook for new migrants to the UK, the aim being to promote integration and understanding of British society, including its political institutions. The Handbook, *Life in the United Kingdom: A Journey to Citizenship* (Home Office 2005) was compiled by a sub-committee of the 'Life in the United Kingdom' Advisory Group (chaired by Professor Sir Bernard Crick) with the help of the Citizenship Foundation. The Handbook, of which currently Chapters 2, 3 and 4 form the basis of the citizenship test (for those at higher levels of English language), consists of the following eight chapters:

1  The making of the United Kingdom (providing a concise history)
2  A changing society (including demography, immigration patterns, role of women, family, children and young people)
3  Britain today: a profile (population, religion, regions, customs and traditions)
4  How Britain is governed (system of government, formal institutions, devolved administrations, relation with Europe and world; role of citizen)

5  Everyday needs (housing, education, health, leisure)
6  Employment (looking for work, rights, children and work)
7  Sources of help and information
8  Knowing the law (citizen rights, human rights, marriage and divorce, children, courts, legal advice/aid).

For those with lower levels of English (at English language levels below ESOL Entry level 3), potential applicants are required to attend combined English and citizenship education classes at a further or adult education college. In January 2004, the Home Office and DfES commissioned the National Institute for Adult and Continuing Education (NIACE) and LLU+ to develop learning materials based on the six headings from the original Life in the UK Advisory Group Report as outlined previously. These learning materials expanded these six categories into 12 sections.[5]

The DfES Diversity and Citizenship Curriculum Review can, in part be understood and contextualized in relation to the Home Office initiatives mentioned above. In the Citizenship part of the review, one of the key considerations was whether to introduce a fourth 'pillar' to the citizenship education curriculum on 'British social and cultural history'. The QCA's revised Programmes of Study for Citizenship at KS3 and KS4 make explicit references to 'Britishness' and 'shared values', and the importance of contextualizing this understanding in relevant historical context. This also suggests that citizenship as legal status (nationality) and citizenship as active participation in an educational context are being brought together in a way that recognizes the importance of considering a diversity of identities – including more explicitly – national identity, in the context of citizenship. I examine these proposals relating to the fourth strand in detail in Chapter 6 on 'identity-based' conceptions of citizenship.

## Theoretical and practical implications for diversity

I have argued that a human rights approach to citizenship is essentially a legal conception, based on a modern liberal conception of the state and citizenship, emerging with doctrines of state sovereignty and individuals being conceptualized as being 'free and equal' with natural rights (Held 1993). The focus with a human rights approach, is the idea of the state protecting individuals; a tradition which can be traced back to Hobbes and Locke (Held 1993).

The case of France was provided as an exemplification of a definition of citizenship, which centres on a universalist conception with the premise that everyone is equal regardless of ethnicity, religion or gender. As such, it does not recognize difference (Kiwan and Kiwan 2005). Indeed, it is argued that it is through the transcendence of difference through citizenship, that individuals can put their cultural, linguistic and/or religious backgrounds aside and become active members of the one and indivisible nation-state (Schnapper 1994, cited in Kiwan and Kiwan 2005). Citizenship education has always been at the heart of the French Republican education project, with the aims of citizenship education being to integrate the diverse population of France into a homogenizing and common culture, based on the values of the Revolution: *liberté, égalité, fraternité* (Osler and Starkey 2001). Since the 1980s, there has been an increased emphasis on human rights within citizenship education (Starkey 2000).

Although this universal and legalistic approach to citizenship, which is based on an abstract notion of equality, could be deemed to be well-intentioned, in reality it does not engage with issues of structural disadvantage (Kiwan and Kiwan 2005). Instead of school being a shelter from the social injustices of the outside world, it is now school itself which is seen by students to be generative of these injustices (Dubet and Martuccelli 1996, cited in Kiwan and Kiwan 2005). As a consequence, students are unlikely to be motivated to take part as active citizens within the school community, if they perceive it to be a factor contributing to their marginalization (Barrère and Martuccelli 1998, cited in Kiwan and Kiwan 2005).

There have been calls for the development of a more inclusive concept of citizenship in an ethnically and religiously diverse society, proposing that this re-conceptualization be based on a human rights foundation (Osler 1999; Osler and Starkey 2005). Such human rights approaches are predicated on a moral argument that all human beings are equal, and therefore all deserve the same rights. While there may be a recognition of the hybrid and plural nature of identities, the focus is on achieving equality for 'minority' groups. So identity is addressed in a relatively static and functional way. Indeed, it has been similarly argued that Kymlicka's approach to minority rights in a liberal framework, although against assimilation, and valuing culture, does not value cultural diversity *per se* (Parekh 2000). I propose that human rights as a universal legalistic approach can not adequately take into account ethnic and religious diversity and may be ineffective in the empowerment and active participation of citizens within their community. This is a result of neglecting the question of the differential motivation to actively participate. I further propose that identity may be a key influence in promoting active participation. This is discussed and developed in Chapter 6 on 'identity-based' conceptions of citizenship, and in Chapter 7, where I develop an inclusive model of active citizenship.

Several interviewees who had been involved in the citizenship development in the educational policy context expressed the view that citizenship defined as a legal status in terms of nationality, and citizenship as participation are two separate conceptualizations and that it is unhelpful to conflate the two. According to 'U', who provided a submission to the Crick Advisory Group – a senior employee of a key organization in the field of citizenship education, the linking of citizenship with the immigration and asylum agenda has been detrimental: 'I think the citizenship brand, if you will, has been received considerable harm in recent months with the way it's been associated with the asylum refugee agenda and with the notion that … you know, of citizenship tests for "foreigners"' (Interview with 'U': 6). He argued that moving from a model of citizenship that is participative to one that is based on nationality is a move towards a potentially exclusive model of citizenship. This concern regarding citizenship as a legally defined status being conflated with the citizenship education agenda was also voiced by a member of the Citizenship Advisory Group:

> That distinction is difficult to explain to people … I kind of wish we could have a different word. I don't know what, we used to call it education for civil society, but then people don't know what civil society is either
>
> (Interview with 'K': 14)

One interviewee argued that the 'integration agenda' and the focus on 'community cohesion' is a separate issue from citizenship education. She argued that citizenship education had been 'almost hijacked or ambushed by people who think it's all about integration because it's actually not and that's a real danger because then you will turn off people from even touching it' (Interview with 'S', Developer of resources, ActionAid: 7).

In contrast to the concerns expressed by some of those key players involved regarding the perceived conflation of citizenship as a 'legal status' and citizenship as 'active participation', Sir Bernard Crick argues explicitly for the bringing together of the two senses of citizenship. In the foreword of the Annual Report 2005/6 for the Advisory Board on Naturalization and Integration (ABNI),[6] he states:

> Since the children of immigrants now have learning for active citizenship in school, it would be anomalous and unhelpful if their parents and new arrivals did not have the same requirement and entitlement. So the two senses of citizenship were to come together: that of being a legal citizenship of a state and also a participative citizen
>
> (ABNI/Home Office 2006)

The recent announcement to introduce the same requirements (i.e. 'sufficient' language and 'sufficient' knowledge of life in the UK) for those seeking to settle in the UK in April 2007 could also be perceived as blurring the distinction between citizenship as 'nationality' and citizenship as 'active participation' (Home Office press release, 4 December 2006). Although cumbersome in practice for those having to go through the process, at a theoretical level this could be construed quite positively in the sense that it emphasizes active participation and integration on the basis of a commitment to permanently settle in a given community, rather than solely in terms of the legal status of nationality. While the course route has the potential to promote integration, it could be argued that the route of taking the test does not allow for any meaningful participation. However, there have been calls for more meaningful forms of participation, including requiring applicants to collect portfolios providing evidence of participatory or community activities, and also the provision of citizenship courses for those deemed to have 'sufficient' levels of English (ABNI/Home Office 2006). If these participatory aspects were to be introduced, I would suggest that the proposed settlement requirements could potentially support a more inclusive form of citizenship by providing the relevant knowledge and skills for individuals to participate locally, and indeed nationally, as well as improve their job prospects and life chances for their children.

# 5 'Participatory' conceptions

## Introduction

Although the works of Bentham and Mill are often cited as laying the foreground for liberal democracy, neither were strong advocates of participatory democracy, unlike John Stuart Mill, James Mill's son. John Stuart Mill was committed to the notion of representative government (of every citizen having a voice), as he saw this as key to enhancing individual liberty in all domains, and that it 'promotes a better and higher form of national character' (J. S. Mill, cited in Held *et al.* 1983: 98). He perceived that participation in political life was the basis for developing informed citizens and hence was part of self-development (Held 1993).

In contrast to liberal discourses on the relationship of the individual to the state being framed in terms of individual rights, there is an extensive literature that conceptualizes this relationship quite differently. This philosophical line of thought developed in the historical context of the reception of Locke in eighteenth-century France when there was growing frustration in the French middle and labouring classes at a time when French society was structured very much in terms of privilege (Sabine 1951). By the mid-eighteenth century, Jean-Jacques Rousseau talked of the importance of community and shared values. Rousseau can be said to contrast with Hobbes and Locke in that he was a proponent of 'participatory' democracy, and an active citizenry, an idea which subsequently had an influence on ideas during the French revolution (Held 1993). While Hobbes and Locke argued for state laws to be minimal so as not to encroach on individuals' natural rights, Rousseau perceived laws as enhancing an individual's liberty, as he argued that laws, are by definition, just, and 'an expression of the general will' (Cranston 1968: 36). For Rousseau, liberty and virtue are inter-related, and human beings can only really be free and develop virtue in civil society (Rousseau 1968). He argued that once human beings enter civil society, this provides them with the environment to develop their capacity, and it is only in such a context that the notion of liberty can be utilized meaningfully, and also, as a consequence, that we can talk of human beings as moral beings, whose humanity is realized through active participation in civil society.

Civic republicanism can be traced back to Rousseau (Delanty 2003). With civic republicanism, the emphasis is on civic bonds, and is based on an active concept of citizenship. France is often cited as the classic example of the 'civic republican'[1] model, where citizenship is formulated in abstract universal terms, with no reference to personal or group attributes, such as ethnicity or religion (Brubaker 1998).

Gamarnikow and Green (2000) situate the current approach to citizenship education in England in the context of New Labour's 'Third Way' politics, where the concept of social capital is a central component. They argue that citizenship education is perceived to be instrumental in addressing social fragmentation and exclusion. Social capital is associated with the notion of 'trust', and is located in social institutions, such as the family and other dense social networks within local communities (Gamarnikow and Green 2000). The theoretical roots of social capital theory can be traced back to de Tocqueville's *Democracy in America*, which noted America's rich associational networks in comparison to the elitism of then contemporary mainland Europe (Green and Preston 2001). Green and Preston (2001) trace the development of the social capital tradition, highlighting two key strands – the first strand which aimed to extend rational choice theory into the social domain looking at the role of trust in the context of collective action (Coleman 1988, cited in Green and Preston 2001); the second strand is associated with Putnam who studied civic association in Italy and subsequently social capital (and its assumed decline) in America (Putnam 1993, 2000, cited in Green and Preston 2001). Green and Preston (2001) and Green *et al.* (2003) make the important point that social capital and societal cohesion should not be considered synonymous. They argue that it does not necessarily follow, that education resulting in raised levels of *community* participation will also result in increased *societal* cohesion. Giddens (2004) similarly critiques the concept of social capital, arguing that a distinction must be made between the notion of trust within communities and trust in state institutions.

## Citizenship as 'active participation'

Citizenship education in the Crick Report has been conceptualized in terms of three 'strands' or components: a moral component, a political literacy component and an active participatory component, with particular weight being placed on this third component (QCA 1998). This conception draws on T. H. Marshall's social democratic conception of citizenship developed within the socialist tradition in the context of class struggle (Marshall and Bottomore 1992), although it lacks Marshall's emphasis on rights. Citizenship was conceived as a principle of equality, and categorized into three types: civil, political and social; he argued that the sequence of acquiring these rights ideally, is in that order (drawing this conclusion from his examination of the British context in a historical perspective) (Marshall and Bottomore 1992). This focus on active participation is also evident in the academic writings of Crick, the Chair of the Advisory Group on Education for Citizenship and the Teaching of Democracy in Schools. Crick (2000) defines politics as an *activity*, distinguishing it from democracy. His conception of politics and its relationship to democracy has implications for diversity, which I consider later in this chapter.

The theme of 'active participation' is arguably the most central theme of the Crick Advisory Group's Final Report (QCA 1998): 'Active citizenship is our aim throughout' (QCA 1998: 25). In the introduction to the report, para. 1.5 is a pivotal paragraph in explicitly stating its ambitious aims:

> We aim at no less than a change in the political culture of this country ... for people to think of themselves as active citizens, willing, able and equipped to have an influence in public life ... and to extend radically to young people the best in existing traditions of community involvement and public service, and to make them individually confident in finding new forms of involvement and action among themselves
>
> (QCA 1998: 7–8)

The above quote has several keywords: 'active', 'influence', 'confident', 'involvement' and 'action', which all relate to a conception of citizenship in terms of participation. This conception not only advocates participation, but laudably looks beyond to the results of that participation – namely, having influence and being able to bring about change. This is made explicit where the report elaborates that citizenship education in schools should benefit pupils in that it 'will empower them to participate in society effectively as active, informed, critical and responsible citizens', with the result that society will have 'an active and politically-literate citizenry convinced that they can influence government and community affairs at all levels' (QCA 1998: 9).

The Advisory Group's conception of Citizenship is elaborated in Section 2: 'What we mean by Citizenship' (QCA 1998: 9–13), where active participation is elucidated theoretically. Several political traditions throughout history are referred to, starting with a reference to the Greek and Roman conceptions of citizenship as 'involvement in public affairs' (QCA 1998: 10). Both Plato and Aristotle conceived of human beings[2] as primarily political beings, who could only be fulfilled by actively participating in the affairs of the city-state (Heater 1990; Sabine 1951). John Stuart Mill is explicitly mentioned, in the context of encouraging voluntary and community activity; he argued that active participation enables the development of informed citizens, and was also committed to the notion of representative government (J. S. Mill, cited in Held *et al.* 1983: 98). Crick (2002) argues that J. S. Mill's support for representative government rather than a pure form of democracy comes from being influenced by Tocqueville's concerns of the potential dangers of democracy, based on the French aristocrat's classic study of democracy in nineteenth century America (Tocqueville 1956). J. S. Mill was also influenced by Tocqueville's advocation of intermediary groups between individuals and the state, which, according to Crick, stemmed from his appreciation of diversity, which he argued is important in maintaining liberty in a democracy (Crick 2002).

The concept of 'active citizenship' is related to the three proposed strands zenship, social and moral responsibility, political literacy and community ement, explained in terms of it being a 'habitual interaction between all QCA 1998: 11). This is an interesting theoretical proposition: participation is presented as the pervading concept, or 'glue' of citizenship that links together its different components. The KS3 Programme of Study is divided into three sub-headings, with the third sub-heading devoted to 'Developing skills of participation and responsible action' (QCA 2000). Several aspects are referred to, including the notion of empathy, learning to express a range of views, developing skills of negotiation, taking part in school and community activities, and reflecting on the activity of participation itself. The idea that participation is all-pervasive is coherently reflected in the KS3 Schemes of Work (QCA 2001), with many of the units referring to the 'active participation and responsible action' Programme of Study sub-heading (QCA 2000). In addition, there are also several units that specifically focus on the notion of active participation and related conceptions, which I discuss below.

The stated aims of the KS3 Schemes of Work in the first unit: 'Citizenship – what's it all about?' are to introduce pupils to 'key ideas that are central to developing an understanding of what active citizenship is all about' (QCA 2001, Unit 1: 1). Under the theme, 'what is school like?' it is expected that pupils reflect on ways they already participate in their school and communities. This is then linked to notions of democratic decision-making, and an understanding of the idea of a 'democratic community', which I elaborate on in the following section in a consideration of the relationship between participation and democracy.

Unit 14: 'Developing skills of democratic participation' focuses on issues of decision-making and representativeness in the school context. Pupils are asked to identify different ways of making decisions, and what might constitute 'fair ways' of making decisions (QCA 2001, Unit 14: 3). The idea of pupils' voices being heard on school issues is considered, and compared with decision-making processes in the wider societal context. With regard to the notion of 'representation', in the introduction to the unit, it states that 'Pupils explore … how to ensure representation for diverse groups within society' (QCA 2001, Unit 14: 1). However, in the section 'Where the unit fits in', where it relates the Schemes of Work to the relevant components of the Programme of Study, it does not include 1b 'the diversity of national, regional, religious, and ethnic identities in the United Kingdom'. It could be that this was an oversight, yet the issue of representation for a diversity of identities, and in particular, ethnic and religious identity is not referred to at all under the theme 'How am I represented in my school'. Instead, this issue is presented as a straightforward issue, treated mainly in terms of the types of skills 'they would want somebody representing their views to have, e.g. listening skills, communication skills, organizational skills, leadership skills' (QCA 2001, Unit 14: 5).

The focus of Unit 18: 'Developing your school grounds' is on the practicalities and skills of pupils' 'planning, devising and implementing ways' (QCA 2001, Unit 18: 1) to make improvements in their school. Under the theme, 'How can you meet the needs of people using the school grounds?', it is positive that there is reference to 'the diversity of religious and ethnic identities within the school'. However, this is only considered in relation to 'thinking how this can be reflected in the features and usage of the school grounds' (QCA 2001, Unit 18: 5). Although it is positive that the curriculum is promoting sensitivity to the needs of others, this is not the same as ensuring that there are mechanisms to enable those 'others' (e.g. those with special needs) to participate so that they themselves are empowered to bring about change, and 'speak' for themselves.

## The relationship with democracy

Of note, is the linking of participation with democracy, explicitly evident from the outset in the title of the Report, 'Education for Citizenship and the Teaching of Democracy in Schools' (QCA 1998). While active participation and democracy are presented as being inextricably linked, this relationship is presented with differing emphases throughout the policy and curriculum documentation. There are two main 'arguments' regarding the relationship between active participation and democracy, which can be conceptualized as being on a continuum. At one end of the continuum, democracy is understood in terms of it being a political system, which will be upheld if more people actively participate in the political domain, with voting in elections being the most formalized expression of this active participation. The other end of the continuum is concerned with the *activity* of active participation, which it sees as a democratic activity, with this process empowering people to bring about change.

The foreword to the report would seem to focus on the active participation of citizenship, rather than thinking of participation merely in terms of voting (although it should be acknowledged that the two ends of the continuum are not necessarily mutually exclusive, given that voting is an activity). In the foreword to the report, the Speaker of the House of Commons, and Patron of the Advisory Group, Betty Boothroyd expresses her concern that Citizenship as a school subject is of increasingly low status, and argues that this has 'unfortunate consequences for the future of our democratic processes' (QCA 1998: 3). The phrase 'democratic processes' would seem to indicate that Boothroyd is referring to a whole range of activities that involve different views and perspectives. The foreword concludes with Boothroyd congratulating the Group on its work, and expressing the hope that it will promote both 'understanding of and participation in our democratic, legal and other civic processes' (QCA 1998: 3).

The terms of reference for the Advisory Group, set out by David Blunkett, then Secretary of State for Education and Employment explicitly focus on education for citizenship to include 'the nature and practices of participation in democracy' (QCA 1998: 4). On interviewing David Blunkett, he explicitly linked citizenship education and democracy arguing that it is:

> crucial to the life of a democracy, that people are both well informed and are active participating citizens ... the more people know, the more they do, the more they know and do, the more likely they are to participate formally in things like voting, but more crucially than that, the more likely they are to
> ~rt in civil and civic activity in terms of their own community
>
> (Interview with David Blunkett: 1)

The Crick Report reiterates this theme, first quoting the Lord Chancellor: 'We should not, must not, dare not, be complacent about the health and future of British democracy. Unless we become a nation of engaged citizens, our democracy is not secure' (QCA 1998: 8). The conclusion of a DEMOS pamphlet on politics for 18–34 year olds in Britain is also cited to support the argument that young people's political apathy has 'worrying implications for the future of democracy' (QCA 1998: 16).

The British Youth Council's submission is cited in the Crick Report. With regard to democracy, it proposes that the curriculum should: 'look at what representative democracy is, how it evolved, what it means and what its advantages and disadvantages are. It should also look at other political systems around the world and other representative democracies' (QCA 1998: 19).

This selection of this quote is interesting, as it differs somewhat in tone from the unequivocal support for democracy in the other quotes cited. It proposes an objective non-ideological study of democracy as a political system, in the context of studying about other types of political systems. It may be that Crick wanted to include this, given his view that the term, 'democracy' has come to be conflated with related such concepts as liberty, individualism, and equality, rather than a necessary, but not sufficient component of government (Crick 2002). While Crick (2000) defines politics as an *activity*, he distinguishes politics from democracy however, and warns that politics needs 'defending' against democracy as if democracy 'seeks to be everything, it destroys politics' and can lead to despotism and anarchy (Crick 2000: 73). Crick (2002: 8) explains that the term, 'democracy', has come to mean '"all things bright and beautiful": democracy as a civic ideal, as representative institutions, and as a way of life'. He also notes that democracy is sometimes taken as synonymous with liberty, liberalism, equality and even individualism, rather than a necessary but not sufficient component of government (Crick 2002: 73). He suggests that Tocqueville in part misread democracy in nineteenth-century America as a synonym for equality. He argues that for democracies to be just and stable, they must act *politically* – that is, by conciliating all the main interest groups within a state. In support of this argument, he cites Aristotle's critique of Plato – that Plato makes the mistake of reducing everything in the polis (or state) to a unity, thus destroying politics, and turning 'harmony into mere unison', reducing 'a theme to a single beat'.

Crick's warning against lack of conceptual clarity also has practical implications at the level of pedagogy. It is important that teachers have conceptual clarity with regard to democracy and related concepts, with an understanding both of how they relate to one another and how they differ. This relates to Davies (2000: 104) emphasizing the importance of teaching pupils about such 'procedural concepts' – 'shifting philosophical debates into pedagogical ground', which I consider in the concluding Chapter 8.

There are also several units in the KS3 Schemes of Work (QCA 2001) that all address democracy or democratic processes. Democracy is placed centrally in an understanding of what is meant by citizenship. One of the expectations at the end of Unit 1: 'Citizenship – what's it all about?', is for most pupils to 'recognise the importance of rules and democratic decision-making at school, at home, and in their communities' (QCA 2001, Unit 1: 1). One theme of the unit, entitled 'What is a democratic community?' encompasses a consideration of 'what rights are and how they relate to responsibilities', that 'fairness and social justice are key to democratic communities', and that 'groups and individuals can make decisions in different ways within a democratic society' (QCA 2001, Unit 1: 5). Democracy is being presented both in terms of values and in terms of processes. Unit 6: 'Government, elections and voting' in contrast, focuses on the more formalized aspects of political participation and focuses on democracy as a political system (QCA 2001). One learning objective is to learn about the advantages and disadvantages of different voting systems, with a consideration of different political systems, including dictatorship and oligarchy (QCA 2001, Unit 6: 4). This is positive as it allows an objective, non-ideological study of democracy as a political system, rather than what Crick (2000, 2002) refers to as an 'all things bright and beautiful' approach to democracy – conflating democracy with other related, yet distinct concepts. Unfortunately, however, this seems to be relatively underdeveloped in the remainder of the unit.

Unit 7: 'Local Democracy' focuses on students' local communities, with the themes of 'What do I know about my local community?', 'What is my community concerned about?' and 'How can we influence change?' (QCA 2001, Unit 7). Learning expectations are presented predominantly in pedagogical terms of 'understanding', 'awareness' and 'reflection', with no notion of 'challenging', or 'critiquing'. In addition, while the 'understanding' of the local community includes different approaches to participation in local life, this does not include anything on demonstrations, or illegal protest, or the notion of struggle, nor is there any consideration of the broader issue of unequal power relations and what may contribute to this.

The issue of unequal power relations in relation to democracy is taken up, however, in Unit 12 in the historic context of 'Why did women and some men have to struggle for the vote in Britain? What is the point of voting today?', with the first theme titled 'How can we start to think about power and exclusion?' (QCA 2001, Unit 12). This is then applied to the contemporary context with most pupils being expected to be able 'to identify the principles that underpin exclusion today', and those pupils who 'have progressed further' are expected to use their knowledge to 'discuss the challenges of providing representative government for minority groups' (QCA 2001, Unit 12: 2). However, engagement with these issues is in terms of 'identifying' and 'discussing', rather than in terms of developing participative skills in relation to these issues.

Active participation remains central to the conception of citizenship in the revised QCA Programmes of Study for Citizenship at KS3 and KS4 (QCA 2007): 'Education for citizenship equips young people with the knowledge, understanding and skills to play an effective role in public life' (p. 1). Under 'democracy and justice', the first-mentioned key concept, it explains that pupils need to develop their knowledge, skills and understanding of 'actively participating in different kinds of decision-making and voting in order to influence public life' (p. 2).

The accompanying guidance notes explain that democracy is both a 'political system', and linked to holding certain values, such as 'freedom', 'justice' and 'respect'. It states that 'in a democracy, not everyone gets what they want' (p. 2). However, this is not explicitly linked or discussed in terms of unequal power relations and exclusion. Similarly, skills of taking action and 'advocacy and representation' are presented as pupils merely developing and using such skills, without acknowledging the imbalances of power in society, and institutional processes that can implicitly sustain social exclusion. There is recognition of individual and group identities in relation to political participation signaled under 'range and content' of the subject, where it states that the subject should address 'how individuals, groups and organisations can influence decision-making (locally, nationally and globally) through action' (p. 5). There is also reference to the notion of 'political rights', which is explained in terms of including a study of the 'development of universal suffrage and equal opportunities' (p. 5). KS4 goes further in developing the theme of the inter-relatedness of identity and participation, where it proposes that in a democracy, 'sometimes justice means treating everyone the same, sometimes it means treating people differently' (p. 2). It also proposes that students consider 'the action that has been, or could be taken, to improve conditions of life for different groups' (p. 3).

## Theoretical and practical implications for diversity

The Crick Report, in highlighting the important role of education in promoting active participation, implicitly relies on what Pattie *et al.* (2004) call a choice-based approach to understanding political participation, and in particular 'cognitive engagement theory', which hypothesizes that participation depends on access to information. Pattie *et al.* (2004) propose that the importance of education in promoting active participation is largely based theoretically on what they refer to as a 'choice-based' approach to understanding political participation. They theorize that there are two meta-categories: choice-based and structural approaches. Choice-based theories reflect a liberal conception of society, and are basically utilitarian, with citizenship 'emerging from the choices which agents make' (Pattie *et al.* 2004: 138). This is in comparison to structural approaches where individuals are socialized into the norms and values of the community (communitarian and civic republican theories come under this category). Pattie *et al.* (2004) empirically tested these rival theories as explanations of citizenship, and while no one theory could fully explain participation, what emerged was that choice-based theories better explain participation than structural theories. It would seem that the Crick Report draws strongly on cognitive engagement theory, in its focus on acquiring knowledge, rather than socializing to certain norms and values. However, a weakness of cognitive engagement theory is that it does not address what motivates people to participate.

I suggest that identity may be a significant component in understanding what motivates participation. What is not sufficiently addressed in a participatory-based conception of citizenship is the question of whether a focus on active participation without a concomitant focus on people's diversity of identities can achieve an inclusive empowerment of all types of young people. The rationale for this is that in order to be motivated to participate, one must be able to identify or relate one's own personal identity/ies with those reflected in the larger community. Osler and Starkey's (2005) definition of citizenship as 'a status, a *feeling* and a practice' is useful in this regard, where citizenship as 'feeling' refers to a sense of belonging to the larger community. I propose that citizenship as 'feeling' and citizenship as 'practice' are inextricably linked, and mutually enhancing, given that motivation to actively participate is logically predicated on a sense of belonging to or 'identification' with, the context in which they are participating. Similarly, just as a sense of belonging or identity may promote participation, the experience of participating can enhance a sense of belonging. This may pose a challenge to traditional conceptions of maintaining democracy which typically rely on preserving the public/private sphere distinction, in contrast to the aim of promoting equality and diversity, which calls for 'inclusiveness rather than neutrality' of the public sphere (Modood 2005: 20). While these aims need not necessarily be in tension, the use of terms such as 'maintaining' and 'upholding' in conjunction with democracy and public political institutions suggests a 'maintaining the status quo' approach, rather than being open to a truly more inclusive approach.

Citizenship education must logically therefore incorporate this aspect explicitly in its participatory conception of citizenship in an active and constructive manner, pedagogically going beyond advocating a mere 'awareness' of diversity. Crick's conception of politics and its relationship to democracy logically have implications for diversity. Indeed, Crick (2000) has defined politics as an activity of reconciling the views of different groups, arising 'from the problem of diversity, and does not try to reduce all things to a single unity' (p. 31). He warns that democracy is an element of politics rather than synonymous with it, and that 'if it seeks to be everything, it destroys politics, turning "harmony into mere unison", reducing "a theme to a single beat"' (p. 73). While he proposes that there must be some shared notion of some 'common good', he makes the point that this common good should itself be 'the process of practical reconciliation of the interests of the various ... groups which compose a state' (p. 24). Diversity is inherent in this conceptualization of a participatory politics, however it does not consider issues of unequal power relations, or unequal access to resources and information. Nor does this conception explicitly address the issue of how or whether to accommodate ethnic and religious diversity in the public sphere.

In contrast to Crick, Young's (2000) conception of 'deliberative democracy' attempts to address the problem of differential power and motivation to participate for members of traditionally disempowered groups, and the issue of how to accommodate ethnic and religious diversity in the public sphere. She calls for a 'democratic fix' through the norms of deliberative democracy, where democracy is actually 'deepened through enabling more inclusivity of plural claims and perspectives and empowering for less privileged participants' (p. 35). This is discussed further in Chapter 7.

The focus of the original Crick Report (QCA 1998) and subsequent Programmes of Study and Schemes of Work (QCA 2000, 2001) on the accessibility to information and developing participatory skills is certainly necessary, but it is not sufficient, as it does not address the impact of differential power between groups, which can lead to disempowerment and lack of motivation to participate for those historically marginalized groups. In addition, there is a lack of conceptual clarity, and indeed tensions between, the conceptions of participation, democracy and diversity. Most importantly, the dominant participatory-based conception of citizenship does not substantively accommodate the diversity of identities, which I propose is necessary to achieve an inclusive empowerment of all types of young people. It is positive, however, that the revised QCA KS4 Programme of Study goes some way towards acknowledging the inter-relationship between participation and issues of diversity in its proposal that students consider 'action that has been, or could be taken, to improve conditions of life for different groups' (QCA 2007: 3).

It is important, though, for citizenship education to go beyond merely learning about issues of structural disadvantage and instead explicitly challenge issues of structural disadvantage (Kiwan and Kiwan 2005), and examine how this may be related to ethnic and religious identity.[3] Drawing on the example of citizenship education in the French educational system whereby its civic republican approach means that ethnic and religious identity are explicitly confined to operating only within the personal sphere (Kiwan and Kiwan 2005), citizenship education may fail to achieve a more substantive participation of young people of different ethnic and religious identities.

I suggest that there are two key themes: the public/private sphere distinction, and the extent to which we can meaningfully talk about 'shared values' when talking about participative, inclusive and democratic citizenship. Young's (2000) concept of deliberative democracy engages with both of these themes, where she argues that the public/private sphere distinction is a false dichotomy, and that a 'thick' or 'maximal' notion of shared values can be a means of exclusion and silencing of voices. I would conclude by proposing that citizenship education must logically therefore accommodate a consideration of a diversity of identities explicitly in its participatory conception of citizenship in an active and constructive manner, pedagogically going beyond advocating a mere 'awareness' of diversity. A pedagogy emphasizing active communication and problem-solving should be an important part of developing a process towards inclusive participative citizenship.

# 6    'Identity-based' conceptions

## Introduction

This chapter examines what I have called 'identity-based' conceptions of citizenship, which I explain below. This set of conceptions were considered to be 'underplayed' by interviewees, and also are relatively less evident in the policy and curriculum documentation, in contrast to the more frequently utilized 'moral', 'legal' and 'participatory' conceptions of citizenship examined in the previous chapters.

When asked what dimensions of citizenship they perceived to be underplayed in the conceptualization of citizenship throughout the policy development process, interviewees referred most frequently to categories that relate to a cluster of 'identity-based conceptions': covering diversity, identity, anti-racism, multiculturalism, nationality and global and European aspects of citizenship. I have called these types of conceptions, 'identity-based', because they are inherently concerned with identity, or forms of identification at different levels, e.g. at the local, national, European, or global level.

The first section of this chapter examines how diversity is presented as being both politically and conceptually problematic, drawing both on interviewee data and policy and curriculum documentation (QCA 1998, 2000, 2001). Second, this is followed by an analysis of the various conceptions of citizenship that are perceived to be underplayed by interviewees. These 'identity-based' conceptions are sub-divided into the following four categories: 'national', 'global/European', 'anti-racist' and 'multicultural'.[1] Drawing on theories of citizenship and diversity, and set in contemporary social, political and educational context, I show the extent to which these categories are also reflected in the policy and curriculum documentation, illustrating discontinuities in the conceptualizations between the policy and curriculum development stages of the process. Third, drawing on the DfES Diversity and Citizenship Curriculum Review (Ajegbo et al. 2007), I discuss our proposals for a fourth strand in the Citizenship curriculum: 'Identities and diversity: living together in the UK' and its implications for QCA's revised Programmes of Study at KS3 and KS4. Finally, I consider the implications of these different identity-based categorizations for the practice of active citizenship. I propose that a 'multicultural' conception – as a basis for active citizenship in the

British multicultural context is necessary; this is because identification with the community is crucial in any meaningful active participation in that community, regardless of the level of that identification – that is, identification and participation at a local, national or global level. In the following chapter, I propose a model of active citizenship, underpinned by a more 'institutionally-embedded' multiculturalism.

## Diversity: politically 'difficult' and conceptually 'problematic'

In many of the interviews, the issue of diversity did not arise unless, as the interviewer, I specifically raised it as an issue for discussion. A key theme that emerged was that diversity was perceived to be 'too difficult' to deal with, and in addition, not a primary objective in the context of citizenship education.

Although the Crick Report takes T. H. Marshall as its starting point for his conceptualization of citizenship[2] (QCA 1998), the issue of social inclusion is not substantively addressed, even though T. H. Marshall's primary concern was with social inclusion (Marshall and Bottomore 1992). Crick explained that he does not find diversity as a concept 'morally difficult' or 'philosophically difficult', but that dealing with diversity in the citizenship curriculum as a compulsory component would be 'pedagogically extremely difficult' (Interview with Crick: 8).

This downplaying of diversity in the Crick Report's conceptualization of diversity seems paradoxical in theoretical terms, given Crick's (2000) conceptualization of the nature of politics. As discussed in the previous chapter, Crick (2000: 18) in his book, *In Defence of Politics* states that 'Politics arises from accepting the fact of the simultaneous existence of different groups, hence different interests and different traditions, within a territorial unit under a common rule'.

The above clearly defines politics in terms of difference, or diversity. Crick (2000: 33) goes on to explain that 'politics is a way of ruling divided societies without undue violence', and that politics can be defined as a 'process of discussion' between different groups. One explanation for the relative downplaying in particular of ethnic and religious diversity in the Crick Report may be that this was an act of politics itself – a compromise based on perceived political sensitivities at the time. 'L', an academic, who provided a submission to the Crick Advisory Group during its broader consultation process, suggests that diversity was not dealt with in any significant way by Crick's Advisory Group, because 'Crick took a semi-political decision to side-step and not make it as central as it deserved to be' (Interview with 'L': 4). Similarly, Tony Breslin of the Citizenship Foundation, who contributed a submission to the Crick Report, suggests that 'the underplayed strands in Crick are the European dimension and anti-racist dimension' and that this is because 'Crick is a very astute politician himself' who 'was sensitive to the potential hijacking of the agenda' (p. 4). Another explanation may be that Crick is referring to political diversity, rather than ethnic or religious diversity. While Crick's civic republican approach can accommodate political diversity, it does not explicitly accommodate ethnic or religious diversity.

Referring to the text of the Crick Report (QCA 1998: 17), diversity is presented as a potential problem, with cultural diversity being linked to 'the apparent loss of a value consensus', a quote attributed to the Citizenship Foundation. Diversity is conceptualized as a potential barrier to citizenship, rather than as an integral aspect of citizenship. The framing of diversity as a problem is also evident in the way it is explicitly linked to dissent and social conflict – with the 'knowing and understanding' of 'the nature of diversity, dissent and social conflict' outlined as an expected learning outcome for students by the end of compulsory schooling (QCA 1998: 44).

When asked about this conceptualization of diversity in the context of citizenship, Crick referred to 'the naturalness of conflict, societies do find conflict sometimes in religion, in ethnicity' (Interview with Sir Bernard Crick: 8). But he added: 'I celebrate diversity but I also see the difficulties of diversity, it's a tragedy and a comedy, it's the two masks, it's the two sides of the coin, it's always there' (p. 9). However, while Crick here referred to the potential benefits that diversity can bring, the dominant message in the Crick Report is one in which diversity is a potential problem (QCA 1998, 3.13, 3.14, 3.16: 17–18).

The Crick Report proposes that the way to deal with the 'problem' of diversity is to: 'find or restore a sense of common citizenship, including a national identity that is secure enough to find a place for the plurality of nations, cultures, ethnic identities and religions long found in the United Kingdom' (QCA 1998: 17). The solution being proposed is to come up with *one* version of citizenship, and *one* national identity. I would argue that this proposed sense of common citizenship does not necessarily invoke an assimilationary model, whereby different ethnic and religious groups are expected to assimilate into the dominant culture, shedding the specificity of their ethnic and religious identities. However, integration into a shared *political* culture, with a focus on shared commitment to political institutions and laws is proposed: 'minorities must learn and respect the laws, codes and conventions as much as the majority ... because this process helps foster common citizenship' (QCA 1998: 17–18).

The Crick Report's reference to the binary conceptualization of diversity as majority/minority in the excerpt above might suggest that the political integration of 'minorities' into the mainstream 'majority' is relatively unproblematic and is mainly an issue of minorities acquiring political knowledge and abiding by the law. As discussed in Chapter 4, education is invoked here as a key component, in what Pattie *et al.* (2004) refer to as the cognitive engagement model. However, the presentation of integration as a one-way process has been criticized for assuming a deficit model of minorities (Osler 2000). What Osler argues is that not only is diversity often presented negatively, but that young people, in particular of ethnic or religious minority background, are considered a potential problem.

Over the last 5 years, there has been a shift with an increased focus on issues of identity and diversity (Kiwan 2006a). As discussed in Chapter 2, issues relating to diversity, 'race' and immigration were rarely linked to the aims of citizenship education, in contrast to recent media and policy discourses. It is in this context that the DfES Diversity and Citizenship Curriculum Review Report can be situated, as discussed later in this chapter.

### *Flexibility of the curriculum*

Although it was generally acknowledged by interviewees that diversity was not sufficiently addressed in the citizenship education policy development process, interviewees pointed out that the curriculum has enough flexibility that diversity issues could be addressed by citizenship education teachers in the classroom. David Kerr, NFER researcher seconded to QCA as Professional Officer to the Crick Advisory Group, referred to this as 'a light touch flexible framework which is there for schools to actually interpret' (Interview with David Kerr: 6). Tony Breslin, Director of the Citizenship Foundation talked of the curriculum 'opening up a space for work around diversity, anti-racism' (Interview with Tony Breslin: 4). There is a notion that the development of the curriculum and the experience of teachers in the classroom need not rigidly adhere to the formulation of policy in the Crick Report (QCA 1998), but rather, there is a notion that this process is one which 'evolves' (Interview with David Kerr: 8). Yet although reference is made to the flexibility of the curriculum, what is also expressed is a worry that too many different lobby groups are trying to take ownership of citizenship, and that this may ultimately lead to conceptual confusion:

> I do think there is a fundamental difficulty with citizenship education in that so many people see it as their area and you can make a list of all those … global, diversity, political people, historians, values people, all those sorts of things, there a real danger that if they all had their bit, the whole thing gets de-stabilised
>
> (Interview with David Kerr: 8)

While this is a valid theoretical point, of note is that this issue was being raised specifically in the context of talking about diversity and citizenship. This would suggest that diversity can be seen as just one more issue for citizenship to address, rather than considering that, both conceptually and in practice, diversity may actually be inherent to thinking about citizenship in a multicultural society.

## From policy to curriculum: a changing conception?

While diversity is primarily perceived to be a problem in relation to the outlined conception of citizenship in the Crick Report (QCA 1998), this is not so apparent in the subsequently developed KS3 Programme of Study (QCA 2000), which outlines expected learning outcomes, and the KS3 Schemes of Work (QCA 2001), which provide fuller guidance for teachers. In the KS3 Programme of Study, diversity is not presented as problematic, but is presented in terms of 'the need for mutual respect and understanding' (QCA 2000). However, in pedagogical terms, it is only explicitly addressed under the 'knowledge and understanding' learning outcome in terms of pupils being 'taught about' such 'diversity of … identities', rather than in terms of acquiring skills (QCA 2000). This suggests a rather passive acceptance of a description of the status quo, rather than an active engagement with the issues. With regard to the KS3 Schemes of Work, there are several units that address or include components relating to identity and diversity. These include: Unit 4: 'Britain – a diverse society?'; Unit 10: 'Debating a global issue'; Unit 11: 'Why is it so difficult to keep the peace today?'; Unit 12: 'Why did women and some men have to struggle for the vote in Britain? What is the point of voting today?' and Unit 13: 'How do we deal with conflict?' (QCA 2001). These units reflect a range of conceptualizations of identity, which are discussed in the four sections below: 'national', 'global/European', 'anti-racist' and 'multicultural'. In the following four sections, the differences between the conceptualizations of diversity in the Crick Report, the KS3 Programmes of Study and the KS3 Schemes of Work are elucidated, and pedagogical implications suggested.[3]

### A national identity?

While the Crick Report acknowledges national, regional, ethnic and religious diversity (QCA 1998), it takes a civic republican approach whereby it separates ethnic and religious identity from citizenship (Brubaker 1998), relegating these forms of identity to the personal sphere. This conception of citizenship is underpinned theoretically by the conception of a civic identity, framed primarily in legal terms, rather than in social or cultural terms. In this 'territorial-civic' model, the state precedes the nation, in contrast to an 'ethnic' or 'ethnocultural' model of citizenship where the 'nation' exists before the state (Brubaker 1998; Miller 1995).

'O', a former senior employee of the Qualifications and Curriculum Authority (QCA) emphasized the importance of political national identity in the context of citizenship, arguing for a civic republican approach. 'O' was quite adamant that individuals' other identities are kept out of the public political sphere: 'I think that political national identity is terribly, terribly important and needs to be detached from one's sense of ethnic cultural identity' (Interview with 'O': 9). Examples of France and the USA were cited: 'where people are clearer about the distinction between their identity as citizens and their identity as Roman Catholics or Jews or Muslims' (p. 6). 'O' argued that 'in citizenship terms, probably what we need in this society is a greater emphasis on our unity than on our diversity' (p. 6).

'O' framed the 'problem' of diversity, and in particular, religious diversity, in terms of a discourse around a lack of 'shared values' in the context of a national identity.[4] 'O' proposed that one of the aims of citizenship education should be to inculcate 'some sense of identity with the country of which they are citizens' (Interview with 'O': 7), linking this with the perceived problem of alienated British Muslim youth whose 'loyalty to [British] society were so non-existent really that they could go off and fight for the Al-Qaeda' (Interview with 'O': 6–7). In this account, education is perceived to create those myths of comment descent and common culture, what Smith (1988) referred to as the paradoxical problem of the territorial-civic model, given that the state precedes the nation, and the nation has to subsequently be constructed to create that 'imagined community' (Anderson 1983).

Tom Bentley, former Director of Demos, and a member of the Crick Advisory Group suggested that although it is generally recognized that diversity is a feature of contemporary society, citizenship continues to be framed in traditional terms: 'as a dominant civic identity identified with nationhood ... but equating nationhood with a body of institutionalised identity and practice, body of law' (p. 7), in contrast to different kinds of social and cultural identities. Identity is acknowledged primarily in terms of legal conceptualizations of identity – how it relates to public sphere institutions, rather than in more sociocultural forms of identity – typically ascribed by liberalism to the personal private sphere (Rawls 1971).

This raises the question of whether public institutions can equally represent citizens with diverse identities, if they do not actually recognize 'our particular identities, but only our more universally shared interests in civil and political liberties' (Gutmann 1995: 3–4). In theoretical terms, it is assumed that public institutions are neutral by not recognizing difference, however, in practice, liberalism will result in 'particularism masquerading as the universal', unless there are systems and processes that are 'authored' by those from a diversity of different identities (Taylor 1995: 44). Building on this, I propose the concept of 'institutional multiculturalism', which I develop in the following chapter.

### Global/European citizenship

In contrast to citizenship being situated in the nation-state context, several interviewees argued for identifications above the national level to be given more emphasis in conceptualizations of citizenship. There has been a long tradition of an alternative to the state-oriented types of citizenship – of a more universalist approach to citizenship. In Greece, there were alternative conceptions put forth by the Stoics, which put an emphasis on the rationality of human beings, and argued that because of all human beings having this common attribute, this made them equal (Heater 1990). The notion of a universal community is also central to many world religions, including Christianity and Islam (Delanty 2003).

This universalist approach to citizenship was revived in the seventeenth and eighteenth centuries, partly in response to development of the European nation-state (Williams 2002), with Kant advocating an international system based on 'principles of mutual respect' (Kant 1949). Most recently, a range of more universalist theories have emerged in reaction to liberal and communitarian theories, due to a number of influences, such as the assertion of cultural rights, globalization, the decoupling of citizenship and nationality, and the conflation of the public and private spheres (Williams 2002).

There is a wide range of what are sometimes referred to as 'post-national' (Soysal 1998) conceptions of citizenship, including transnational, global and multiple citizenships (Delanty 2000) and 'diasporic', 'cultural' and 'sexual' citizenship (Isin and Wood 1999). An example of a 'post-national' model is proposed by

Soysal (1998), who, drawing on the German context of Turkish 'guestworkers', argues for citizenship being more universal, based on personhood rather than nationhood, referring to the increasing power of transnational bodies (in legal terms), as well as the forces of globalization. Osler and Vincent (2002: 123) propose that with globalization and increased interdependence, it is important to educate young people 'to participate as cosmopolitan citizens', stressing that local, national and international citizenship are not mutually exclusive. Osler and Starkey (2003) propose that human rights can provide the basis for this education for cosmopolitan citizenship, stating that this is extended from Held's model of cosmopolitan democracy.

That global and European issues be given sufficient emphasis was 'frequently-expressed' (QCA 1998: 76), a theme that emerged from the Crick Advisory Group's own consultation process. The terms of reference of the Crick Advisory Group make reference to the relationship of active citizenship in the local and national, regional and indeed global contexts: 'the teaching of civics, participatory democracy and citizenship ... to include some understanding of democratic practices and institutions, including ... the relationship of formal political activity with civic society in the context of the UK, Europe and the wider world' (QCA 1998: 4). There are references to the regional and global levels in the context of pupils learning about and developing skills to effect change, with a quote from the British Youth Council advocating that 'the curriculum should show how ordinary citizens have been the catalysts for change and improvement at a local, national and international level' (QCA 1998: 19). The concept of 'learning through action' is referred to as a teaching approach where pupils' experiences acting at a local level may help to enable them 'to make the connection between learning and acting locally to thinking globally' (QCA 1998: 37).

In his interview, however, Crick expressed scepticism regarding globalism in the context of citizenship, adding that David Blunkett is also of the same view:

> I mean, Blunkett and I both share the view that sometimes ... global concerns are way of avoiding nasty neighbourhood concerns that can annoy the local council and annoy school governors and can annoy parents. It's actually easier to be terribly concerned to do things about starvation in Southern Africa or the deforestation in Brazil or the East Indies, but you can end up with a kind of fantasy politics
>
> (Interview with Sir Bernard Crick: 12)

Marianne Talbot, a member of the Advisory Group, refers to Crick's scepticism of globalism, explaining that as a group, they believed that a focus on the local was the most appropriate starting point: 'I think we all felt that actually if you start local, it would filter out, and I'm sure that's got to be right. Local ought to be the school' (Interview with Marianne Talbot: 10).

It may be that Crick's scepticism is not just a practical one, where he is concerned that a focus on global issues may direct attention away from local and national levels. It also reflects theoretical arguments that globalization has undermined national forms of citizenship (Stevenson 2002). His concern is also a conceptual concern, where Crick is anxious for citizenship to remain within a national framework, as stated in the Crick Report: 'A main aim for the whole community should be to find or restore a sense of common citizenship, including a national identity' (QCA 1998). This implies that local citizenship is acceptable insofar as it encourages active participation on a small-scale, with the potential to trickle up to the national level. While there are references to global dimensions of citizenship, these are framed as being particularly important in order to give 'due regard to the homelands of our minority communities' (QCA 1998).

The KS3 Programme of Study refers to the European and global community under the 'Knowledge and understanding' (heading, 1i), where it is proposed that pupils be taught about 'the world as a global community, and the political, economic, environmental and social implications of this, and the role of the European Union, the Commonwealth and the United Nations' (QCA 2000). This contains two aspects, the first is the idea that the world is a shared political community, and the second aspect refers to existing regional and international organizations.

Unit 4: 'Britain – a diverse society?', in the KS3 Schemes of Work, contains a theme entitled 'What is a global citizen? Is there a global community?' (QCA 2001: 7), where pupils learn about globalization, and how it impacts on local and national communities. In addition, Unit 10: 'Debating a global issue' is devoted to global dimensions of citizenship, with a specific focus on environmental issues (the consequences in the Amazon rainforest given as the example). Pupils are expected to 'make connections between their own actions and choices and the effects these have on other communities locally, nationally and globally' (QCA 2001, Unit 10: 9). Demaine (2002) notes that the rise of 'global citizenship' in the school curriculum does not address the issue that both the terms 'globalization' and 'citizenship' are contested concepts, and argues that for global citizenship education to be successful, it must acknowledge that individuals operate from within the legal and political structures of the nation state. He also argues that global citizenship education will have to address economic, social and political inequalities between citizens both within and between nation states.

Indeed, while the relationship between the local and global is made in the Crick Report, there is evidence that the relationship between the national and global levels is often relatively neglected. Indeed, Kymlicka (2003) has provided examples from democratic 'multicultural' societies, where the different groups have relatively minimal contact between one another, yet exhibit a 'cosmopolitan interculturalism', where individuals of these groups develop skills for participation at a more global level, rather than at the local or national level. I return to this theme in the following Chapter 7. This relative tentativeness with regard to the national level, and its implications, are often not addressed.

### Anti-racism

The relationship between anti-racism and citizenship is fraught with tension in academic discourse, and this is also reflected in the views of interviewees.

One expressed concern by those working in the anti-racism field is that a focus on citizenship could potentially detract from work on anti-racism. Yasmin Alibhai-Brown was critical of this stance, arguing: 'Black and Asian people feel that if you concentrate only on citizenship, then you're taking away from people's commitment to anti-racism' (Interview with Yasmin Alibhai-Brown: 2). She asserted that there has not been support for citizenship from those working in the anti-racism field – which may in part explain why there is no reference to any consultation with the Commission for Racial Equality (CRE) in the Crick Report (QCA 1998). Alibhai-Brown further explains that:

> struggles for equality should be embedded in collective citizenship and human rights which are universal and not conditional. So far too many anti-racists have failed to understand the developing sense of citizenship entitlement in the UK and how that gives race equality a different and more profound framework
> (e-mail communication, 20 February 2007)

When asked about this issue, the CRE employee said:

> I would have thought it would have been within our scope to contribute. It would be important that we contributed but I would guess that they didn't contact us; that would be my assumption. It's quite possible given that there wasn't an education specialist that it could have fallen through the net, if you like, but I would think it's more likely they didn't contact us, and I think the reality is that with citizenship, race was seen as an issue, but very much sort of in isolation, I think it would be an afterthought to be honest
> (Interview with CRE employee: 4)

Here, the CRE employee made the point that racism is not generally perceived to be an integral component of citizenship. However, what also emerged was that some of those in the anti-racism field, likewise, are not particularly interested in citizenship, but instead view it as a convenient place in which to package anti-racism initiatives. The CRE employee argued that anti-racism should be incorporated throughout the whole curriculum, rather than standing as a separate component. She argued, however, that pragmatically, having citizenship as a separate subject in the curriculum provides a space for race issues to be dealt with: 'the value of having citizenship is that it is an area where you can actually see a clear location for race policy issues' (Interview with CRE employee: 6).

It is interesting to note that this position has changed over the last 2–3 years, with identity, nationality and citizenship having been made a significant focus of work in the CRE (CRE 2006).

There are no references linking anti-racism to citizenship in the Crick Report (QCA 1998). This is particularly striking in Figure 1: Overview of essential elements, made up of a long list key concepts, values and dispositions, skills and aptitudes and knowledge and understanding, which does not contain any reference to anti-racism (QCA 1998: 44). The question of the relationship of anti-racism to citizenship was explicitly raised by Crick in his interview, when discussing approaches to diversity in the context of citizenship. It would appear that the absence of any reference to anti-racism in the Crick Report was a political decision: 'Lots of people said, well, you haven't got anti-racism … I said, well, no, but we've got tolerance and we need to understand diversity' (Interview with Sir Bernard Crick: 8).

Crick argued that his main objection to including anti-racism was that it is a pedagogically difficult issue, and that including such a component may have worried teachers. In addition, he argued that even with the eradication of racism from society, one could still have 'a bloody awful society' (Interview with Crick: 11). Talbot also argued that citizenship is 'about more than [racism]' (Interview with Marianne Talbot: 6), and that 'I don't think that racism is the be all and end all of citizenship' (Interview with Marianne Talbot: 9).

The Crick Report has been critiqued for its lack of any reference to race equality or racial discrimination (Osler and Starkey 2001). The Crick Report instead refers to 'diversity' and how this has the potential to be problematic, as discussed in the first section of this chapter (QCA 1998). 'Equality and diversity' and 'fairness, justice, the rule of law, rules law and human rights' are presented as 'key concepts' in Figure 1: Overview of essential elements, with 'the practice of tolerance' listed under 'values and dispositions' (QCA 1998: 44). This reflects the tradition of liberalism, with Rawls' 'justice as fairness' clearly reflected (Rawls 1971), and the notion 'free and equal individuals', commitment to tolerance, and a clear delineation between private and public sphere (Held 1993).

As in the Crick Report, there is no explicit reference to anti-racism in the KS3 Programme of Study (QCA 2000). In the KS3 Schemes of Work, anti-racism is referred to in Unit 4: 'Britain – a diverse society?', although it is not developed substantively. The learning expectations in Unit 4 for 'most pupils' do not contain any explicit reference to anti-racism; instead there is the concept of 'the importance of respect for all' (QCA 2001, Unit 4: 1). Anti-racism is included implicitly in recommended resources, through references to websites such as 'Kick racism out of football campaign'; 'Show racism the red card' and the QCA 'Respect for All' – where diversity and anti-racist education through the curriculum are listed. In addition, the language and literacy section which lists words that pupils are expected to be able to use and understand includes such terms as 'racism' and 'discrimination'. In terms of the content of the unit, there is only one reference to the issue of racism under the theme 'what are my identities?', with learning outcomes including that pupils 'recognise' that different identities can result in 'bullying, racism and stereotyping' (QCA 2001, Unit 4: 4). Here, pupils 'learn about' rather than critically engage with these issues.

There is a focus on conflict in Units 11: 'Why is it so difficult to keep the peace in the world today?' and 13: 'How do we deal with conflict?', where it could be expected that racism might arise as a relevant concept. However, there are only fleeting references, mainly in terms of language usage of such terms as 'racism' and 'xenophobia' (QCA 2001, Unit 11: 3). There is no substantive content around the theme of anti-racism in Unit 11, and similarly in Unit 13, there is only one reference to 'racial conflict' for pupils to consider under the theme 'what do we mean by conflict?' (QCA 2001, Unit 13: 3). Unit 12: 'Why did women and some men have to struggle for the vote in Britain? What is the point of voting today?' addresses issues relating to power and exclusion, in relation to voting and democracy, yet racism is not referred to in this context. Racism is only mentioned under the theme 'what is the point of voting today?' with reference to anti-racist campaigns as an example of voting for change. What emerges is that while the Schemes of Work do refer to racism (QCA 2001) – in contrast to the Crick Report (QCA 1998) and Programme of Study (QCA 2000), these references are not substantively developed.

The DfES Diversity and Citizenship report explicitly engages with issues relating to racism, at both personal and structural levels. The recommendations relating to the fourth strand of citizenship state that a key conceptual component entails: 'critical thinking about ethnicity, religion and race', with the study of the following areas to be included: 'immigration', 'commonwealth and legacy of Empire' and 'extending the franchise (legacy of slavery universal suffrage, equal opportunities legislation)' (Ajegbo *et al.* 2007: 97). In addition, a scheme of work using an 'enquiry, question-oriented approach' around the theme of slavery is included in the Report Appendix. In the lead-up to the launch of this report, it was widely reported in the media that Secretary of State for Education, Alan Johnson had proposed that schools should focus on 'core British values of justice and tolerance' in the wake of alleged racism in the reality television programme 'Big Brother', where thousands of viewers complained (BBC News, 21 January 2007). The revised QCA Programme of Study at KS3 and KS4 does not however contain any explicit reference to anti-racism, although it states that 'Citizenship addresses issues relating to … inequalities and discrimination' (QCA 2007: 1). In addition, it states that the study of political rights includes understanding the 'development of universal suffrage and equal opportunities' (p. 5).

A dominant theme that emerged from the interviews is concern that 'race issues' are approached in terms of a 'celebratory' model that tends to exoticize ethnic minorities, as opposed to 'really getting to the real hard issues' (Interview with CRE employee: 8). This reflects the critique of multiculturalism in anti-racist discourses that has been ongoing over the last two decades (Gillborn 2004), with one of the most well-known catchphrases critiquing multiculturalism coined by Troyna – 'the three S's – saris, samosas and steelbands' (Troyna 1984). This refers to the exoticization of minority cultures presenting only a superficial characterization of the given minority culture(s). This critique of 'celebrating' diversity is also referred to by 'P', from the Refugee Council:

> I think there might be a tendency to go towards a sort of multicultural celebratory model instead, this is my point … personal point of view, and I think possibly the Refugee Council, instead of one in terms of anti-racist pro-active point of view
>
> (Interview with 'P' of Refugee Council: 4)

Anti-racist critiques of multiculturalism have highlighted multiculturalism's use of 'softer' terms like 'culture', 'equality' and 'prejudice', as opposed to anti-racism's link with 'harder' language, like 'conflict', 'oppression' and 'exploitation' (Gillborn 2004). In the interviews, it can be seen that the coupling of 'harder' terms like 'pro-active', and 'real hard issues' is used in the context of anti-racism, as a contrast to multiculturalism which is perceived to be passive and soft by implication. In these accounts, multiculturalism is framed as 'celebratory', and perceived to be passive, as opposed to a 'pro-active' anti-racist approach. Furthermore, multiculturalism is seen to be ineffective, as well as tokenistic. There have been attempts by multiculturalists to respond to these criticisms – a field now referred to as 'critical' multiculturalism (May 1994; Watson 2000), which aims to be more pro-active and less 'celebratory' in its emphasis. The following section examines the 'multicultural' approach to identity in relation to conceptions of citizenship.

### Multiculturalism

In the Crick Report, diversity is first referred to in section 3: Citizenship: the need and aims; it does not appear in section 2: what we mean by citizenship (QCA 1998). As discussed in the first section of this chapter, diversity is framed predominantly in terms of a potential problem. While there is a reference to Modood's (1997) proposal that an explicit idea of 'multicultural citizenship needs to be formulated for Britain' (Modood 1997, cited in QCA 1998: 17), this is not developed further in the report. The following paragraph, in contrast, talks in terms of 'majorities' and 'minorities'. Discourses utilizing binary oppositions have been critiqued on a number of grounds, including reflecting a 'mainstream liberalism inhospitable to "difference"' with potentially 'normalising assumptions' (Stevenson 2002: 7). This is not to say that references to minority groups should not be made in any circumstance; but that discourses that consistently polarize 'majority' and 'minority' should be avoided. In addition, issues of structural disadvantage are masked in utilizing conceptions of diversity in terms of the binary oppositional terms, 'majority' and 'minority'. In contrast, multiculturalism aims to move beyond a focus on minorities, and instead to study identity as a fluid and hybrid conception (Stevenson 2002). The potential impact of people's identities on how they relate to political institutions and laws is not taken into account in the Crick Report, in what Stevenson (2002) calls a 'sociology of minorities' approach. This approach implies a relatively static conception of identity, and it ignores the relevance of cultural diversity to achieving a common citizenship through a shared political culture – a civic republican conceptualization of citizenship (Brubaker 1998). It has been argued that an understanding of identity is especially necessary in a multicultural society, where identity is seen not as static, but rather as in a state of flux (Joppke and Lukes 1999).

The Crick Report cites from The British Youth Council submission regarding how the curriculum should approach diversity: 'develop an awareness of community and cultural diversity' and to 'gain an understanding of the diversity of community and society and awareness of equal opportunities issues, national identity and cultural differences' and to 'consider the factors that lead to exclusion ... such as bullying, colour and other forms of "difference"' (QCA 1998: 19). The use of terms like 'awareness' and 'understanding' imply a *'learning about'* pedagogical approach to citizenship. While such awareness is important in understanding the context, this proposal does not consider how diversity relates to active participation, nor does it consider issues of structural disadvantage. This implied passive, rather than active approach is evident in Figure 1, which provides an overview of essential elements, categorized into key concepts, values and dispositions, skills and aptitudes and knowledge and understanding. Diversity is referred to under key concepts, values and knowledge and understanding, but is not framed in relation to active participation under the theme of skills and aptitudes (QCA 1998).

In contrast to the language of the Crick Report, in his interview, Blunkett illustrated a more nuanced conceptualization of culture as in a state of flux: 'The nature of citizenship in the nineteenth century, or in the mid twentieth century, would have been very different to what it is now because our society is absorbing cultural change all the time' (Interview with David Blunkett: 3).

While the Crick Report refers to minorities obeying laws as a 'process' that helps to foster common citizenship, it is nevertheless focusing on a simplistic binary categorization of people into two groups, rather than how a range of identities can influence both the process and outcome of a common citizenship (QCA 1998). Blunkett's key phrase, 'diversity through integration', is used in the White Paper, *Secure Borders, Safe Haven: integration with diversity in modern Britain* (Home Office 2002). Here, there is an acknowledgement that diversity is an integral part of living in modern Britain, and that there can be both integration and diversity: these concepts are not mutually exclusive, and that there is a dynamic process of interaction between the two. Yet, implicit throughout this document is the public/private sphere distinction, with no consideration of the process by which ethnic and religious minorities can contribute to a process of developing a 'shared' public culture.

When asked how 'shared values' might be achieved in practice in a multicultural setting, David Blunkett emphasized that values are not static, and change over time. He proposed that the way we teach citizenship in schools, and also the new plans for citizenship classes for the naturalization of new citizens should reflect Britain's diversity:

> We should actually reflect that diversity and I call it diversity through integration, so that it's more than pretending that all we are is a kind of porridge of multiculturalism, it's that each blends and adds something to the other without losing the essence of what we are and who we are, and that's true of religious diversity as well as cultural diversity
>
> (Interview with David Blunkett: 4)

From the above, it can be seen that Blunkett understands identity as something fluid rather than as something fixed. This understanding of identity would

seem to correspond to what Hall (1992) conceptualizes as identity
text of the 'sociological subject', where the identity of the subjec
in relation to other subjects and their surrounding context, with
'inner' self or essence being modified by relationships beyond the sen.
also how communitarianism frames its conception of human beings (Mulhall and
Swift 1994).

Yet what is also evident here, however, is Blunkett's hostility to the term,
'multiculturalism', reflecting the contestation and public debates surrounding the
term, as discussed in Chapter 1. One form of this critique – typified by anti-racist
discourses is that multiculturalism is ineffective. Another argument in effect is
really terminological confusion over the term, where it has erroneously come to
be understood by some as a number of different communities or cultures living
side by side one another, but where differences are kept distinct. Anthias and
Yuval-Davis (1993) have described this misconstrual as supporting an image of
a homogeneous majority and small pockets of 'unmeltable' minorities who do
not share the same values. This conception of multiculturalism corresponds to
Joppke and Luke's (1999) 'mosaic' multiculturalism, in contrast to 'hodgepodge'
multiculturalism, which is conceptualized in terms of hybridity and mixing, and
where there is an acknowledgement that culture is not static, but rather, is in a
state of flux.

The current debates surrounding the establishment of faith schools illustrates a more 'critical' form of multiculturalism (Watson 2000), as discussed in
Chapter 1. These debates have centred around such themes as whether religious schools are antithetical to the liberal aims of education (Brighouse 2005;
Pring 2005) and whether such schools are divisive (Mason 2005). On asking
Blunkett on his views on faith schools and their implications for shared values and community cohesion, he argued for bringing faith schools into the state
sector:

> Well, mine is a very pragmatic view. Faith schools exist. What we therefore
> have to do is to persuade, cajole and incorporate faith schools in the broader
> purpose of sharing, of engaging, of opening up to others. What I mean by
> incorporate is that if you don't have faith schools in the state sector, they
> will flourish in the private sector and that is just a fact ... I would prefer to
> get to a standard where they could enter the state sector, embrace the broad
> liberal curriculum, be part of the process of stability and integration, so it's
> not a choice of whether we do away with it it's a choice as to whether it's
> inside or out, and whether it engages with the curriculum, the broader issues
> of involvement
>
> (Interview with David Blunkett: 6)

The above suggests that Blunkett might prefer that faith schools were not a
feature of British society. He argued, however, that the existence of separate groups
operating within the larger community does not detract from a shared culture and
community cohesion, so long as these groups engage with the larger community,

and indeed contribute to its shared culture and community cohesion. There have been proposals suggesting a multi-faith approach by building partnerships between different communities and schools, and that faith schools be required to accept a quota of pupils from other faiths (Home Office 2001a). However, the government failed to secure such an agreement from faith schools in 2006, and in what has been seen as a compromise, the Education and Inspections Act 2006 has put a duty on schools to promote community cohesion with OFSTED required to inspect schools in relation to the duty from September 2007.

The KS3 Programme of Study's approach to identity can be broadly categorized as 'multicultural', where there is recognition of 'the diversity of national, regional, religious and ethnic identities in the United Kingdom and the need for mutual respect and understanding' (QCA 2000). This is presented under the 'knowledge and understanding' heading, rather than in the context of more actively developing 'skills of enquiry and communication', or of 'participation and responsible action'. Hence identity and diversity are being presented as something that pupils learn about, as opposed to actively engage with – what has been critiqued as a 'soft' multiculturalism.

The KS3 Schemes of Work, Unit 4: 'Britain – a diverse society?' is the main unit addressing identity and diversity, with the focus being on 'respect for diversity in our society' (QCA 2001, Unit 4: 1). The theme of a plurality of national identities in the context of a range of other types of identities is reflected in this unit with the expectation for most pupils at the end of this unit is to 'recognise that there are many different identities locally and nationally' (QCA 2001, Unit 4: 1). There are five themes in this unit: (1) 'what are my identities?', (2) 'what is my local community like?', (3) 'what images do we have of Britain?', (4) 'what is a global citizen?' and (5) 'taking responsible action' (QCA 2001). In contrast to the Crick Report's emphasis on the potential problem of diversity, the Schemes of Work refer to both the 'benefits and challenges of living in a diverse society' as a learning expectation for most pupils (QCA 2001, Unit 4: 1). In addition, identity is conceived of as being fluid and multiple, with learning objectives for pupils including that they 'explore their identities and develop their understanding of multiple identities and diversity' (QCA 2001, Unit 4: 3). This conception of identity is influenced by cosmopolitan conceptions that view people's identities as increasingly fragmented, and multiple, rather than a single unified conception of the individual (Hall 1992). Teaching activities also engage pupils in considering how their identity has changed over time and also in considering how it might change in the future (p. 3). These conceptualizations of identity reflect Joppke and Lukes (1999)'s 'hodgepodge' multiculturalism, emphasizing hybridity and mixing, and where there is an acknowledgement that culture is in a state of flux.

However, the learning outcomes are framed predominantly in terms of pupils being able to 'describe', 'recognise' and 'understand'. Under the KS3 Programme of Study 'knowledge and understanding' (heading, 1b), it is proposed that 'pupils should be *taught about*' 'the diversity of national, regional, religious and ethnic identities in the United Kingdom and the need for mutual respect and understanding' (QCA 2000). One of the themes in Unit 4 entitled 'What images do we have of Britain?', again is framed in terms of '*celebrating* diversity' as a learning outcome (QCA 2001, Unit 4: 5). Phrases and terms such as 'taught about' and 'celebrating' do not encourage an active engagement with diversity as an issue, nor does it recognize the conceptual or practical challenges its poses. This suggests a 'pedagogy of acceptance', being passive rather than active, engaging or challenging. Similarly, while local, national and international levels of community are considered, learning outcomes emphasize the notion of 'celebrating diversity' (pp. 4–5), with the notion of struggle or conflict not significantly referred to, except in relation to considering how the media represents different ethnic groups, and the issue of stereotyping (QCA 2001, Unit 4: 6). The final theme of the unit, 'taking responsible action', is important in that it explicitly links identity and diversity with active participation. Its learning objectives include that pupils 'identify how they might influence change and take responsible action' (p. 7), with learning outcomes that pupils 'describe how individuals and groups can make a difference'. However, an inclusion of issues of exclusion and structural disadvantage is not referred to, which is important to engage with in order to understand factors involved in differential participation of different individuals and groups.

Units 11 and 13 focus on the link between conflict and diversity, with learning expectations at the end of Unit 11 including that 'most pupils appreciate that issues of diversity contribute to conflict situations' (QCA 2001, Unit 11: 2), and be able to 'describe and where appropriate, explain significant social, cultural, religious or ethnic differences in the societies studied' (QCA 2001, Unit 11: 6). Unit 13 focuses on religious values and attitudes with regard to conflict, with the learning expectation that most pupils understand that some 'religions share some beliefs and values' (QCA 2001, Unit 13: 2). These two units reflect more closely the conceptual approach to diversity of the Crick Report – the linking of diversity with conflict and the role of shared values in citizenship. Unit 12: 'Why did women and some men have to struggle for the vote in Britain? What is the point of voting today?', provides an ideal opportunity to link identity and active participation, given its focus on power and exclusion. Under the first theme, 'how can we start to think about power and exclusion?', a Rawlsian teaching activity is proposed where pupils are asked to design a political system that they will live in, but they do not yet know what their personal characteristics are, e.g. their ethnicity, religion, sex or age (QCA 2001, Unit 12: 4). This teaching activity perpetuates the conception of a clear divide between the public and private sphere, and also the idea that the application of justice can be context-free. Liberalism underestimates the impact of the community on the identity of the individual (Mulhall and Swift 1994), which develops through inter-relations with others (Taylor 1990). This implies that individuals need a 'secure cultural context', which should be considered to be a 'primary good' (like religious freedom, or right to vote) (Gutmann 1995). This would require public institutions to recognize difference rather than ignore it.

While the Programmes of Study and Schemes of Work use a relatively more 'multicultural' approach to citizenship than the Crick Report, it could be argued that this takes the form of a 'soft' multiculturalism, rather than a more 'critical' multiculturalism (Watson 2000). In the following section, I discuss the proposals we made in the DfES Diversity and Citizenship Curriculum Review Report (Ajegbo *et al.* 2007), and the implications for QCA's KS3 review, in particular the changes made to the KS3 and KS4 Citizenship Programmes of Study.

## New developments

The remit for the DfES Diversity and Citizenship Review was to 'review the teaching of ethnic, religious and cultural diversity across the curriculum to age 19, and in relation to Citizenship, exploring particularly whether or not "modern British social and cultural history" should be a fourth pillar of the Citizenship curriculum' (Ajegbo *et al.* 2007). This was launched publicly in May 2006, by Minister Bill Rammell, and linked to issues of 'community cohesion', identity and diversity and 'shared British values'.

In our report, we recommended a fourth strand, entitled 'Identity and Diversity: Living Together in the UK'. Five sub-themes are highlighted as important areas to include:

1  Understanding that the UK is a 'multinational' state, made up of England, Northern Ireland, Scotland and Wales
2  Immigration
3  Commonwealth and the legacy of Empire
4  European Union
5  Extending the franchise (e.g. legacy of slavery, universal suffrage, equal opportunities legislation) (Ajegbo *et al.* 2007).

The rationale behind this proposed fourth strand is to highlight the importance of addressing issues of identity and diversity in the context of inclusive citizenship, explicitly linking these issues to active participation and political literacy. As noted earlier, while the Crick Report presents diversity under 'key concepts, values and knowledge and understanding', diversity is not considered in relation to active participation under 'skills and understanding' (QCA 1998). While there are references in both the KS3 and KS4 Programmes of Study (QCA 2000) to pupils learning about the 'diverse national, regional, religious and ethnic identities of the United Kingdom',[5] these issues are not substantively situated in relevant historical and political context. And like the Crick Report, issues of identity and diversity are not considered in relation to active participation.

The Crick Report's approach to citizenship framed citizenship in terms of 'a skill, a knowledge, an attitude for citizenship' (Interview with Sir Bernard Crick: 10), and deliberately avoided addressing the issue of the relationship between citizenship and national identity. The recommendations formulated in the DfES Diversity and Citizenship Report propose that issues of identity, including a historically-contextualized understanding of national identity is central to developing both the knowledge and skills for a participative and inclusive citizenship. Indeed, Kymlicka (1999: 94) has argued that the promotion of 'shared allegiance to political principles' alone is not sufficient and should not occur in isolation from examining issues of identity and history, which he argues are crucial components of citizenship education. These recommendations drew on the Home Office work on naturalization, discussed in Chapter 4, which emphasizes the active experience of 'living in the UK', as opposed to attempts to define abstract notions of 'Britishness'. Our report also made pedagogical suggestions with regard to providing more explicit learning opportunities for pupils in relation to identity and diversity. I discuss these issues in the final Chapter 8.

Alan Johnson, Secretary of State for Education welcomed the Citizenship curriculum recommendations of the report (25 January 2007), stating that he has asked QCA to incorporate the proposed strand into the new Citizenship Programmes of Study at KS3 and KS4. QCA has introduced the proposed fourth strand, 'identities and diversity: living together in the UK' as a 'key concept', alongside 'democracy and justice', 'rights and responsibilities', and 'critical thinking' (QCA 2007). In the accompanying notes for the KS3 Programme of Study, there is reference to how 'migration has shaped communities' and how 'living together in the UK has been shaped and continues to be shaped by political, social, economic and cultural change' (QCA 2007: 2). There is also a reference to taking account of the historical context 'where appropriate'. At KS4, there is an explicit reference linking issues of identity and diversity to active participation and examining this in historical context: 'Students consider the action that has been, or could be taken, to improve conditions of life for different groups. Sometimes it is important to consider the historical context for such changes and how this relates to the values and traditions of the UK' (QCA 2007: 3). There is a section entitled 'Range and Content', indicating to teachers the 'breadth of the subject' on which they should draw. There are three bullet points relating to the proposed fourth strand:

- the shared values and changing nature of UK society, including the diversity of beliefs, cultures, identities and traditions
- reasons for migration to, from and within the UK and the impact of movement and settlement on places and communities
- the UK's role and interconnections with the European Union and the rest of Europe, the Commonwealth, the United Nations and the world as a global community and the political, economic, environmental and social implications of this (QCA 2007: 5 KS3 Citizenship Programme of Study).

Under the detailed notes, there is an explicit reference to 'the four nations of the UK, with a note saying that this links with 'the study of the origins of the UK in history' (QCA 2007: 5). At KS4, there is an explicit reference to pupils examining these issues in relation to issues of cohesion and integration' (QCA 2007: 7). In the concluding section of this chapter, I briefly outline the theoretical and practical implication for diversity, which are further developed in Part 3.

## Theoretical and practical implications for diversity

In Huntingdon's (2004) most recent book on American national identity, entitled *Who Are We? America's Great Debate*, he argues strongly against diversity: 'multiculturalism is in its essence anti-European civilization' (p. 171). He asserts that all ...

> Americans should recommit themselves to the Anglo-Protestant culture, traditions and values that for three and a half centuries have been embraced by Americans of all races, ethnicities, and religions and that has been the source of their liberty, unity, power, prosperity, and moral leadership as a force for good in the world
>
> (Huntingdon 2004: xvii)

His calls for a preservation of the dominant Anglo-Protestant culture – the maintenance of the status quo seems to be based only on his assertion that race and ethnicity 'are now largely eliminated' (2004: xv), and that the majority of Americans want the preservation of the dominance of Anglo-Protestant culture. This is predicated on his assertion that settlers differed from immigrants in that they came to create a new community in the USA because it was a tabula rasa, in contrast to immigrants who should not expect to create, or contribute to the creation of a new society – rather they should assimilate into a national identity assumed to be unchanging and static. While Huntingdon's (2004) proposition that political principles alone can not provide 'the deep emotional content and meaning provided by kith and kin, blood and belonging, culture and nationality' (2004: 339) is potentially convincing, his argument for this national identity to be the Anglo-Protestant culture is at best ideological and not supported by any empirical evidence.

In contrast to Huntingdon's (2004) assumption that a multiplicity of identities undermines national citizenship, proponents of 'multicultural' citizenship argue that incorporating diversity is necessary for the development of an inclusive citizenship (Gutmann 1995; Kymlicka 1995; Osler 1999; Young 2000). Liberalism has been critiqued for its sharp distinction between the public and private sphere. The practical implications for diversity are that there may indeed be significant diversity within the private sphere, and possibly at local community level, however, there is little scope for diversity within the public political sphere, where there is clearly a single political culture. It has been argued that it is not the aim of public institutions to represent or account for difference, and that the assumed neutrality of our public institutions is the price citizens must pay in order to be treated as equals, regardless of ethnicity, 'race', religion, or sex. However Gutmann (1995) argues that individuals need 'a secure cultural context', and that it should be considered a 'primary good' (like religious freedom, freedom of conscience, free speech, right to vote, etc.), and therefore should require public institutions to recognize difference, rather than ignore it.

In the following chapter, I argue that a 'multicultural' model of diversity holds the most potential and is the most appropriate 'identity-based' conception of citizenship, given that identity is conceptualized as fluid, hybrid and multiple (Stevenson 2002). I propose a model of citizenship drawing together the 'participative' (as discussed in Chapter 5) and 'multicultural' conceptualizations of citizenship, and drawing on our proposals in the DfES Report on Diversity and Citizenship (Ajegbo *et al.* 2007).

# Part 3

# Developing theory and practice

# 7 Developing a theory of inclusive citizenship[1]

## Introduction

It has been argued that political philosophy 'should apply itself more often to clarifying and criticising the idea behind policies affecting the public' (Crick 2003: Preface). Throughout this book, my analysis has drawn on the politico-philosophical literature on citizenship, examining conceptions of citizenship in the citizenship education policy and curriculum development process, and the implications of these conceptions of citizenship for ethnic and religious diversity. On reviewing the politico-philosophical literature, what becomes overwhelmingly evident is that citizenship is a highly contested concept, with competing conceptualizations based on different philosophical understandings of what it is to be a human being, and the perceived relationship between a human being and the political community or state. This chapter attempts to draw together the analysis of my key findings with the politico-philosophical literature on citizenship and diversity, where I propose a model of inclusive and participative citizenship.

## A model of inclusive citizenship

This model consists of two main components: first, I propose the concept of 'institutional' multiculturalism, constituted as a process. Second, I propose that citizenship education must redirect its emphasis to the citizen-state relationship, relative to the emphasis on the relationship between individuals and groups from different backgrounds and cultures which is the predominant focus of 'interculturalism' (Gundara 2003; Kymlicka 2003).

### Institutional multiculturalism

In Part 2 of the book, a recurrent theme from the interviews was a questioning of the limits of the public/private sphere distinction, a theme that has been raised by the feminist and politics of recognition literature (Gutmann 1995; Jones 1998; Taylor 1995; Young 2000). In Chapter 2 on interviewees' perceptions of the aims and outcomes of citizenship, it was noted that typically, interviewees perceived that the citizenship initiative served more than one aim. Yet it emerged that there may be inherent tensions between some of these aims, which in part relate to the public/private sphere distinction. For example, traditional conceptions of maintaining democracy may rely on preserving the public/private sphere distinction, in contrast to the aim of promoting equality and diversity, which calls for 'inclusiveness rather than neutrality' of the public sphere (Modood 2005: 20). While these aims need not necessarily be in tension, the use of terms such as 'maintaining' and 'upholding' in conjunction with democracy and public political institutions suggests a 'maintaining the status quo' approach, rather than being open to a truly more inclusive approach.

From Chapter 3, it can be seen that the contestation regarding whether values referred to more procedural, or more personal, social or cultural values also relates to the debate regarding the public/private sphere distinction. While the distinction made in the Crick Report is useful in that it promotes the political nature of citizenship and the relationship between the individual to the state or political community, the distinction in practice is not such a simple one, and indeed misrepresents the public sphere as culturally neutral. Indeed, in Chapter 6, I argue that the liberal premise of equality should in fact require public institutions to recognize difference, rather than ignore it (Gutmann 1995). It is important that the institutions and processes of the public sphere are 'authored' by those from ethnically and religiously diverse backgrounds (Taylor 1995).

This theme of 'shared values' also came up frequently in the interviews, linked to the notion of supporting democracy. Young (2000: 40) criticizes the assumption made by some democratic theorists that there must be a 'common good' or 'shared values' – the idea of 'privileging unity'. She says that this can silence some views and be a means for exclusion, as a result of either competition amongst competing interests, or having to put aside one's affiliations to form a deliberative public (public/private sphere dichotomy). According to Young (2000: 35), such commonality should be neither a precondition nor a goal, saying that this does not fit the reality of plural and structurally differentiated societies. Instead, she argues for a thin or 'minimal' notion of 'common good' only so far as a commitment to an inclusive collective problem-solving. She calls for a 'democratic fix' through the norms of deliberative democracy where democracy is actually 'deepened through enabling more inclusivity of plural claims and perspectives and empowering for less privileged participants'. I have argued that shared values are not necessarily problematic in an ethnically and religiously diverse society, however what has typically been neglected is a consideration of the *process* by which these shared values are reached – both at societal level and at school level. The workings of the Crick Advisory Group, discussed in Chapter 2, also illustrated a reluctance to engage with the issue of accommodating a diversity of views in reaching consensus, both in terms of its selection of 'like-minded' individuals, and the lack of truly inclusive and democratic decision-making processes.

What is needed, is to be able to operationalize 'multiculturalism' within the concept of citizenship. Multiculturalism is not about *describing* a societal context; for it to be meaningful, it must be about how we *operate* within society. Furthermore, recent attempts to discredit multiculturalism by equating it with different communities living 'parallel lives'[2] – but what Amartya Sen more accurately calls 'plural monoculturalism' (Sen 2006), are misleading. Just as there has been an acknowledgement of the concept of 'institutional racism', I would propose that the concept of 'institutional multiculturalism' is a means to go beyond the problem that multiculturalism is generally perceived to be about and for 'minorities'. By 'institutional multiculturalism', I mean that multiculturalism is not merely about an aesthetic or cosmetic experience, or encounters with 'different' cultures.[3] It is a political reconstituting of society itself, so that diversity is not a passive concept to be 'celebrated', but rather is a proactive process, with outcomes not only at the level of the individual, but at the level of society itself. It entails two inter-related key features. First, it requires that public institutions recognize difference rather than ignore it (Gutmann 1995). This is a recognition that the theoretical public/private sphere distinction is in fact a misrepresentation of the reality, as in practice, personal attributes, including ethnicity and religion implicitly do shape the assumed 'culture-neutral' practices in the institutions of the public sphere – what Taylor (1995: 44) has called 'particularism masquerading as the universal'. I propose that this recognition may in part be facilitated by its second feature – a focus on the *process* of 'authoring' (Taylor 1995) by those from a diverse range of ethnic and religious backgrounds.

As a member of the subsequent Crick Advisory Group on immigrants and citizenship education ('Life in the UK' Advisory Group), a group also appointed by Blunkett, then Home Secretary, I drafted the section of text which aimed to invoke this model of 'institutional' multiculturalism in its published report (Home Office 2003). This group had the following terms of reference: to advise on 'the method, conduct and implementation' of the naturalization test, in light of legislative requirements of the Nationality, Immigration and Asylum Act (NIA) 2002. The definition of 'multicultural' in the context of being British, which I drafted is given on p. 10:

> We see a multicultural society as one made up of a diverse range of cultures and identities, and one that emphasises the need for a continuous process of mutual engagement and learning about each other with respect, understanding and tolerance – whether in social, cultural, educational, professional, political or legal spheres. Such societies, under a framework of common civic values and common legal and political institutions not only understand and tolerate diversities of identity but should also take respect and take pride in them
> (Home Office 2003: 10)

This definition incorporates my conception of 'institutional multiculturalism'. The above was an attempt to implicitly challenge the assumption that ethnic and religious identities operate only in the private sphere, as well as emphasizing a move beyond a celebratory definition of multicultural, focusing on mutual learning in all spheres. The word, 'process' was chosen to indicate that active participation and contribution is inherent to an understanding of operation in all the above-mentioned domains – political, legal and professional, as well as the less problematically perceived social and cultural domains. There is nevertheless a commitment to shared values, achieved and developed through contribution from all those actively participating through the 'continuous process of mutual engagement', however, there is an implicit recognition that shared values can indeed change. Shared values must not be privileged over and above the expression of a wide range of views, which can result in a means of exclusion (Young 2000). By emphasizing process and collective problem-solving, this enables more inclusivity which Young (2000) argues actually 'deepens' democracy. The fluidity of identity is also recognized: 'We do not imply that identities are ever fixed; in fact identities are often more fluid than many people suppose' (p. 10).

The concept of 'institutional multiculturalism' is also reflected in the formulation of the proposed fourth strand: 'Identity and diversity: Living together in the UK', as outlined in the DfES Diversity and Citizenship Report (Ajegbo *et al.* 2007). Our remit was to consider how to 'provide pupils with more explicit learning opportunities around the contrasting but complementary themes of diversity on the one hand, and unity or "shared values" on the other' (p. 89). The rationale for the proposals is that issues of identity and diversity must be explicitly recognized and contextualized in relation to political issues, systems and values. Again, as in the Home Office report described above, the assumption that ethnic and religious identities operate only in the private sphere is directly challenged. The argument is made that identity is central to the relationship between the citizen and their political community in a model of participatory and inclusive citizenship, as motivation to participate is logically predicated on identifying with that context.

Issues of process are also highlighted in relation to the proposed fourth strand. The title of the fourth strand contains the phrase 'living in the UK'. The choice of these words was deliberate, and drew on the Home Office policy work on citizenship as legal status, discussed in Chapter 4. The Handbook, *Life in the United Kingdom*, which forms the basis of the test and courses required by those applying for British citizenship,[4] emphasizes the contextualized experience of living in the UK, rather than promoting any abstract conceptions of 'Britishness'. This emphasis on process is also central to the pedagogical approaches advocated, where a contextualized 'process of dialogue and communication' (p. 96) is seen as central to the teaching of the five areas proposed within the fourth strand: the UK as a multinational state, immigration, the Commonwealth and the legacy of Empire, the European Union and extending the franchise. The examples of fourth strand pedagogical approaches in Appendix 1 illustrate a politically and historically contextualized question-oriented approach that emphasizes the process of collective debate around contemporary issues of identity and citizenship (see Ajegbo *et al.* 2007).

For an inclusive model of citizenship in a multicultural society like the UK, I propose that a model of 'institutional multiculturalism' must supplement the 'participatory' model of citizenship advocated in the Crick Report (QCA 1998). In Chapter 4, I argued that, while human rights are an important component of citizenship, theoretically they cannot underpin citizenship (Kiwan 2005). Similarly, while political knowledge and skills are important for citizenship, a 'participatory' model alone is not sufficient for a model of active citizenship in a multicultural. society. The Crick Report's dominant conception of citizenship as active participation, is inherently influenced by the legacy of the political literacy movement in which Crick was involved (Crick and Porter 1978; Davies 1999b). This was informed by Crick's understanding of politics in a very practical sense as an activity involving negotiation between different political interest groups (Crick 2000), and a commitment at a theoretical level to civic republicanism's civic identity conceived primarily in terms of legal and political conceptualizations of identity, relegating ethnic and religious identity to the private sphere.

In Chapter 5, I argue that the focus of the original Crick Report (QCA 1998) and subsequent Programmes of Study and Schemes of Work (QCA 2000, 2001) on the accessibility to information and developing participatory skills is certainly necessary, but it is not sufficient, as it does not address the impact of differential power between groups, which can lead to disempowerment and lack of motivation to participate for those historically marginalized groups. This raises the question of how individuals from such groups may be motivated to participate. The rationale for the 'participative' model relies on cognitive engagement theory (Pattie *et al.* 2004) – that participation depends on access to information, rather than what motivates people to participate. Yet understanding what motivates people to participate is crucial to developing an inclusive conception of citizenship. In order to actively participate, individual citizens from a diverse range of backgrounds must be able to *identify* with their community – the inextricable link between citizenship as 'practice' and citizenship as 'belonging'. Therefore citizens' identities and experiences are necessarily central to an inclusive conception of citizenship. The example of citizenship education in the French educational system, illustrates that, by not explicitly addressing ethnic and religious diversity and how this relates to issues of structural disadvantage (Kiwan and Kiwan 2005), citizenship education may fail to achieve a more inclusive participation of young people from a range of different ethnic and religious backgrounds. It is hoped, that the newly drafted QCA Programmes of Study – by explicitly linking issues of identity and diversity to political literacy and active participation, will enable a more inclusive participation of young people of different ethnic and religious identities.

## *Focusing on the citizen-state relationship*

From Chapter 6, it can be seen that there were identity-based conceptions of citizenship at local, national and international levels. Although the Crick Report did not explicitly address the relationship between citizenship and nationality (QCA 1998), citizenship is framed implicitly in terms of a civic identity – a political national identity. Consultations carried out and reported in the Crick Report noted that there was a general perception that European and global citizenship were relatively neglected (QCA 1998). In addition, it was noted that Crick, in his interview, expressed reticence with respect to global conceptions of citizenship, perhaps reflecting a concern that a focus on the global might direct attention away from more local and national framings of citizenship.

xt of globalization, there are trends of simultaneous strengthening of
both above and below the national level, with decreased identifica-
nal level (Hall 1992). Osler and Starkey (2005) propose the concept
n citizenship, where participation at local, national and international
ited. However, it is important that such conceptions acknowledge
...at individuals operate from within the legal and political structures of the nation
state (Demaine 2002). While the KS3 Schemes of Work provide teachers with
examples to illustrate the relationship between local and global levels of citizenship (QCA 2001), elucidating the relationship between the local and national
levels, and the national and international levels must therefore be a priority.

The remit of the DfES Diversity and Citizenship Review to explore whether
or not to add a fourth pillar of 'modern British social and cultural history' to the
existing Citizenship curriculum illustrates a governmental concern to address more
explicitly the inter-relationship between diversity and national identity contextualised politically and historically. Indeed, when the review was publicly launched
by Minister Bill Rammell in 2006, this was linked to conceptions of community
cohesion, 'Britishness' and 'shared values' (DfES 2006). Similarly, the House of
Commons Education and Skills Select Committee Inquiry into Citizenship Education also collected evidence around the key themes of 'Britishness', 'shared
values', an understanding of identity and diversity (Education and Skills Select
Committee 2006). In addition, this concern is increasingly framed in relation not
only to community cohesion at more local levels, but in relation to identification at the nation-state level. I highlighted, in Chapter 6, how our 'fourth strand'
proposals in the DfES Diversity and Citizenship Review place an explicit consideration of diversity and citizenship in a 'national' framework. The first theme
highlighted under the fourth strand proposes that it is important for pupils to have
a 'contextualised understanding that the UK is a "multinational" state, made up of
England, Northern Ireland, Scotland and Wales' (p. 97). This situated approach to
citizenship in the UK is also reflected in the newly drafted Programmes of Study
at KS3 and KS4 by QCA, reflected in the key concept phrase 'identities and diversity: living in the UK', and accompanying notes that propose that pupils develop
this understanding by drawing on relevant historical examples where appropriate (QCA 2007). Links between national and global levels are highlighted under
'Range and Content', referring to the UK's 'interconnections with the European
Union and the rest of Europe, the Commonwealth, the United Nations and the
world as a global community' (QCA 2007: 5).

Enhancing links between local, regional and national levels of citizenship are
considered in the DfES Diversity and Citizenship Review (Ajegbo *et al.* 2007).
A key recommendation is made in the development of 'school links' around curriculum objectives between schools of different demographic make-up within the
UK. This linking can be between schools in the same town or area, across regions,
and also across the 'nations' of the UK. This is further discussed in Chapter 8.

However, the development of relationships between local, national and global
levels is not necessarily straightforward in practice. Kymlicka (2003) has argued
that there is an inherent tension between what he refers to as 'local interculturalism'

and 'cosmopolitan interculturalism'. He cites examples of groups living side-by-side one another in multicultural societies, where individuals may have intercultural skills and interests in others at some distance from themselves – in another part of the world, for example; yet have no interest in those other groups within their own local community or state. His basic argument is that intercultural education typically focuses on developing individuals' attitudes and skills for living in an ethnically and religiously diverse context, however it does not advocate which groups, or what level (local, national, or global) should be the priority. This may be due, in part, to the inherent aims of intercultural education, where the primary goal is personal self-development through engagement with a diversity of other cultures and ideas (Gundara 2000, 2003; Leeman 2003). Consequently, intercultural education has typically been linked with discourses of human rights, and has been located in personal, social and health education (Johnson 2003). The emphasis of intercultural education is on engagement and dialogue *between* cultures (evident from the term, itself – intercultural – literally meaning between cultures). However, political education and the relationship between the individual and the political community or state is relatively less of a focus in this model (Wylie 2004).

The rationale behind promoting the idea of engaging with others from a diversity of backgrounds is that it reduces prejudice and undermines negative stereotypes, and therefore improves inter-group relations (Forbes 1997, cited in Spinner-Halev 2003). However, there is little empirical evidence in support of this 'contact' hypothesis (Spinner-Halev 2003; Wylie 2004). It was also noted in Chapter 5 that a distinction must be made between social capital's notion of trust within communities and trust in state institutions (Giddens 2004). It has been argued that education resulting in raised levels of community participation does not necessarily lead to increased societal cohesion (Green and Preston 2001; Green *et al.* 2003). Spinner-Halev (2003) distinguishes between identity in the form of the 'vertical' relationship between the citizen and the state, and identity in terms of the priority given to the 'horizontal' relationship between individuals. He suggests that the former be cultivated relative to the latter, as he argues that identity and belonging can be inculcated through developing 'a sense of loyalty and identification with the polity, and not necessarily with one's fellow citizens' (Spinner-Halev 2003: 63). While it is important to develop reasonably good individual relationships between citizens so that inter-group conflict does not arise, it is not sufficient that intercultural education focus primarily on inter-group relations. Kymlicka (2003: 164) extends this critique, arguing that models of intercultural education stressing the importance of understanding the content of others' beliefs 'miss the target'. He proposes *acceptance* that others may hold different beliefs, rather than necessarily engaging substantively with these beliefs, is more appropriate. This is especially the case in divided societies such as Northern Ireland and Israel (Spinner-Halev 2003; Wylie 2004), where it is more realistic to develop a strong 'vertical' relationship between the citizens and state, while accepting that 'horizontal' relations between individuals of different groups show tolerance and a level of acceptance, rather than deep understanding and mutual respect.

This raises the question of what approaches might be most appropriate in terms of promoting community cohesion. Since the summer of 2001, when there were a number of inter-ethnic disturbances in Bradford, Burnley and Oldham, we have witnessed an increased policy focus around community cohesion, starting with the publication of the Cantle and Denham Reports (Home Office 2001a,b). After the London bombings in July 2005, the government announced its intention to set up a Commission on Cohesion and Integration in order to consider practical ways to promote community cohesion and integration. In May 2006, there was a re-structuring of the Home Office, with all departments with a remit relating to community cohesion, moving into the newly created Department for Communities and Local Government (DCLG), under the responsibility of Secretary of State, Ruth Kelly. The following month in June 2006, Ruth Kelly set up the Commission and its report is due in July 2007. In a parallel development, a new statutory requirement has been introduced, the Education and Inspections Act 2006, imposing a duty on schools to promote community cohesion, and which will be inspected by OFSTED from September 2007 (DfES 2006).

References to integration have also been made in relation to policy developments in the Immigration and Nationality directorate at the Home Office in the domain of expected legislative changes from April 2007 to the requirements for those applying to settle permanently in the UK:

> The Government today strengthened its commitment to integration by announcing that from 2 April next year (2007) all those seeking to live in the UK permanently will have to pass English language and knowledge of life in the UK tests before being granted permanent settlement rights
>
> (Home Office press release, 4 December 2006)

In light of Kymlicka's (2003) argument above, I would propose that community cohesion must not only address aspects relating to the promotion of 'intercultural understanding' – the 'horizontal' relationship (Spinner-Halev 2003), but must also crucially address the quality of the 'vertical' relationship between citizens and the legal and political institutions and processes of the political community or state. Community cohesion not only depends on good relations between individuals from different communities, but on individuals from all communities having trust in the legal and political systems in the society in which they live. In many cases, disturbances between different communities can be attributed to perceptions of injustice, or that other groups receive preferential treatment. These perceptions reflect the quality of trust in the 'vertical' relationship with the state. It is important that greater efforts to improve this 'vertical' relationship are made – in part, through a promotion of 'institutional multiculturalism'. In the DfES Diversity and Citizenship Review, we make a number of more 'structural' recommendations. These include: proposing that schools ensure that they have set up mechanisms 'to ensure that pupil voice is heard and acted upon' (p. 9), a number of recommendations relating to leadership, systems infrastructure and also teacher training (Ajegbo *et al.* 2007). These proposals are discussed in Chapter 8, on practical implications.

In conclusion, I am suggesting that the concept of 'institutional' multiculturalism, which I characterize as an inclusive process could in part support strengthening the quality of the citizen-state relationship by developing citizens' trust in the state's legal and political institutions – what Spinner-Halev has called the 'vertical' relationship between the citizen and state. I conceive of these two components – 'institutional multiculturalism' and a re-balancing of focus to the 'citizen-state' relationship as mutually reinforcing. In the final chapter, I provide an outline of implications for policy, curriculum and pedagogic practice of this theory of an inclusive participative citizenship.

# 8 Practical implications for policy, curriculum and pedagogy

## Introduction

Before outlining some suggestions for policy, curriculum and pedagogy, it must be recognized that schools do not operate in a sociopolitical vacuum, and therefore what schools and teachers can achieve must be realistically framed within this context. For students to be personally motivated to participate, society's institutional structures and processes must also reflect its diversity of identities. As discussed in the previous section, for this 'vertical' relationship to flourish, I proposed the term, 'institutional' multiculturalism to describe a *process* towards achieving an inclusive participation of a diversity of identities into the public political sphere.

## Ethnicity and religion in the public sphere

Pattie *et al.* (2004) compared political participation between different ethnic groups and found no statistically significant differences in terms of extent of participation between ethnic groups. However political engagement is dominated by those already 'well-resourced' – the rich, the highly educated, and professionals (Pattie *et al.* 2004). With regard to the nature and form of political participation, ethnic group differences were not statistically significant – that is, whether these acts of participation are 'individual' (e.g. voting, or signing a petition), 'contact' (e.g. contacting an MP or the media), or 'collective' (e.g. attending a political meeting). Across ethnic groups, the most common form of participation is 'individualistic', with two-thirds of participants in this study claiming to have donated money to a political organization – a finding that challenges the assertion that citizens in the UK are politically apathetic (QCA 1998). However, Pattie *et al.* (2004: 275) interpret the rise of individualistic forms of participation (at the expense of more collective forms) to be related to 'a weakening of the institutions which support collective action, such as political parties', and they coin the term, 'the atomised citizen' to describe this phenomenon. This may have negative consequences for ethnic groups working to advocate their interests in a system that is weakened by increased forms of individualistic actions.

Chapter 2 discussed how, with regard to the variable of ethnicity, ethnic minorities are relatively more satisfied with how democracy works than are those of 'white/European' ethnic designation; however, with regard to religion, the 'religious' tend to be less satisfied than the 'non-religious', although this trend was not statistically significant (Pattie *et al.* 2004). I suggested that this finding could be interpreted in terms of the public/private sphere distinction being less accommodating of religion than ethnicity, resulting in those designated as 'religious' in this study, being relatively more dissatisfied than the 'non-religious'. In addition, it would be of particular interest to examine whether there are differential attitudes between religious groups to democracy and trust in legal and political institutions, given that public discourses have been increasingly focused on Islam, especially since 11 September 2001.

There is an anomaly with regard to how the relation between religion and the state is conceptualized, in comparison to the relationship between ethnicity and state. While Kymlicka (1995) argues against the separation of ethnicity and state, he seems to accept the liberal position that religion and state be separated. The rationale for this argument is not self-evident, and in addition seems to be problematic in that 'religion' and 'culture' would seem to be conceived as self-contained distinct entities, rather than acknowledging the dynamic interplay between religion, culture, politics and identity.

There is emerging evidence that, in the UK context, there is a trend of increased religiosity with the younger generation of Muslims, expressed in a politicized form, rather than in more traditional cultural forms like their parents (Mirza *et al.* 2007). Wearing the 'hijab' for example, is one means of expressing a religious identity in the public sphere. However, there are a significant number of British Muslims who have adopted a more secular approach to religion, with 59 per cent of Muslims feeling that they have more in common with British non-Muslims than Muslims abroad, and 51 per cent of Muslims feeling that no Muslim organization represents their views (Mirza *et al.* 2007). Indeed, Modood (2005) argues that moderate Islam and moderate secularism are in fact philosophically closer to one another, paradoxically, than either of their more radical alternatives. This raises the question of whether representativeness of Muslim viewpoints through the current mechanisms of 'community leaders' in fact serves the needs of British Muslims, including those who identify culturally with Islam. Reflecting this lack of representation, a London-based group calling themselves 'Progressive British Muslims' was launched in November 2005, and another group called 'Muslims for Secular Democracy' was launched in June 2006 illustrating attempts to redress this imbalance (Mirza *et al.* 2007).

At the level of broader public policy, there is a need to develop mechanisms to achieve institutional multiculturalism and to support the 'vertical' citizen-state relationship. Building on Modood's (2005) proposal of a moderately, rather than a radically, secular state being the best mechanism for claims of recognition by different religious groups, I propose that an 'inclusive citizenship' policy task force could consider, as one its key tasks, how to incorporate into the mainstream, the 'moderately' religious, and also the 'culturally' religious – those individuals who identify themselves with a religious tradition in predominantly cultural terms, across all religions. This group has been largely overlooked, and not

explicitly recognized. The empowerment of this group may be particularly important, in that it may facilitate achieving a sustainable process of 'shared values',
as well as provide role models for young people. This proposal is not intended to
promote the concept of 'community leader', but to reflect the diversity of views
within and across individuals and groups, and to explicitly recognize that religion
does indeed operate in the public sphere, although this has tended to present itself
as the 'particular masquerading as the universal' (Taylor 1995: 44).

## Educational policy, curriculum and practice

### Head teachers and school leadership

Kerr *et al.* (2004) in the DfES-funded Citizenship education longitudinal study
identified a number of key factors that are correlated with successful citizenship
education in schools. These include that there is strong school leadership and senior
management support for citizenship education, as well as a supportive school ethos.
This in turn, provides a supportive context and ethos through which to establish
democratic systems and processes that promote effective pupil voice. Indeed, there
is international research evidence to support this from the International Association
for the Evaluation of Educational Achievement (IEA) Civic Education Project,
one of the most high profile large cross-national empirical studies on citizenship
education covering 24 countries (Torney-Purta *et al.* 1999). Kerr (2001) found that
schools that promote a democratic school ethos and have democratic practices are
most effective in promoting civic knowledge and participation (measured by 'civic
knowledge' and 'expectations to vote'). Senior management support is also crucial
in terms of commitment to continuing professional development (CPD) for staff.

The DfES Diversity and Citizenship Report recommended that schools deliver
Citizenship Education discretely, given the evidence that citizenship education is
most effectively delivered using this model (OFSTED 2006). If more schools move
towards adopting this preferred model over the next 5 years, then this will increase
the demand for trained Citizenship teachers, which in turn will necessitate that the
DfES review the number of initial teacher training places for Citizenship (Ajegbo
*et al.* 2007). Although we recommended that Citizenship be delivered discretely,
we nevertheless recognized the importance of establishing substantive, workable
and effective links between other subjects, especially History, Geography and
Religious Education. It is therefore important that school leaders prioritize cross-
curricular planning, are committed to nurturing an inclusive and participative
ethos in school for both staff and pupils and develop authentic links to the larger
community.

There is evidence that some school leaders do not sufficiently address issues of
inclusion and participation, nor do they show an explicit commitment to combat-
ing institutional racism. In a survey of 14 schools, it was found that 'No school
in this sample had a fully developed strategy for preparing pupils through the
curriculum for life in a diverse society' (Cline *et al.* 2002, cited in Ajegbo *et al.*
2007: 94). According to the CRE, up to one-third of all schools in England do not

have a 'race' equality policy, which is a basic requirement of the Race Relations (Amendment) Act (RRAA) 2000 (Ajegbo *et al.* 2007). While having such a policy does not necessarily mean that these schools have translated into practice an inclusive and participative school ethos, it signals intent, and could be seen as a first step towards implementing inclusive processes and practices. In addition, schools will be inspected from September 2007, with regard to their duty to promote community cohesion (DfES 2006). It is the responsibility of school leaders to ensure that there are inclusive policies and practices in place both within the school community, as well as between the school and its supporting local community. School leaders must be supported to promote 'institutional multiculturalism' through adequate training. The DfES Diversity and Citizenship Report recommends that the National Professional Qualification for Headship (NPQH) be revised so that this training contains as an essential component, developing an 'understanding to tackle the combinations of identity, "race" and religion' (p. 37), and which relates 'to the curriculum, school ethos, pupil voice and the community' (p. 38). This training must recognize the diverse demographic make-up of schools, where the agenda and issues may vary significantly. It is important that inclusive practices are not solely associated with multi-ethnic schools or seen as irrelevant in monocultural schools, but seen as important for majority pupils to equip them with the knowledge and skills to operate successfully in a multicultural society. Gaine (2005) argues that, school leaders, in developing policies for inclusive practice in a mainly white school, should ensure that the needs of the majority should not be overlooked at the expense of minorities present. By doing this, 'institutional multiculturalism' avoids being reduced to 'language provision, celebrating the ethnic diversity present within the school, catering for different religious diets, practices and sensitivities or dealing with specific kinds of bullying' (p. 48).

*Teacher training*

Promoting inclusive citizenship in practice also critically requires that teachers are effectively trained so that they are confident and substantively equipped to address issues relating to ethnicity, 'race', religion and culture (Ajegbo *et al.* 2007). Indeed, before the introduction of citizenship education as a statutory subject, Kerr (1999) identified lack of teacher commitment and confidence and lack of appropriate teacher training to be key obstacles in developing citizenship education; this continues to be the case, especially in relation to developing an inclusive citizenship curriculum that adequately deals with issues relating to ethnic and religious diversity.

There is a relatively small, although growing literature investigating the views of teachers and student teachers and their understandings of a variety of issues relating to citizenship, including social and political attitudes, attitudes towards 'race' and diversity, and how this impacts on their teaching. For example, there have been studies conducted investigating the social and political attitudes of PGCE students in the UK context (Wilkins 1999, 2001; Walkington and Wilkins 2000), and also in the Australian context (Allan and Hill 1990).

Wilkins (1999) carried out a study examining the understandings that primary and secondary postgraduate certificate of education (PGCE) students had of 'citizenship' and diversity-related issues, by sending questionnaires to 669 students at two large teacher education institutions in the UK just prior to starting their PGCE course, followed by a second phase in which 26 students were randomly chosen and interviewed, initially, at the end of their first term of the PGCE course, and then on completion of their PGCE course. This study found that PGCE students did not have a clear understanding of the term, 'citizenship', and in addition, many trainee teachers were politically disengaged and perceived themselves to have low political efficacy, and were highly cynical of the political process and of democracy in the UK. Although disengaged from mainstream politics, these PGCE students showed interest in 'single-issue' politics (e.g. animal rights, environmentalism) (Wilkins 1999). With regard to perceptions relating to social class, many participants perceived that such divisions are still a strong feature of British society. Participants expressed beliefs that there are high levels of racism within British society, but that their generation is more tolerant and that racism is on the decrease. Wilkins (1999) noted that participants showed awareness of racism at the level of the individual, but did not show such awareness at the institutional level, suggesting that these trainee teachers did not have an understanding of the complexity of racism in terms of its expression through social structures within society; in addition the author noted a 'political correctness backlash' (Wilkins 1999).

In a second study, Wilkins (2001) found that most PGCE students expressed positive attitudes towards a diverse society, and believed that education is important in developing civic virtues and respect for diversity. However, there was a minority of students expressing negative attitudes towards 'race' issues, including the perceptions that black people are responsible for most crime, and that ethnic minorities are given favourable treatment. It is not clear how widespread such views were nor whether they continue to be a significant feature, but Wilkins (2001) cites findings from an earlier study that echo his findings (Cohen 1989, cited in Wilkins 2001); he argues that anti-racism must be a key component of citizenship education, that schools must recognize that racism is more than prejudice on an individual level – that it must be addressed at the institutional level, and that the recruitment of ethnic minorities to teaching must be a priority. Indeed, Cline *et al.* (2002, cited in Ajegbo *et al.* 2007) have shown that, while intentions may be good, this may not translate into appropriate practice, with many teachers arguing for a 'colour-blind' approach, which can result in denying difference and which may inadvertently contribute to institutional racism.

According to the Training and Development Agency for Schools (TDA), only 36 per cent of newly qualified teachers were satisfied that their training adequately equipped them to teach in multicultural schools (Ajegbo *et al.* 2007). This suggests that the TDA should urgently evaluate the effectiveness of initial teacher training (ITT) providers with respect to their delivery of issues relating to diversity. Our DfES Diversity and Citizenship Report found that there is a widespread perception that diversity-related issues are more relevant, and more highly prioritized in multi-ethnic schools, as there is a general assumption that such issues are more pertinent to the daily lives of pupils in multi-ethnic schools. However, the evidence from the DfES Diversity and Citizenship review suggests that, while teachers in multi-ethnic schools may have confidence in addressing diversity issues and may consider them to be 'second nature', in practice, these schools do not necessarily have established diversity strategies in place; nor are they necessarily equipped with substantive knowledge or skills to address issues relating to diversity either in curricular context, or in relation to classroom or school practices and ethos (Ajegbo *et al.* 2007).

This evidence is supported by findings from an international project, entitled 'What education for what citizenship?', which was launched by UNESCO in 1994, with the aim of improving educational strategies for citizenship education (Albala-Bertrand 1997). The first phase consisted of a comparative survey of teachers and secondary school students across 34 countries; the second phase aimed to evaluate key findings from phase 1, in order to develop effective curriculum and pedagogic strategies for citizenship education in different countries, and finally the third phase aimed to disseminate the findings internationally via the web, and to develop an 'expert system' to provide increased access to research evidence on citizenship education (Albala-Bertrand 1997). Being in a multi-ethnic school seemed to encourage interest in civic studies, and propensity toward civic participation in the community; however, multi-ethnicity appeared to be associated with low participation in school group activities. This may in part be explained in terms of teachers in multi-ethnic schools taking diversity for granted, and in fact not necessarily being equipped with the appropriate knowledge and skills, nor putting into practice explicit diversity strategies in the class and school context.

The DfES Diversity and Citizenship Report recommended that, as a first step, that schools audit and evaluate – across curriculum subjects and school practices, the extent to which and how they currently teach pupils issues relating to diversity (Ajegbo *et al.* 2007). This could then be seen as a building block, in developing a shared database of resources, and to identify where there may be gaps, and to develop new resources. Schools could be supported by national subject associations, and in the case of England, the Qualifications and Curriculum Authority (QCA), who will be providing guidelines and case studies to support the KS3 revised curriculum (QCA 2007). There is also the issue of the methodology of transferring good practice from one institutional setting to another, and I also recommend research supporting the transfer of good practice be supported in this regard.

It is also important that training for diversity is also seen as an imperative for continuing professional development (CPD). The DfES Diversity and Citizenship Report highlighted the issue that teachers will be working in very different contexts, and that location clearly has implications for classroom experience: 'teaching in cosmopolitan London is different from Bradford or Oldham' (Ajegbo *et al.* 2007: 67), or indeed Suffolk or Cornwall. The DfES has approved the roll-out of a Citizenship CPD programme – the Certificate of the Teaching of

Citizenship, evaluated by OFSTED. The DfES has made available up to 600 places, with bursaries available covering most of the cost. The Certificate is being offered by Higher Education institutions in England, in partnership with non-governmental organizations and local authorities.[1] Given that the standards for the certification of the teaching of Citizenship were drafted prior to the publication of the DfES Diversity and Citizenship Report, and the revised QCA Programmes of Study at KS3 and KS4, it is perhaps understandable, although disappointing, that issues of identity and diversity are not explicitly referred to at all. Addressing issues of identity and diversity must be a crucial component of these courses, given the recommendations of the DfES Diversity and Citizenship Report.

### Teacher recruitment and retention

Clearly, it is important that there is an ethnically and religiously diverse staff, in order to represent a diverse student population. Having an ethnically and religiously diverse workforce should be valued as an important resource, not only so that ethnic minority teachers can take up positions in multi-ethnic schools – and hence provide a source of motivation to participate for pupils through providing role models from a range of different backgrounds, but it is important to ensure that all pupils come into contact with a variety of ideas and beliefs as part of their personal development (Johnson 2003). Yet the practical reality for many ethnic minority teachers is that they encounter what they perceive to be discriminatory practices and attitudes both at individual and structural levels (Ajegbo *et al.* 2007), which discourages many ethnic minorities from teaching in predominantly 'white areas' or 'white schools', and indeed may lead them to drop-out of teaching altogether.

The DfES Diversity and Citizenship Report recommended that developing knowledge and skills specifically relating to issues of diversity should be key criteria for Advanced Skills Teachers (AST) status (Ajegbo *et al.* 2007). This will encourage and reward the development of skills in this domain. In addition, it was proposed that promotion should also be based on expertise in relation to inclusive practice, and where teachers have significant responsibility within their schools for enhancing the skills of other staff.

### National and system infrastructure

For processes of inclusive citizenship to become embedded within schools, it is important that there is a systematized approach and national coordination of DfES, QCA, OFSTED, local authorities and also examination boards. As mentioned previously, OFSTED from September 2007, will have a responsibility to inspect and report on schools regarding their duty to promote community cohesion (DfES 2006). It is expected that OFSTED will give recommendations for improvement for schools, which in turn will need to be supported by their local authorities (DfES 2006). Coordination between QCA and examination boards will also be important to ensure that issues of diversity are studied and assessed more systematically in GCSE Citizenship, with GCSE subject criteria substantively addressing issues of diversity.

### School linking

Given my arguments regarding the importance of emphasizing the relationship between and within local and national levels, as well as national and international levels, I suggest the introduction of schemes linking the local and the national. In the DfES Diversity and Citizenship Report, the importance of 'harnessing' the local context is emphasized. This provides pupils with a contextualized starting point for understanding and becoming interested in issues of citizenship and diversity, which can then be extended to the national and international levels. In addition, such an approach avoids tokenism, by allowing for an examination of issues that are relevant and authentically interesting to the pupils – a focus on the particular before moving to the general. Crucially, in the DfES Diversity and Citizenship Report, it was emphasized that linking between schools should be organized around curriculum objectives, with links including electronic links, relationships with other schools, parents, community groups and business (Ajegbo *et al.* 2007). In addition, I would also advocate schemes linking schools between England and Wales, Scotland and Northern Ireland. Furthermore, activities whereby pupils shadow representatives from local organizations in national fora, could also be systematically introduced. A school coordinator could be appointed to oversee these local–national networks.

### Pupil voice

This is a growing area of research and practice, where it has been proposed that pupils participate in policymaking and practice (Osler and Starkey 2005; Noyes 2005). While there are debates relating to whose aims such participation or 'consultation' may serve, it is important that schools encourage pupil participation by having in place appropriate mechanisms to ensure expression of views. Not only can this encourage pupil motivation to participate, and therefore develop a more inclusive citizenship ethos, but it also enables the development of a more appropriate and 'tailor-made' curriculum for a given class of pupils. It has been shown that schools who have been most successful with respect to developing and implementing citizenship education have a supportive school ethos with active involvement of pupils through school and class councils and other school systems and processes and good relations between teachers and pupils (Kerr *et al.* 2004). Yet the power dynamic between teachers and pupils should be recognized, and pupil participation framed realistically, in terms of teachers providing the scaffolding and 'authoritative' direction or process as opposed to an 'authoritarian' pedagogy (Kalantzis and Cope 1999).

## Curriculum

In the context of the IEA study, Kerr (1999) identified a lack of tradition in explicitly dealing with such themes as 'democracy', 'national identity', 'social diversity and cohesion' as a key obstacle in developing citizenship education. This study also found that England scored below the international mean on positive attitudes towards immigrants, and also on national identity and patriotism, with girls more supportive of immigrants' and women's rights in all countries (Kerr 2001). If the UK aims for an inclusive and participative model of citizenship, then this finding might suggest that how citizenship is conceptualized in the new citizenship education policy and curriculum may provide an opportunity to play a potentially important role in influencing attitudes to identity and diversity in the context of citizenship.

In addition, Buckingham's (1999a,b) studies on political socialization found that young people are alienated and cynical about politics, stemming from feelings of exclusion, rather than ignorance or immaturity. He argues that crucially, 'micro-politics of personal experience' needs to be connected with the 'macro-politics of the public sphere' in a realistic and relevant way (Buckingham 1999b: 113), for the effects of citizenship education to be sustainable. Young people must be able to be political actors in their own right, if citizenship education is to be authentic. This will require addressing the issue of ethnic and religious identity in the public as well as the private sphere, in addition to other forms of identification.

Extending this idea, I would argue that it is important that multiculturalism is politicized and clearly located within a local and national framework. By this, I mean that multiculturalism is explicitly addressed in the context of the public political sphere, and is framed in terms of an inclusive and participative process. This requires clear conceptual understanding, first and foremost by teachers – what Davies (2000: 104) has referred to as 'shifting philosophical debates into pedagogical ground'. He has advocated the idea of 'procedural concepts', in order to provide pupils with the conceptual understanding and language to think, talk and act politically. Banks *et al.* (2006), in their 'Democracy and Diversity' Report, provide a coherent set of principles and concepts for teachers to use in further developing their citizenship education curricula to explicitly balance unity and diversity in the local, national and global contexts. These include emphasizing interconnectedness and human rights, in relation to diversity and unity. Banks *et al.*'s (2006) set of principles and concepts provide a useful framework to structure and further develop teachers' expertise.

For example, there should be an explicit examination of the relationship between a range of related concepts, such as immigrants, refugees, asylum-seekers, citizenship, human rights, and democracy.

## Pedagogy

With regard to teaching and learning methodology, a more 'liberal' (as opposed to more 'authoritarian') relationship between teachers and students has been shown to be significantly correlated with the development of cosmopolitan values, positive attitudes towards religions, ethnic and cultural diversity at the school level, and also with active participation at school and at the level of the community (Albala-Bertrand 1997). It did not, however, appear to be significantly correlated with such content knowledge as awareness of human rights or understanding of political or institutional institutions and processes. Mode of presentation did not seem to be significantly correlated in developing awareness of citizenship issues, but it was significantly correlated with civic participation (i.e. active methods, e.g. debates, role-play, outside school visits correlate more positively with civic participation), and also civic tolerance; furthermore, realistic activities outside school were significantly associated with student participation in civic activities in real life (Albala-Bertrand 1997). This suggests that pedagogical approach is correlated with attitudes and participative skills (or intention to participate), but not with content knowledge.

Osler and Starkey (1999) reviewed the findings of a 1997 European Commission study across 18 European countries, which aimed to identify features of projects in education, training and youth programmes which contribute effectively to political education and 'active citizenship'. Information was collected on the quality of information provided to participants relating to the projects' aims, the capacity to provide for students to engage in democratic activities and opportunities to explore multiple identities. The authors identified themes, such as women's citizenship needs, challenging racism and understanding exclusion, by exploring a number of case studies, and based on this, they provided suggestions for best practice in terms of content, pedagogy and organization. Four key suggestions were: individuals should learn the process of seeking out relevant information, rather than being provided with it (whether working individually or collectively); that projects must address identities and feelings not just information and rights, and must also address structural inequalities (Osler and Starkey 1999); projects are most successful when they are designed and implemented by those who are marginalized, rather than a project merely designed for them; and finally, projects are most successful when they provide opportunities for participants to develop skills for participation (Osler and Starkey 1999).

With regard to pedagogical approaches that take into account the issue of diversity, Walkington and Wilkins (2000) also report on a study in which they compared two groups of primary school teachers – the first group consisted of teachers who had taught abroad through VSO and had returned to teaching in the UK, while the second group consisted of primary teachers with no experience of teaching abroad. All teachers completed a questionnaire followed by a semi-structured interview asking them about their aims and practices with regard to teaching about developing countries in the geography curriculum. The findings showed that all teachers fulfilled Geography curriculum aims, however, those from the first group combined these aims with Global Citizenship education. The authors suggest that these reflect different models of the purpose of education, with Group 1 using a 'process-oriented' model, developing critical thinking and personal development through participative pedagogical approaches, in contrast to Group 2, who tended to utilize a more 'transmission-based' model, focusing on the transmission of particular geographical knowledge and skills (Walkington and Wilkins 2000). It is suggested that curriculum reform is not sufficient to change the teaching of citizenship values, but that there must be an intervention at the level of teacher-training: that it is important to 'educate the teacher's world-view', and teachers need to be 'equipped with strategies for participatory teaching styles' (Walkington and Wilkins 2000: 77). The authors call for more research in this area of teacher education, and in particular, relating to citizenship education.

While content knowledge is clearly important, a 'pedagogy of acceptance' must be avoided. This approach was evident in the KS3 Programme of Study and KS3 Schemes of Work (QCA 2000, 2001), with proposals that pupils 'learn about' diversity, rather than operationalizing this with respect to participative skills. Kalantzis and Cope (1999) have proposed a 'pedagogy of process', which they characterize as a 'post-progressivist pedagogy'. Inherent in this pedagogy is not a fixed set of strategies, but that teachers respect and care for their pupils (Nieto 1999) and create a supportive environment, conducive to an active and inclusive participation. They argue that it is important that teachers are explicit that multiculturalism is not 'culturally agnostic', but is a 'value-laden response to diversity' (p. 262). Rather than merely 'learning about' or even critiquing the status quo, this pedagogy advocates that pupils learn about cultures and discourses of power in order to open up social and political access. The importance of recognizing asymmetric power relations is necessary for a 'critical' curriculum (Parker 2004), a theme that is also highlighted in relation to curriculum work in Brazil (Gonçalves e Silva 2004), Palestine (Moughrabi 2004) and South Africa (Moodley and Adam 2004). This pedagogy is both consciousness-raising and learning how to operate within, and learning how to potentially change structures and processes.

DeWitt's (2003) proposal of an 'inquiry-based multicultural democracy' (MCD) entails this concept of democracy as a 'path', where this process is dynamic and critical of the status quo. In addition, diversity is conceptualized in a multi-dimensional way, accommodating cultural and socioeconomic diversity within the framework of political diversity. DeWitt (2003) suggests that the internet is a particularly useful resource in that it provides multiple perspectives and viewpoints that are inherent to the concept of a multicultural democratic pedagogy.

In the DfES Diversity and Citizenship Report, there are three curricula 'schemes of work' examples included in Appendix 1, around the fourth strand sub-themes of (1) the UK as a 'multinational' state, (2) migration and (3) extending the franchise (slavery).[2] These examples aim to illustrate an enquiry, question-oriented approach using relevant historical examples to develop contextualized 'citizenship thinking', relating to contemporary and relevant issues in the UK. They indicate to teachers the range, content and skills relevant to these particular examples. This pedagogical approach advocated illustrates what we argued to be the appropriate role of History in relation to Citizenship, drawing on its methodological 'use of evidence and processes of enquiry' (p. 84) to develop participative citizenship.

# Conclusions

Key issues raised from the empirical literature illustrate that England scored below the international mean on attitudes to diversity and national identity (Kerr 1999). I have also discussed how research on pedagogical approaches highlights the importance of active participation both within school and in the community for improving strategies for citizenship education (Albala-Bertrand 1997; Osler and Starkey 1999; Walkington and Wilkins 2000). In addition, issues relating to identity, structural disadvantage and empowerment must be addressed (Buckingham 1999b; Osler and Starkey 1999), in order to tackle cynicism stemming from feelings of exclusion and disempowerment (Buckingham 1999b). Finally, if these issues are to be addressed, teachers must have sophisticated conceptual understandings of the inter-relationship between citizenship and diversity. However, there is some research evidence to suggest that this is lacking (Wilkins 1999), and moreover, there is evidence to suggest that there may in fact be a minority of PGCE students who actually have negative views with regard to diversity (Wilkins 2001).

Kerr (1999) made the important point that the knowledge and research base underpinning the field of citizenship education in England is relatively sparse; and more importantly, that policy and curriculum development are taking place to a large extent separately from the aims and practices occurring at the school level, and without clear theoretical understanding, or empirical evidence of the potential impact of these policies at the student level. This emphasizes the need for policy and practice relating to citizenship education to be informed by reliable evidence. For citizenship education to be effective, Kerr (1999) proposes that there must first be a clear theoretical elucidation of what is meant by the concept of citizenship; second, the development of policy and curriculum and implementation must be based on reliable research evidence, and third, that policy, curriculum and implementation must be 'joined up' – they must not be considered as discrete, independent stages, but rather, as mutually inter-dependent processes. This would suggest that fundamental issues, such as accounting for diversity cannot be added on at the implementation stage, but instead, must be developed and articulated theoretically throughout the whole cycle from policy development through to implementation.

# Notes

## Introduction

1 It could be argued that the exception to this is the nationalist literature on citizenship, although this takes a 'negatively' construed view of diversity, as there is explicit emphasis on bonds of ethnicity. According to Miller (1995), ethnicity did not really figure in conceptions of citizenship prior to the nineteenth century; the 'ethnic' model of nationalism reflects nineteenth-century roots in German romanticism and its organic view of society, where the 'nation' exists before the state. The German politics of citizenship reflects this 'ethnocultural' understanding of nationhood (Brubaker 1998).

2 I did not aim for this group to be representative of those who have formulated policy in this field; rather, the aim was to reflect, to as great an extent as possible, a range of views, beliefs and values held by some of those who have been involved to varying degrees in the field. Nine of the 15 women were from 'ethnic minorities', whereas none of the men were.

3 It should be noted that some of the participants are involved in more than one 'stage' of the process.

4 For full details of data analysis, please refer to Kiwan (2006b).

5 KS3 refers to the school age range 11–14, with the Programme of Study outlining expected learning outcomes, and the Schemes of Work providing fuller guidance materials for teachers.

## 1 Citizenship education in England: setting the scene

1 It should be noted that the UK has a longer history of mass immigration (see, e.g. CRE 1996).

## 2 Key players' perceptions: influences, processes, aims and contributions

1 This chapter draws on Kiwan, D. (2006c). 'Constructing citizenship in the education policymaking process in England: an act of citizenship?', *International Journal of Learning* 13(6): 131–8.

2 These issues are examined in more detail in Chapter 6, which focuses on the 'underplayed' conceptions of citizenship.

3 Based on the survey question: 'Thinking about Britain, how satisfied are you with the way democracy works?' (Pattie *et al.* 2004).

4 Pattie *et al.* (2004) divide political participation into three categories: individualistic, contact and collective. Examples of individualistic actions include donating money or signing a petition; contact refers to, e.g. contacting a politician, and collective refers to, e.g. going on a demonstration.

5  See Gewirtz and Cribb (2002) for a discussion of tensions between different facets of justice, and their implications for policy sociology.
6  Referred to by four members of the Crick Advisory Group.
7  This may not necessarily have any significance given that the sample did not attempt to achieve representativeness.
8  This could be construed more negatively as illustrating discriminatory and exclusionary assumptions with regard to the relationship between ethnicity and nationality.
9  According to David Kerr, Secretary to the Crick Advisory Group.
10  See earlier section in this chapter.

## Part 2  Conceptions of citizenship

1  Interviewees were asked: 'What understanding of citizenship is being presented? What aspects do you think are being emphasized, and what aspects are not being emphasized, and why? What do *you* think of this conceptualization?'.

## 3  'Moral' conceptions

1  See Chapter 4 for discussion of liberalism in relation to 'legal' conceptions of citizenship.
2  A project with the remit of raising the quality of PSE in schools.

## 4  'Legal' conceptions

1  With full citizenship entailing six privileges, four of which were public rights (service in the army, voting in the assembly, eligibility to public office and the legal right of action and appeal), and two of which were private rights (rights of intermarriage and trade with other Roman citizens).
2  It should be noted that I am characterizing the *education curriculum* as 'legal', as opposed to citizenship at the political institutional level, which is typically characterized as 'civic republican' in the literature (Brubaker 1998).
3  It should be noted that I was a member of this Advisory Group, 2002–3.
4  For those at or above English for Speakers of Other Languages (ESOL) Entry level 3.
5  Sections: (1) What is citizenship? (2) Parliament and the electoral system. (3) The United Kingdom in Europe, the Commonwealth and the United Nations. (4) The United Kingdom. (5) The United Kingdom as a diverse society. (6) Human rights. (7) Working in the United Kingdom. (8) Health. (9) Housing. (10) Education. (11) Community Engagement. (12) Knowing the law.
6  ABNI, a non-departmental public body, was set up in November 2004 to carry forward the recommendations of the 'Life in the UK' Advisory Group. Its first chair was Sir Bernard Crick, and I was its first Head of Secretariat.

## 5  'Participatory' conceptions

1  Delanty (2003) proposes that civic republicanism illustrates a particular focus on *participation* in the community, as it is based on the notion of *positive* freedom (in contrast to liberalisms's negative freedom) – illustrated in the notion of a self-governing political community.
2  Or more specifically, men.
3  As well as gender and social class.

## 6  'Identity-based' conceptions

1  Based on the coding of the interview data.
2  See Chapter 5 for a discussion relating to this.

3 It should be noted that the categorizations based on the coding of the interview data are not always mutually exclusive, hence, my decision to locate the discussion of a particular unit in one section rather than in another, is to some extent a pragmatic decision.

4 This is discussed in Chapter 3 – 'moral' conceptions of citizenship, as discourses on 'shared values' tend to be framed in moral terms.

5 Learning about 'the *origins* [italics added] and implications of the diverse national, regional, religious and ethnic identities of the United Kingdom' (KS4).

## 7 Developing a theory of inclusive citizenship

1 Significant sections of this chapter have been reprinted by permission of Sage Publications Ltd., from Kiwan (2007a) 'Developing a model of inclusive citizenship: "institutional multiculturalism" and the citizen-state relationship', *Theory and Research in Education* 5(2): 225–40, Sage Publications and the Slovene Society of Researchers in the School Field, 2007.

2 Cited in Cantle Report (Home Office 2001a).

3 For example, eating out at 'ethnic' restaurants, or going to see a 'foreign language' film.

4 And from April 2007, those applying for indefinite leave to remain (Home Office 2006).

## 8 Practical implications for policy, curriculum and pedagogy

1 For example, Birkbeck College, University of London, in association with the Citizenship Foundation is offering the certificate from April 2007.

2 These were initially developed by Andrew Wrenn and adapted by Lee Faith, Head of Citizenship at Deptford Green School, with comments from the Citizenship Foundation.

# Bibliography

ABNI/Home Office (2006) *2005/6 Annual Report of the Advisory Board on Naturalisation and Integration (ABNI) November 2004 – April 2006*, London: TSO.

Ajegbo, K., Kiwan, D. and Sharma, S. (2007) *Curriculum Review: Diversity and Citizenship*, London: DfES.

Albala-Bertrand, L. (1997) 'What education for what citizenship? Preliminary results', *Educational Innovation and Information* 90: 2–8. (UNESCO Survey).

Alderson, P. (2000) 'Citizenship in theory and practice: being or becoming citizens with rights', in D. Lawton, J. Cairns and R. Gardner (eds.) *Education for Citizenship*, London: Continuum.

Alibhai-Brown, Y. (2000) *After Multiculturalism*, London: Foreign Policy Centre.

Allan, R. and Hill, B. (1990) 'The political awareness of some Australian primary teachers in training: implications for the primary social education curriculum', *Social Science Teacher* 20(1): 17–20.

Anderson, B. (1983) *Imagined Communities*, London: Verso.

Annette, J. (2005) 'Faith schools and communities: communitarianism, social capital and citizenship', in R. Gardner, J. Cairns and Denis Lawton (eds.) *Faith Schools: Consensus or Conflict?*, Abingdon: RoutledgeFalmer.

Anthias, F. and Yuval-Davis, N. (1993) *Racialized Boundaries*, London: Routledge.

Aristotle (1976 edn.) *Ethics* (Translated by J. A. K. Thomason), London: Penguin Books Ltd.

Ball, S. (1994a) 'Political interviews and the politics of interviewing', in G. Walford (ed.) *Researching the Powerful in Education*, London: UCL Press.

Ball, S. J. (1994b) *Education Reform: A Critical and Post-structuralist Approach*, Buckingham: Open University Press.

Ballance, J. (1995) ' "A Union without cohesion": religion, national identity and the "British Constitution" in the nineteenth century', in M. Dunne and T. Bonazzi (eds.) *Citizenship and Rights in Multicultural Societies*, Keele: Keele University Press.

Banks, J. A. (2004) 'Introduction: Democratic Citizenship Education', in J. A. Banks (ed.) *Diversity and Citizenship Education: Global Perspectives*, San Francisco: Jossey-Bass.

Banks, J. A., McGee Banks, C. A., Cortes, C. E., Hahn, C. L., Merryfield, M. M., Moodley, K. A., Murphy-Shigematsu, S., Osler, A., Park, C. and Parker, W. C. (2006) *Democracy and Diversity: Principles and Concepts for Educating Citizens in a Global Age*, Seattle: Center for Multicultural Education, University of Washington.

Barrère, A. and Martuccelli, D. (1998) 'La Citoyenneté à l'école: vers la définition d'une problématique sociologique', in *Revue française de Sociologie* 39(4): 651–71, cited in

Kiwan, D. and Kiwan, N. (2005) 'Citizenship education: the French and English experience', in C. Pole, J. Pilcher and J. Williams (eds.) *Young People in Transition: Becoming Citizens*, Basingstoke: Palgrave Macmillan.

Barker, M. (1981) *The New Racism: Conservatives and the Ideology of the Tribe*, London: Junction Books, cited in Gillborn, D. (1999) 'Race, nation and education: New Labour and the New Racism', in J. Demaine (ed.) *Education Policy and Contemporary Politics*, Basingstoke: Macmillan Press Ltd.

Batho, G. (1990) 'The history of the teaching of civics and citizenship in English schools', *The Curriculum Journal* 1(1): 91–100.

BBC News (2007) 'Schools "must act on Brother row"'. Online. Available: www.bbc.co.uk/1/hi/education/62833.stm (accessed 19 February 2007).

Beck, J. (1998) *Morality and Citizenship in Education*, London: Cassell.

Ben-Porath, S. R. (2006) *Citizenship under Fire: Democratic Education in Times of Conflict*, Princeton: Princeton University Press.

Billig, M., Downey, J., Richardson, J., Deacon, D. and Golding P. (2006) ' "Britishness" in the last three general elections: from ethnic to civic nationalism', Report for the Commission for Racial Equality.

Blair, T. (2006) 'Our Nation's Future – multiculturalism and integration'. Online. Available: www.number-10.gov.uk/output/Page10563.asp (accessed 12 December 2006).

Blum, L. (1999) 'Race, community and moral education: Kohlberg and Spielberg as civic educators', *Journal of Moral Education* 28(2): 125–43.

Blunkett, D. (2005) 'A New England: An English Identity within Britain', Speech to the Institute for Public Policy Research (IPPR), 14 March.

Board of Education (1905) *Handbook of Suggestions for the Consideration of Teachers and Others Concerned in the Work of Public Elementary Schools*, cited in Stow, W. (2000) 'History: values in the diversity of human experience', in R. Bailey (ed.) (2000) *Teaching Values and Citizenship across the Curriculum*, London: Kogan.

Brighouse, H. (2005) 'Faith-based schools in the United Kingdom: an unenthusiastic defence of a slightly reformed status quo', in R. Gardner, J. Cairns, and D. Lawton (eds.) *Faith Schools: Consensus or Conflict?*, Abingdon: RoutledgeFalmer.

Bron, J. (2005) 'Citizenship and social integration: educational development between autonomy and accountability', in CIDREE/DVO (eds.) *Different Faces of Citizenship: Development of Citizenship Education in European Countries*, Belgium: CIDREE/DVO.

Brown, G. (2004) Speech to British Council annual lecture. Online. Available: www.hm-treasury.gov.uk/newsroom_and_speeches/press/2004/press_63_04.cfm (accessed 20 February 2007).

Brown, G. (2006) 'The future of Britishness', Speech to Fabian Society 2006 Annual Conference (14 January). Online. Available: www.fabian-society.org.uk/press_office/display.asp?id=520&type=news&cat=43 (accessed 20 February 2007).

Brubaker, R. (1998) 'Immigration, citizenship and nation-state in France and Germany', in G. Shafir (ed.) *The Citizenship Debates*, Minneapolis: University of Minnesota Press.

Buckingham, D. (1999a) 'Young people, politics and media: beyond political socialisation', *Oxford Review of Education* 25(1–2): 171–84.

Buckingham, D. (1999b) 'Electronic citizens? Young people, television news and the limits of politics', *The School Field* 10(1/2): 101–15.

Cline, T., Guida de Abreu, G., Fihosy, C., Gray, H., Lambert, H. and Neale, J. (2002) *Minority Ethnic Pupils in Mainly White Schools*, London: DfES, cited in Gaine, C. (2005) *We're all White, Thanks: The Persisting Myth about 'White' Schools*, Stoke on Trent: Trentham Books.

Cohen, L. (1989) 'Ignorance, not hostility: student teachers' perceptions of ethnic minorities in Britain', in G. Verma (ed.) *Education for All: A Landmark in Pluralism*, Lewes: Falmer Press, cited in Wilkins, C. (2001) 'Student teachers and attitudes towards "race": the role of citizenship education in addressing racism through the curriculum', *Westminster Studies in Education* 24(1): 7–21.

Coleman, J. (1988) 'Social capital and the creation of human capital', *American Journal of Sociology* 94(Suppl.): S95–S120, cited in Green, A. and Preston, J. (2001) 'Education and social cohesion: re-centring the debate', *Peabody Journal of Education* 76(3/4): 247–84.

Colley, L. (1992) *Britons: Forging the Nation 1707–1837*, London: Pimlico, cited in Grillo, R. D. (1998) *Pluralism and the Politics of Difference*, Oxford: Clarendon Press.

Commission for Racial Equality (CRE) (1996) *Roots of the Future: Ethnic Diversity in the Making of Britain*, London: CRE.

Commission for Racial Equality (CRE) (2006) Draft Corporate Plan 2006–9. Online. Available: www.cre.gov.uk/policy/corporateplan.html (accessed 16 February 2007).

Cookson, Jr. P. W. (1994) 'The power discourse: elite narratives and educational policy formation', in G. Walford (ed.) *Researching the Powerful in Education*, London: UCL Press.

Corbin, J. and Strauss, A. (1990) 'Grounded theory research: procedures, canons and evaluative criteria', *Qualitative Sociology* 13(1): 3–21.

Council of Europe (2006) European Youth Campaign for Human Rights, Diversity and Participation. Online. Available: http//alldifferent-allequal.info/ (accessed 16 February 2007).

Cranston, M. (1968) 'Introduction', in Rousseau, J. - J. (ed.) *The Social Contract* (Translated and introduced by Maurice Cranston), Harmondsworth, Middlesex: Penguin Publishers Ltd.

Cresswell, J. W. (1998) *Qualitative Inquiry and Research Design*, London and Thousand Oaks, CA: SAGE.

Crick, B. (2000) *In Defence of Politics*, 5th edn, London and New York: Continuum.

Crick, B. (2002) *Democracy: A Very Short Introduction*, Oxford: Oxford University Press.

Crick, B. (2003) 'Preface', in A. Lockyer, B. Crick and J. Annette (eds.) *Education for Democratic Citizenship: Issues of Theory and Practice*, Aldershot: Ashgate.

Crick, B. and Porter A. (eds.) (1978) *Political Education and Political Literacy*, London: Longman.

Crittenden, B. (1999) 'Moral education in a pluralist liberal democracy', in J. M. Halstead and T. H. McLaughlin (eds.) *Education in Morality*, London and New York: Routledge.

Davies, I. (1999a) 'What has happened in the teaching of politics in schools in England in the last three decades, and why?', *Oxford Review of Education* 25(1/2): 125–40.

Davies, I. (1999b) *Good Citizenship and Educational Provision*, London: Falmer Press.

Davies, I. (2000) 'Implementing citizenship education: can it be done?', *School Field* 11(3/4): 91–109.

Delanty, G. (2000) *Citizenship in a Global Age*, Buckingham: Open University Press.

Delanty, G. (2003) *Community*, London and New York: Routledge.

Demaine, J. (2002) 'Globalisation and citizenship education', *International Studies in Sociology of Education* 12(2): 117–28.

Department for Education and Employment (DfEE) (1997) *Excellence in Schools*, Cmnd. 3681, London: HMSO.

DfES (2006) 'The Education and Inspections Act'. Online. Available: www.dfes.gov.uk/publications/educationandinspectionsact/ (accessed 16 February 2007).

DeWitt, S. (2003) 'Multicultural democracy and inquiry pedagogy', *Intercultural Education* 14(3): 279–90.

Dubet, F. and Martuccelli, D. (1996) *A l'École: sociologie de l'expérience scolaire*. Paris: Seuil, cited in Kiwan D. and Kiwan, N. (2005) 'Citizenship education: The French and English experience', in C. Pole, J. Pilcher and J. Williams (eds.) *Young People in Transition: Becoming Citizens*, Basingstoke: Palgrave Macmillan.

Education and Skills Select Committee (2006) Inquiry into Citizenship Education Press: Notice 22. Online. Available: http://www.parliament.uk/parliamentary_committees/education_and_skills_committee/espn070206b.cfm (accessed 16 February 2007).

Etzioni, A. (1995) *The Spirit of Community*, London: Fontana Press.

Fogelman, K. (1997) 'Education for democratic citizenship in schools', in D. Bridges (ed.) *Education, Autonomy and Democratic Citizenship*, London: Routledge.

Forbes, H. D. (1997) *Ethnic Conflict: Commerce, Culture and the Contact Hypothesis*, New Haven, CT: Yale University Press, cited in Spinner-Halev, J. (2003) 'Education, reconciliation and nested identities', *Theory and Research in Education* 1(1): 51–72.

Freeman, M. (1994) 'The philosophical foundations of human rights', *Human Rights Quarterly* 16: 491–514.

Gaine, C. (2005) *We're all White, Thanks: The Persisting Myth about 'White' Schools*, Stoke on Trent: Trentham Books.

Gamarnikow, E. and Green, A. (2000) 'Citizenship, education and social capital', in D. Lawton, J. Cairns and R. Gardner (eds.) *Education for Citizenship*, London: Continuum.

Gates, B. (2005) 'Faith schools and colleges of education since 1800', in R. Gardner, J. Cairns and Denis Lawton (eds.) *Faith Schools: Consensus or Conflict?*, Abingdon: RoutledgeFalmer.

Gewirtz, S. and Cribb, A. (2002) 'Plural conceptions of social justice: implications for policy sociology', *Journal of Education Policy* 17(5): 499–509.

Giddens, A. (2004) 'Challenging social capital', in FPS (eds.) *The Global Exchange Forum Social Capital: A Policy Tool for North and South?* Conference Report, London: Foreign Policy Centre.

Gillborn, D. (1999) 'Race, nation and education: New Labour and the New Racism', in J. Demaine (ed.) *Education Policy and Contemporary Politics*, Basingstoke: Macmillan Press.

Gillborn, D. (2004) 'Anti-racism: from policy to practice', in G. Ladson-Billings and D. Gillborn (eds.) *The RoutledgeFalmer Reader in Multicultural Education*, London: RoutledgeFalmer.

Gilroy, P. (2002) *There Ain't No Black in the Union Jack*, London and New York: Routledge.

Glaser, B. and Strauss, A. (1967) *The Discovery of Grounded Theory*, Chicago: Aldine.

Goncalves e Silva, P. B. (2004) 'Citizenship and education in Brazil: The contribution of Indian Peoples and Blacks in the struggle for citizenship and recognition', in J. A. Banks (ed.) *Diversity and Citizenship Education: Global Perspectives*, San Francisco: Jossey-Bass.

Gordon, P. and Lawton, D. (1978) *Curriculum Change in the Nineteenth and Twentieth Centuries*, London: Hodder & Stoughton, cited in Batho, G. (1990) 'The history of the teaching of civics and citizenship in English schools', *The Curriculum Journal* 1(1): 91–100.

Goulbourne, H. (1991) *Ethnicity and Nationalism in Post-imperial Britain*, Cambridge: Cambridge University Press.

Green, A. and Preston, J. (2001) 'Education and social cohesion: re-centring the debate', *Peabody Journal of Education* 76(3/4): 247–84.

Green, A., Preston, J. and Sabates, R. (2003) 'Education, equality and social cohesion: a distributional approach', *Compare* 33(4): 453–70.

Griffiths, M. (1998) *Educational Research for Social Justice: Getting off the Fence*, Buckingham: Open University Press.

Grillo, R. D. (1998) *Pluralism and the Politics of Difference*, Oxford: Clarendon Press.

Guba, E. G. and Lincoln, Y. S. (1998) 'Competing paradigms in qualitative research', in N. K. Denzin and Y. S. Lincoln (eds.) *The Landscape of Qualitative Research*, London and Thousand Oaks: SAGE.

Gundara, J. S. (2000) *Interculturalism, Education and Inclusion*, London: SAGE.

Gundara, J. S. (2003) 'Intercultural education: world on the brink?', Professorial lecture, London: Institute of Education, University of London.

Gutmann, A. (1995) 'Introduction', in A. Gutmann (ed.) *Multiculturalism: Examining the Politics of Recognition*, Princeton: Princeton University Press.

Hall, S. (1992) 'The question of cultural identity', in S. Hall, D. Held and T. McGrew (eds.) *Modernity and its Futures*, Milton Keynes: Open University.

Halstead, D. and Pike, M. (2006) *Citizenship and Moral Education: Values in Action*, London and New York: Routledge.

Händle, C., Oesterreich, D. and Trommer, L. (1999) 'Concepts of civic education in Germany based on a survey of expert opinion', in J. Torney-Purta, J. Schwille and J. -A. Amadeo (eds.) *Civic Education across Countries: Twenty-four National Case Studies from the IEA Civic Education Project*, Amsterdam: International Association for the Evaluation of Educational Achievement.

Hargreaves, D. H. (1994) *The Mosaic of Learning: Schools and Teachers for the Next Century*, London: Demos, cited in Beck, J. (1998) *Morality and Citizenship in Education*, London: Cassell.

Haydon, G. (1999) 'The moral agenda of citizenship education', *School Field* 10(3/4): 47–54.

Haydon, G. (2000) 'The moral agenda of citizenship education', in D. Lawton, J. Cairns and R. Gardner (eds.) *Education for Citizenship*, London: Continuum.

Heater, D. (1990) *Citizenship: The Civic Ideal in World History, Politics and Education*, London: Longman.

Held, D. (1993) *Political Theory and the Modern State*, Cambridge: Polity Press.

Home Office (2001a) 'Community Cohesion': A Report of the Independent Review Team (Cantle Report), London: Home Office.

Home Office (2001b) *The Report of the Ministerial Group on Public Order and Community Cohesion (Denham Report)*, London: Home Office.

Home Office (2002) *Secure Borders, Safe Haven: Integration with Diversity in Modern Britain*, London: Home Office.

Home Office (2003) *The New and the Old*. The Report of the 'Life in the United Kingdom' Advisory Group, London: Home Office.

Home Office (2005) *Life in the United Kingdom: A journey to Citizenship*, Published on behalf of the Life in the United Kingdom Advisory Group, London: TSO. Second imprint.

Home Office (2006) 'English language ability to be required for visas', Press release. Online. Available: www.homeoffice.gov.uk/about-us/news/learning-english (accessed 11 February 2007).

Huntingdon, S. (1993) 'The clash of civilizations', *Foreign Affairs* 72(3): 22–49.

Huntingdon, S. P. (2004) *Who are we? America's Great Debate*, London: Simon and Schuster.

Ipgrave, J. (2003) 'Dialogue, citizenship and religious education', in R. Jackson (ed.) *International Perspectives on Citizenship, Education and Religious Diversity*, London and New York: RoutledgeFalmer.

Irwin, T. (1992) 'Introduction', in Plato, *The Republic* (Translated by A. D. Lindsay and Introduced by T. Irwin), London: J. M. Dent and Sons.

Isin, E. F. and Wood, P. K. (1999) *Citizenship and Identity*, London: SAGE.

Jackson, R. (ed.) (2003) *International Perspectives on Citizenship, Education and Religious Diversity*, London and New York: RoutledgeFalmer.

Jenkins, R. (1967) *Essays and Speeches*, London: Collins, cited in Grillo, R. D. (1998) *Pluralism and the Politics of Difference*, Oxford: Clarendon Press.

Johnson, L. S. (2003) 'The diversity imperative: building a culturally responsive school ethos', *Intercultural Education* 14(1): 17–29.

Jones, K. B. (1998) 'Citizenship in a woman-friendly polity', in G. Shafir (ed.) *The Citizenship Debates*, Minneapolis. University of Minnesota Press.

Joppke, J. and Lukes, S. (1999) 'Introduction: multicultural questions', in C. Joppke and S. Lukes (eds.) *Multicultural Questions*, Oxford: Oxford University Press.

Joshee, R. (2004) 'Citizenship and Multicultural Education in Canada: from assimilation to social cohesion', in J. A. Banks (ed.) *Multicultural Societies in Diversity and Citizenship Education: Global Perspectives*, San Francisco: Jossey-Bass.

Kalantzis, M. and Cope, B. (1999) 'Multicultural Education: Transforming the Mainstream', in S. May (ed.) *Critical Multiculturalism: Rethinking Multicultural and Anti-racist Education*, London: Falmer Press.

Kant, I. [1795] (1949) 'The groundwork of the metaphysic of morals', in H. Paton (ed.) *The Moral Law*, London: Hutcheson, cited in Williams, J. (2002) 'Introduction' in Section 1: 'The ideal of global citizenship', in N. Odwe and J. Williams (eds.) *Global Citizenship: A Critical Reader*, Edinburgh: Edinburgh University Press.

Kastoryano, R. (2006) 'French secularism and Islam: France's headscarf affair', in T. Modood, A. Triandafyllidou and R. Zapata-Barrero (eds.) *Multiculturalism, Muslims and Citizenship: A European Approach*, Abingdon, Oxon: Routledge.

Kekes, J. (1999) 'Pluralism, moral imagination and moral education', in J. M. Halstead and T. H. McLaughlin (eds.) *Education in Morality*, London and New York: Routledge.

Kerr, D. (1999) *Re-examining Citizenship Education: The Case of England*, Slough: NFER.

Kerr, D. (2000a) 'The making of citizenship in the national curriculum (England): Issues and challenges', unpublished paper presented at ECER Conference, Edinburgh, September.

Kerr, D. (2000b) 'Changing the political culture: The Advisory Group on Education for Citizenship and the Teaching of Democracy in Schools', *Oxford Review of Education* 25(1/2): 275–84.

Kerr, D. (2001) *Citizenship and Education at Age 14: A Summary of the International Findings and Preliminary Results for England*, Slough: NFER.

Kerr, D., Ireland, E., Lopes, J. and Craig, R. with Cleaver, L. (2004) *Making Citizenship Education Real, Citizenship Education Longitudinal Study: Second Annual Report, First Longitudinal Survey*, Slough: NFER.

Kerr, D. and Lopes, J. (2006) *Evaluation of the '2005 European Year of Citizenship through Education': 'Learning and Living Democracy'*, *Final Report*. Online. Available: www.coe.int/t/e/cultural_co-operation/education/e.d.c/majour_events/Evaluation_Report_Eng.PDF (accessed 26 September 2006).

Kiwan, D. (2005) 'Human rights and citizenship: an unjustifiable conflation?', *Journal of Philosophy of Education* 39(1): 37–50.

Kiwan, D. (2006a) 'Evidence submitted to House of Commons Education and Skills Select Committee, Inquiry into Citizenship Education', Online. Available: www.publications.parliament.uk/pa/cm200506/cmselect/cmeduski/uc581-v/uc581m03.htm (accessed 9 January 2007).

Kiwan, D. (2006b) 'An inclusive citizenship? Conceptions of citizenship in the citizenship education policymaking process in England', unpublished PhD thesis, University of London.

Kiwan, D. (2006c) 'Constructing citizenship in the education policymaking process in England: an act of citizenship?', *International Journal of Learning* 13(6): 131–8.

Kiwan, D. (2007a) 'Developing a model of inclusive citizenship: "institutional multiculturalism" and the citizen-state relationship', *Theory and Research in Education* 5(2): 225–40.

Kiwan, D. (2007b) 'Citizenship education at the cross-roads: four models of citizenship and their implications for ethnic and religious diversity', *Oxford Review of Education* (in press).

Kiwan, D. (2007c) *Towards a Theory of Inclusive Participative Citizenship*, Council of Europe publication (in press).

Kiwan, D. (2007d) 'Uneasy relationships? Conceptions of "citizenship", "democracy" and "diversity" in the English citizenship education policymaking process', *Education, Citizenship and Social Justice* (forthcoming).

Kiwan, N. and Kiwan, D. (2002) 'Citizenship education in theory and practice: the French and English experience', unpublished conference paper presented at BSA Annual Conference, Leicester.

Kiwan, D. and Kiwan, N. (2005) 'Citizenship education: the French and English experience', in C. Pole, J. Pilcher and J. Williams (eds.) *Young People in Transition: Becoming Citizens*, Basingstoke: Palgrave Macmillan.

Kvale, S. (1996) *Interviews: An Introduction to Qualitative Research Interviewing*, London and Thousand Oaks: SAGE.

Kymlicka, W. (1995) *Multicultural Citizenship*, Oxford: Oxford University Press.

Kymlicka, W. (1999) 'Education for citizenship', in J. M. Halstead and T. H. McLaughlin (eds.) *Education in Morality*, London and New York: Routledge.

Kymlicka, W. (2003) 'Multicultural states and intercultural citizens', *Theory and Research in Education* 1(2): 147–69.

Ladson-Billings, G. (2004) 'Culture versus citizenship: the challenge of racialised citizenship in the United States', in J. A. Banks (ed.) *Multicultural Societies in Diversity and Citizenship Education: Global Perspectives*, San Francisco: Jossey-Bass.

Leary, V. (1990) 'The effect of Western perspectives on international human rights', in A. An-Na'im and F. Deng (eds.) *Human Rights in Africa: Cross-Cultural Perspectives*, Washington, DC: The Brookings Institution.

Lawton, D. (2000) 'Overview: citizenship education in context', in D. Lawton, J. Cairns and R. Gardner (eds.) *Education for Citizenship*, London: Continuum.

Leeman, Y. A. M. (2003) 'School leadership for intercultural education', *Intercultural Education* 14(1): 31–45.

Leganger-Krogstad, H. (2003) 'Dialogue among young citizens in a pluralistic religious education classroom', in R. Jackson (ed.) *International Perspectives on Citizenship, Education and Religious Diversity*, London and New York: RoutledgeFalmer.

Luchtenberg, S. (2004) 'Ethnic diversity and citizenship education in Germany', in J. A. Banks (ed.) *Multicultural Societies in Diversity and Citizenship Education: Global Perspectives*, San Francisco: Jossey-Bass.

McLaughlin, T. (2000) 'Philosophy and educational policy: possibilities, tensions and tasks', *Journal of Education Policy* 15(4): 441–57.

Macpherson, W. (1999) *The Stephen Lawrence Inquiry: Report of an Inquiry by Sir William Macpherson of Cluny*, London: HMSO.

Malen, B. and Knapp, M. (1997) 'Rethinking the multiple perspectives approach to education policy analysis: implications for policy-practice connections', *Journal of Education Policy* 12(5): 419–45.

Marshall, T. H. and Bottomore, T. (1992) *Citizenship and Social Class*, London: Pluto Press.

Mason, M. (2005) 'Religion and schools – a fresh way forward? A rights-based approach to diversity in schools', in R. Gardner, J. Cairns and D. Lawton (eds.) *Faith Schools: Consensus or Conflict?*, Abingdon: RoutledgeFalmer.

May, S. (1994) *Making Multicultural Education Work*, Clevedon: Multilingual Matters

Mertens, D. M. (1998) *Research Methods in Education and Psychology*, London and Thousand Oaks: SAGE.

Mickelson, R. A. (1994) 'A feminist approach to researching the powerful in education', in G. Walford (ed.) *Researching the Powerful in Education*, London: UCL Press.

Mill, J. S. (1983) 'Representative Government' (first published in 1861), in D. Held, J. Anderson, B. Gieben, S. Hall, L. Harris, P. Lewis, N. Parker and B. Turok (eds.) *States and Societies*, Oxford: Blackwell Publishers in association with the Open University.

Miller, D. (1995) *On Nationality*, Oxford: Clarendon Press.

Mirza, M., Senthilkumaran, A. and Ja'far, Z. (2007) *Living Apart Together: British Muslims and the Paradox of Multiculturalism*, London: Policy Exchange.

Modood, T. (1992) 'British Asian Muslims and the Rushdie Affair', in J. Donald and A. Rattansi (eds.) *'Race', Culture and Difference*, London: SAGE and the Open University.

Modood, T. (1997) 'Ethnic minorities in Britain: Diversity and disadvantage. Policy Studies Institute', cited in QCA (1998) *Education for Citizenship and the Teaching of Democracy in Schools (Crick Report)*, London: QCA.

Modood, T. (2005) *Multicultural Politics: Racism, Ethnicity and Muslims in Britain*, Edinburgh: Edinburgh University Press.

Moodley, K. A. and Adam, H. (2004) 'Citizenship education and political literacy in South Africa', in J. A. Banks (ed.) *Diversity and Citizenship Education: Global Perspectives*, San Francisco: Jossey-Bass.

Moughrabi, F. (2004) 'Educating for Citizenship in the New Palestine', in J. A. Banks (ed.) *Diversity and Citizenship Education: Global Perspectives*, San Francisco: Jossey-Bass.

Mouritsen, P. (2006) 'The particular universalism of a Nordic civic nation: common values, state religion and Islam in Danish political culture', in T. Modood, A. Triandafyllidou and R. Zapata-Barrero (eds.) *Multiculturalism, Muslims and Citizenship: A European Approach*, Abingdon, Oxon: Routledge.

Mulhall, S. and Swift, A. (1994) *Liberals and Communitarians*, Oxford: Blackwell.

Nicgorski, W. (1992) 'Amercian pluralism: a condition or a goal?', in F. C. Power and D. K. Lapsley (eds.) *The Challenge of Pluralism*, London and Notre Dame: University of Notre Dame Press.

Nieto, S. (1999) 'Critical multicultural education and students' perspectives', in S. May (ed.) *Critical Multiculturalism: Rethinking Multicultural and Anti-racist Education*, London: Falmer Press.

Noyes, A. (2005) 'Pupil Voice: purpose, power and the possibilities for democratic schooling – a thematic review', *British Education Research Journal* 31(4): 533–40.

OFSTED (2006) *Towards Consensus? Citizenship in Secondary Schools*, London: HMI.

Osler, A. (1999) 'Citizenship, democracy and political literacy', *Multicultural Teaching* 18(1): 12–15.

Osler, A. (2000) 'The Crick Report: difference, equality and racial justice', *The Curriculum Journal* 11(1): 25–37.

Osler, A. and Starkey, H. (1999) 'Rights, identities and inclusion: European programmes as political education', *Oxford Review of Education* 25(1/2): 199–215.

Osler, A. and Starkey, H. (2001) 'Citizenship education and national identities in France and England: inclusive or exclusive?', *Oxford Review of Education* 27(2): 287–305.

Osler, A. and Starkey, H. (2003) 'Learning for cosmopolitan citizenship: theoretical debates and young people's experiences', *Educational Review* 55(3): 243–54.

Osler, A. and Starkey, H. (2005) *Changing Citizenship: Democracy and Inclusion in Education*, Maidenhead: Open University Press.

Osler, A. and Vincent, K. (2002) *Citizenship and the Challenge of Global Education*, Stoke on Trent: Trentham Books.

Papademetriou, D. G. (2006) 'Transatlantic Task Force on Immigrant Immigration', Presentation at the European Conference on Active participation of ethic minority youth in society, Copenhagen, Denmark.

Parekh, B. (2000) *Rethinking Multiculturalism*, Basingstoke and London: MacMillan Press.

Parker, W. C. (2004) 'Diversity, Globalization, and Democratic Education: Curriculum Possibilities', in J. A. Banks (ed.) *Diversity and Citizenship Education: Global Perspectives*, San Francisco: Jossey-Bass.

Parker-Jenkins, M. (2005) 'The legal framework for faith-based schools and the rights of the child', in R. Gardner, J. Cairns and D. Lawton (eds.) *Faith Schools: Consensus or Conflict?*, Abingdon: RoutledgeFalmer.

Pattie, C., Seyd, P. and Whiteley, P. (2004) *Citizenship in Britain: Values, Participation and Democracy*, Cambridge: Cambridge University Press.

Powell, E. (1968) Speech at Eastbourne, 16.11.68, cited in Gilroy, P. (2002) *There Ain't No Black in the Union Jack*, London and New York: Routledge.

Pring, R. (2000) *Philosophy of Educational Research*, London: Continuum.

Pring, R. (2005) 'Faith schools: can they be justified?', in R. Gardner, J. Cairns and D. Lawton (eds.) *Faith Schools: Consensus or Conflict?*, Abingdon: RoutledgeFalmer.

Punch, M. (1998) 'Politics and ethics in qualitative research', in N. K. Denzin and Y. S. Lincoln (eds.) *The Landscape of Qualitative Research*, London and Thousand Oaks: SAGE.

Putnam, R. (1993) *Making Democracy Work: Civic Traditions in Modern Italy*, Princeton, NJ: Princeton University Press, cited in Green, A. and Preston, J. (2001) 'Education and social cohesion: re-centring the debate', *Peabody Journal of Education* 76(3/4): 247–84.

Putnam, R. (2000) *Bowling Alone: The Collapse and Revival of American Community*, London: Simon and Schuster, cited in Green, A. and Preston, J. (2001). 'Education and social cohesion: re-centring the debate', *Peabody Journal of Education* 76(3/4): 247–84.

Qualifications and Curriculum Authority (QCA) (1998) *Education for Citizenship and the Teaching of Democracy in Schools (Crick Report)*, London: QCA.

QCA (2000) Programmes of Study (Citizenship). Online. Available: www.nc.uk.net/ (accessed 30 October 2000).

QCA (2001) Schemes of Work (Citizenship). Online. Available: www.standards.dfes. gov.uk/local/schemes/citizenship/schemes.html (accessed 7 September 2001).

QCA (2004) The non-statutory national framework for religious education. Online. Available: www.qca.org.uk/9817.html (accessed 16 February 2007).

QCA (2005) Programmes of Study (PSHE). Online. Available: www.nc.uk.net/nc/contents/ PSHE-3–POS.html (accessed 13 January 2005).

QCA (2007) Programmes of Study: Citizenship (KS3 and KS4) at the secondary curriculum review. Online. Available: www.qca.org.uk/secondarycurriculumreview/ (accessed 16 February 2007).

Rammell, B. (2006) Speech to Community cohesion event, Southbank University, 16 May. Online. Available: www.dfes.gov.uk/speeches/search_detail.cfm?ID=340 (accessed 16 February 2007).

Rawls, J. (1971) *A Theory of Justice*, Oxford: Oxford University Press.

Rex, J. (1991) 'Ethnic identity and ethnic mobilisation in Britain', *Monographs in Ethnic Relations*, No. 5, Warwick: Centre for Research in Ethnic Relations.

Rex, J. (1995) 'The political sociology of a multicultural society', in M. Dunne and T. Bonazzi (eds.) *Citizenship and Rights in Multicultural Societies*, Keele: Keele University Press.

Rex, J. (1996) *Ethnic Minorities in the Modern Nation State: Working Papers in the Theory of Multiculturalism and Political Integration*, Basingstoke and London: MacMillan Press.

Rousseau, J. -J. (1968) *The Social Contract* (Translated and introduced by Maurice Cranston), Harmondsworth: Penguin.

Runnymede Trust Commission on the Future of Multi-Ethnic Britain (2000) *The Future of Multi-Ethnic Britain: Report of the Commission on the Future of Multi-Ethnic Britain*, London: Profile Books.

Russell, B. (1964) *A History of Western Philosophy*, New York: Simon and Schuster.

Sabine, G. H. (1951) *A History of Political Theory*, London: Harrap.

Schlesinger, A. M. (1992) *The Disuniting of America*, London and New York: W. W. Norton.

Schnapper, D. (1994) *La Communauté des Citoyens: sur l'idée moderne de nation*. Paris: Gallimard, cited in Kiwan, D. and Kiwan, N. (2005) 'Citizenship education: the French and English experience', in C. Pole, J. Pilcher and J. Williams (eds.) *Young People in Transition: Becoming Citizens*, Basingstoke: Palgrave Macmillan.

Scott (2000) 'Editorial – responses to Crick and citizenship education', *The Curriculum Journal* 11(1): 1–8.

Seale, C. (1998) 'Qualitative interviewing', in C. Seale (ed.) *Researching Society and Culture*, London: SAGE.

Sen, A. K. (2006) *Identity and Violence: The Illusion of Destiny*, London: Allen Lane.

Smith, A. (1988) *The Ethnic Origin of Nations*, Oxford: Blackwell.

Soysal, Y. N. (1998) 'Toward a postnational model of membership', in G. Shafir (ed.) *The Citizenship Debates*, Minneapolis: University of Minnesota Press.

Spinner-Halev, J. (2003) 'Education, reconciliation and nested identities', *Theory and Research in Education* 1(1): 51–72.

Starkey, H. (2000) 'Citizenship education in France and Britain: evolving theories and practice', *The Curriculum Journal* 11(1): 39–54.

Stevenson, N. (2002) 'Cosmopolitanism, multiculturalism and citizenship'. *Sociological Research* 7(1). Online. Available: www.socresonline.org.uk/7/1/stevenson.html (accessed 4 August 2004).

Stow, W. (2000) 'History: values in the diversity of human experience', in R. Bailey (ed.) *Teaching Values and Citizenship across the Curriculum*, London: Kogan.

Talbot, M. and Tate, T. (1997) 'Shared values in a pluralist society?', in R. Smith and P. Standish (eds.) *Teaching Right and Wrong: Moral Education in the Balance*, London: Trentham.

Tate, N. (1994) 'The role of the school in promoting moral social and cultural values', *Educational Review* 10(1): 66–70, cited in Stow, W. (2000) 'History: values in the diversity of human experience', in R. Bailey (ed.) (2000) *Teaching Values and Citizenship across the Curriculum*, London: Kogan.

Taylor, C. (1990) *Sources of Self*, Cambridge: Cambridge University Press.

Taylor, C. (1995) 'The politics of recognition', in A. Gutmann (ed.) *Multiculturalism: Examining the Politics of Recognition*, Princeton: Princeton University Press.

TES (*The Times Educational Supplement*) (23 June 2006) 'Analysis: Classes to stop suicide bombs?', by Michael Shaw. Online. Available: www.tes.co.uk/2249991 (accessed 16 February 2007).

*The Guardian* (7 April 2004) 'Why Trevor is right', by Polly Toynbee. Online. Available: www.guardian.co.uk/Columnists/Column/0,5673,1187233,00.html (accessed 21 July 2004).

*The Independent on Sunday* (9 December 2001: 1) 'Blunkett's "British test" for immigrants'.

*The Independent on Sunday* (9 December 2001: 4) 'If we want social cohesion we need a sense of identity'.

*The Independent* (31 October 2006) 'Schools told to promote integration of communities', by Ben Russell. Online. Available: education.independent.co.uk/news/article1943293.ece (accessed 21 February 2007).

*The Times* (3 April 2004) 'I want an integrated society with a difference', by Tom Baldwin: Interview with Trevor Phillips. Online. Available: www.timesonline.co.uk/printFriendly/0,,1-2-1061080,00.html (accessed 21 July 2004).

*The Times* (18 August 2004: 4–5) 'Lothario, no: but he is a romantic', by Mary Ann Sieghart.

de Tocqueville, A. (1956) *Democracy in America* (Translated by R. Heffner), New York: New American Library.

Torney-Purta, J. Schwille, J. and Amadeo, J. -A. (eds.) (1999) 'Civic Education across Countries: Twenty-four National Case Studies from the IEA Civic Education Project', Amsterdam, Netherlands: International Association for the Evaluation of Educational Achievement.

Troyna, B. (1984) 'Multicultural education: emancipation or containment?', in L. Barton and S. Walker (eds.) *Social Crisis and Educational Research*, Beckenham: Croon Helm.

United Nations (UN) (1948) Universal Declaration of Human Rights. Online. Available: www.un.org/Overview/rights.html (accessed 10 September 2004).

United Nations (UN) (1989) Convention on the Rights of the Child. Online. Available: www.unhchr.ch/html/menu3/b/k2crc.htm (accessed 10 September 2004).

Walford, G. (1994) 'Reflecting on researching the powerful', in G. Walford (ed.) *Researching the Powerful in Education*, London: UCL Press.

Walford, G. (2001) *Doing Qualitative Research: A Personal Guide to the Research Process*, London: Continuum.

Walkington, H. and Wilkins, C. (2000) 'Education for critical citizenship: the impact of teachers' world view on classroom practice in the teaching of values', *The School Field* 11(1/2): 59–78.

Watson, C. W. (2000) *Multiculturalism*, Buckingham: Open University Press.

Weisse, W. (2003) 'Difference without discrimination: religious education as a field of learning for social understanding?', in R. Jackson (ed.) *International Perspectives on Citizenship, Education and Religious Diversity*, London and New York: RoutledgeFalmer.

Wilkins, C. (1999) 'Making "good citizens": the social and political attitudes of PGCE students', *Oxford Review of Education* 25(1/2): 217–30.

Wilkins, C. (2001) 'Student teachers and attitudes towards "race": the role of citizenship education in addressing racism through the curriculum', *Westminster Studies in Education* 24(1): 7–21.

Williams, J. (2002) 'Introduction', in Section 1; 'The ideal of global citizenship', in N. Odwe and J. Williams (eds.) *Global Citizenship: A Critical Reader*, Edinburgh: Edinburgh University Press.

Wylie, K. (2004) 'Citizenship, identity and social inclusion: lessons from Northern Ireland', *European Journal of Education* 39(2): 237–48.

Young, I. M. (2000) *Inclusion and Democracy*, Oxford: Oxford University Press.

# Index

n refers to notes, t refers to a table

11 September 2001 1, 14, 27, 58

Advanced Skills Teachers (AST) 122
Advisory Board on Naturalization and
    Integration (ABNI) 72
Afghanistan 58
age, issues of 2, 45
Alderson, P. 64
Alibhai-Brown, Yasmin 17, 39, 40, 66;
    anti-racism 92
Annette, J. 16
Anthias, F. 97
Aristotle, 49, 52, 62, 76, 79
assimilation 15, 86
asylum seekers 67, 68
Australia 119

Ball, S. J. 40
Ballance, J. 15
Banks, J. A. 2, 124
Ben-Porath, S. R. 56
Bentham, Jeremy 62–3, 74
Bentley, Tom 89
Blair, Tony 'Our Nation's
    Future-multiculturalism and
    integration' 18
Blunkett, David 3, 17, 20, 22, 23;
    conception of citizenship 45; influence
    of personal experience 25; on Crick
    Advisory Group 34; on democracy 29,
    78; on empowerment 31; on faith
    schools 97; on multiculturalism 96–7;
    relationship with Crick 38–39
Boothroyd, Betty 78
Brazil 126
Breslin, Tony 85, 87

British citizenship, acquisition of 1, 69,
    110, 114
British Empire 14, 18
British Humanist Association 16
Britishness 1, 14, 24, 35–6, 70, 101,
    110, 112
British Youth Council 50, 65, 79, 95
Bron, J. 56
Brown, Gordon 24, 53
Buckingham, D. 124
Bulger, Jamie 20, 28

Canada 2
Cantle Report 16–17, 18, 114
Catholicism 13, 14–15, 36, 88
Christianity 28, 58–9, 61, 89
Citizenship Foundation 28, 85, 86
Civic Education Project (IEA) 29
civic republicanism 2, 44, 57, 74–5, 85, 88,
    95, 111
class, issues of 13, 75, 120
Cline, T. 120
cohesion 1, 16, 18, 20, 31–2, 69, 113,
    114, 119
Colley, Linda 53
Commission for Racial Equality (CRE) 14,
    26, 33, 92, 118
Commission on Cohesion and Integration
    114
Commonwealth immigrants act 1962.
    Control of immigration 14
Community Service Volunteers (CSV)
    32–3, 46
conflict 61, 99
Conservative administration (1979) 16, 19

Continuing Professional Development
(CPD) 9, 46, 118; Certificate of the
Teaching of Citizenship 121–2
Cookson, Jr. P. W. 6
Cope, B. 126
Council for Curriculum Reform 19
Council of Europe 2
Crick, Sir David 3, 22, 45; *In Defence of
Politics* 38, 39, 85: on democracy 75,
79, 82; on global context 90–1; on
political education 19, 46; on PSHE 51,
52, 57
Crick Advisory Group 3, 20; validation of
expertise 38–40; workings of 32–8,
33t, 41
Crick Report 31, 37; Appendix A 50;
on active participation 76, 111; on
anti-racism 85, 92–3; on democracy 79;
on diversity 85–6; on human rights
65–6; on multiculturalism 95–6;
on national identity 67–70; on values
50–1; 'three strands' conception 20–1,
30, 44–8, 75
Crittenden, B. 59


Davies, I. 79, 124
Delanty, G. 17, 56
Demaine, J. 91
democracy 32, 38, 108, 124, 126;
participatory citizenship and 8, 27, 29,
74–81; school ethos 118
*Democracy in America* (De Tocqueville)
75, 76, 79
Denham Report 114
Dewey 19
DeWitt, S. 126
DfES 3; Appendix 1 126; identity and
diversity 1, 21, 84, 87, 100, 110, 112,
122; local context 123; multiethnic
schools 120–1; racism 94; review
of citizenship 23–4, 43–4, 53,
54, 70, 100–1, 118; structural
recommendations 114; training of
head teachers 119
direct training 19
diversity 4–5, 30, 34–6, 39–40;
conceptualisation of 85–7; integration
and 1–2, 24–5, 32; multiethnic schools
120–1; practical implications 60–1;
religious 35–6; 'shared values' 56–7;
teaching skills 125–6; unity and
1–2, 56–8, 124; views of student
teachers 120

Dunblane school massacre 28
Durkheim, 49

Education and Inspections Act 2006 98,
114
'Education for Citizenship and the
Teaching of Democracy in Schools'
(QCA) 78
Education Reform Act (1988) 19
empowerment 31, 47, 82, 83, 127
England: national identity 68, 127; school
links 123
equality 8; France 70–1; minority groups
71; race 16, 31, 119
ethnicity 7, 27, 33t, 35–6, 71, 68, 83, 94,
116–17; Crick report 85, 86; ethnic
minority underachievement 15
ethnoculturalism 44, 88
Etzioni, A. 56
Europe 2, 89–91; eighteenth-century 63;
multiculturalism 17;
seventeenth-century 62
European Commission study (Osler and
Starkey) 29, 125
European Convention on Human Rights 66
*Excellence in Schools* (DfEE) 16, 20
exclusion 2, 80

faith schools 16–17, 97–8
feminist perspectives 25, 107
flexibility of the curriculum 87
France 2, 13, 44, 74–5, 88; assimilation of
minority cultures 57, 70–1; citizenship
and nationality 68; human rights 64

Gamarnikow, E. 75
GCSE Citizenship 123
gender 2, 33t, 45
geography 19, 125–6
Germany 2, 44, 90, 128n
Giddens, A. 75
Gillborn, D. 16
Glaser, B. 4
global citizenship 84, 89–91, 101, 112, 125
globalization 1, 89, 90–1, 112
Goulbourne, H. 15–16
Greece, Ancient 2, 45, 49, 58, 59, 76, 89
Green, A. 75
Grillo, R. D. 14
Gutmann, A. 102

Halstead, D. 50, 54, 61
Hansard Society 50
Haydon, G. 49–50

head teachers *see* school leaders
Held, D. 90
history 19, 53–4, 126; historical context of citizenship and democracy 70, 80
Hobbes, Thomas 62, 70, 74
House of Commons Education and Skills Select Committee, inquiry into citizenship education 2006 1, 53, 112
human rights 8, 16, 31, 54–5, 63–7, 70–1, 124
Human Rights Act (1998) 66
Huntingdon, S. P. 15, 58, 102

identity, national *see* national identity
identity and diversity 1, 25, 82, 83, 85–6; 'Identity and Diversity: Living together in the United Kingdom' 21, 84, 100, 110
'identity-based' conceptions of citizenship 7, 8, 43, 70, 84–103
immigration 2, 14, 24; 57, 67; acquisition of British citizenship 1, 69; assimilation 15, 86
Immigration and Nationality Directorate, Home Office 114
'Implicit Schools' 60
inclusivity 8, 18, 71, 82, 83, 100; coordination of relevant bodies 122–3; model of inclusive citizenship 107–15; promotion of inclusion in schools 118–19; pupil participation 123; role of curriculum 124; teacher training 119–22
individualism 8, 45, 56
Initial Teacher Training (ITT) 46, 120
integration 2, 15, 18, 72, 86, 114; diversity and 1–2, 25; workplace 2
intercultural education 113
International Association for the Evaluation of Educational Achievement (IEA) 29, 31, 118, 124
internet 126
interviews, methodology 5–6, 23; perceptions of aims and outcomes of citizenship education 29–30, 30t; questions put to interviewees 4–5
Ireland, Northern 13, 68, 113; school links 123
Islam 14–15, 16, 27, 57, 89, 117
Israel 113

Jenkins, Roy 15
Jewish faith 16, 36, 88

Johnson, Alan 94, 101
Joppke, J. 97, 98

Kalantzis, M. 126
Kant, I 89
Kelly, Ruth 114
Kerr, David 26, 28, 29, 37, 60, 87, 118, 124, 127
key players 5–6, 7, 54; explanatory models 26–8; power of individuals 22–4; societal influences 24–6; 24t; understanding aims of citizenship 28–32, 30t
Knapp, M. 30
KS3 5, 44, 46, 51, 121, 128n; anti-racism 93–4; conflict 99; democracy 79–81; diversity and identity 55, 68, 84, 87–8, 98–9, 101, 112, 122, 126; global and European dimensions 91, 101; human rights 54–5, 66–7, 68; multiculturalism 98; participation 77–8; values 54–5, 70
KS4 53–4, 67, 70, 101, 121; anti-racism 94; democracy 80–1, 83; diversity and identity 83, 84, 112, 122
Kymlicka, W. 53, 71, 91, 101, 117; 'local/cosmopolitan interculturalism' 112–13, 114

language test for citizenship 69–70, 114
Lawrence, Philip 28
Lawrence, Stephen 20, 24
Lawton, D. 19
'legal' conceptions of citizenship 8, 43, 62–73
liberalism 17, 25, 56, 58–9, 62–3, 93, 99, 102; history of term 62, 74
liberty 8, 74, 76
*Life in the United Kingdom: A Journey to Citizenship* (Home Office 2005) 69–70, 110
local community: democracy 80; importance of 19
Locke, John 59, 62, 70, 74
London bombings 1, 2, 14, 27, 56, 58, 114
Lukes, S. 97, 98

Malen, B. 30
Marshall, T. H. 13, 20, 44–5, 65, 75; social inclusion 85
McLaughlin, T. 30
media, the 1, 27–8
migration as part of programme of study 101

Mill, James 62–3
Mill, John Stuart 45, 59, 74, 76
Miller, D., 128n
Modood, T. 95, 117
'moral' conceptions of citizenship 7, 43, 49–61
multiculturalism 2, 7, 8, 84; anti-racist discourses 94–5; democracy 126; development of citizen education in the UK 18–21, 84–5; historical background 13–18; identity and 95–100; institutional 60, 89, 107–11, 115, 117, 119; politicization of 124
Muslims 14–15, 28, 57–8, 88, 117
Muslims for Secular Democracy 117

National Curriculum, introduction of 19–20
National Curriculum Council (NCC) 19
National Forum for Values in Education and the Community 20, 51, 53, 59
National Foundation for Educational Research (NFER) 60
national identity 29, 67–70, 84, 88–9, 127
National Institute for Adult and Continuing Education (NIACE) 70
National Professional Qualification for Headship (NPQH) 119
nationalist literature 128n
nationality *see* British citizenship, acquisition of; Britishness; national identity
Nationality, Immigration and Asylum Act (NIA) 2002 109
Netherlands 56
New Labour 16, 23, 56, 75
Newton, Jan 28
non-British culture as part of curriculum 15
Norwood Report 19

OFSTED 122; report 'Towards Consensus? Citizenship in secondary schools' (2006) 60–1
Osler, A. 20, 29, 82, 86, 90, 112, 125

Palestine 126
Papademetriou, D. G. 2
Parekh, B. 17, 58–9
'participatory' conceptions of citizenship 7, 8, 43, 74–83, 110–11; 'active' 72–3, 75–8; identity and participation 81–3; relationship with democracy 27, 78–81

Pattie, C. 27, 30, 81, 86, 116
Personal, Social and Health Education (PSHE) 21, 33; citizenship as module in 60–1; compared to citizenship education 50–2
PGCE 9, 119–20
Phillips, Trevor 17
Pike, M. 50, 54, 61
Plato 49, 62, 76, 79
pluralism 1, 2, 59, 67–8, 86
political education 19, 46–7, 64, 125
political participation, categories of 128n
Portugal 2
Powell, Enoch 15, 36
Preston, J. 75
'Progressing Schools' 60
Progressive British Muslims 117
Protestantism 13, 14, 15, 61, 107
pupil voice 123

QCA 3, 5, 20, 21; introduction of 'identities and diversity: living together in the UK' 101; revised programmes of study KS3, KS4 (2007) 44, 55, 70, 80, 83, 84, 94, 111, 112, 121, 122

race, issues of 13, 59; anti-racist approaches 8, 16, 17–18, 84, 91–5; equality 16, 31, 119; institutional 1, 109, 118–19; views of student teachers 120 *see also* ethnicity
Race Relations Act (1976) 14
Race Relations (Amendment) Act (2000) 119
Rammell, Bill 18, 100, 112
Rawls, J. 63, 93, 99
Refugee Council 33, 94
refugees 67, 68
religion: Crick report 85, 86; DfES report 94; diversity and 7, 27, 35, 71, 68, 83, 85, 86; state and 14–15, 117 *see also* individual faiths
religious education (RE) 19, 61
*Rethinking Multiculturalism* (Parekh) 58–9
Romans 45, 62, 76
Rousseau, Jean-Jacques 45, 74
Runnymede Trust 16
Rushdie, Salman 15

Sacks, Jonathan 36
Schlesinger, A. M. 15
school ethos 118, 119, 123
school leaders 118–19

school linking 112, 123
Schools Curriculum and Assessment
   Authority (SCAA), 20, 51
Scotland 13–14, 68; language 69; school
   links 123
secularism 15
*Secure Borders, Safe Haven: Integration
   with Diversity in Modern Britain*
   (Home Office 2002) 18, 25, 69, 96
Sen, Amartya 109
'shared values' 1, 7, 17, 18, 20, 24, 29, 43,
   108; Brown's view 53; diversity and
   56–8, 59; in the curriculum 55–6, 70,
   101, 112; multiculturalism and 32, 110,
   118; participative citizenship and 83
slavery 94
Smith, A. 88–9
Spinner-Halev, J. 113, 114, 115
social capital theory 75, 113
social studies 19
South Africa 126
Soysal, Y. N. 90
Spens Report 19
Starkey, H. 29, 82, 90, 112, 125
State, the 49, 62–3, 70; multinational 112;
   religion and 14–15; 'vertical'
   relationship between individual and
   state 113, 114, 115, 117
Strauss, A. 4
Sussmuth, Rita 2
Swann Report 'Education for All' 15–16

Talbot, Marianne 90, 93
Tate, Nick 20
teacher recruitment and retention 122
teacher training 9, 46, 118, 119–22
teaching and learning methodology 124–6
*Teaching of History and Civics in the
   Elementary and the Secondary School,
   The* (Bourne) 19

terrorism 15, 57–8 *see also* eleventh
   September 2001; London bombings
Thatcher, Margaret 16
*Theory of Justice, A* (Rawles) 63
*Times Educational Supplement* (TES) 1
Tomlinson, Professor 50
Toynbee, Polly 17
Training and Development Agency for
   Schools (TDA) 120
Transatlantic Task Force on Immigrant
   Integration 2
Troyna, B. 17, 94
Turner, Phil 37

UNCRC (United Nations Convention on
   the Rights of the Child) 63–4, 66
UNESCO 29, 121
unity and diversity 1–2, 56–8, 124
UN Universal Declaration of Human
   Rights (1948) 63, 66–7
USA 2, 6, 75, 79, 88, 102; reform 15

values 48, 54–5, 66 *see also* shared values
Vincent, K. 90
Vitorino, Antonio 2
volunteering 32–3, 46–7, 61, 125
VSO 125

Wales 13–14, 68; language 69; school
   links 123
Walkingon, H. 125
Watson, C. W. 16
*Who are We? America's Great Debate*
   (Huntingdon) 15, 102
Wilkins, C. 120, 125

Young, I. M. 82, 83, 108
Yuval-Davis, N. 97